PERGAMON INTERNATIONAL LIBRARY
of Science, Technology, Engineering and Social Studies

*The 1000-volume original paperback library in aid of education,
industrial training and the enjoyment of leisure*

Publisher: Robert Maxwell, M.C.

Measuring the
Condition of the
World's Poor
(Pergamon Policy Studies-42)

Pergamon Titles of Related Interest

Barney   *The Global 2000 Report to the President of the U.S.*

Carman   *Obstacles to Mineral Development: A Pragmatic View*

Chou/Harmon   *Critical Food Issues of the Eighties*

Diwan/Livingston   *Alternative Development Strategies and Appropriate Technology*

Golany   *Arid Zone Settlement Planning*

Goodman/Love   *Management of Development Projects*

Mushkin/Dunlop   *Health: What Is It Worth?*

Stepanek   *Bangladesh—Equitable Growth?*

PERGAMON
POLICY
STUDIES

Measuring the Condition of the World's Poor

The Physical Quality of Life Index

Morris David Morris

Published for the Overseas Development Council

Pergamon Press
NEW YORK • OXFORD • TORONTO • SYDNEY • FRANKFURT • PARIS

Pergamon Press Offices:

U.S.A.   Pergamon Press Inc., Maxwell House, Fairview Park,
                       Elmsford, New York 10523, U.S.A.

U.K.   Pergamon Press Ltd., Headington Hill Hall,
                       Oxford OX3 0BW, England

CANADA   Pergamon of Canada, Ltd., 150 Consumers Road,
                       Willowdale, Ontario M2J, 1P9, Canada

AUSTRALIA   Pergamon Press (Aust) Pty. Ltd., P O Box 544,
                       Potts Point, NSW 2011, Australia

FRANCE   Pergamon Press SARL, 24 rue des Ecoles,
                       75240 Paris, Cedex 05, France

FEDERAL REPUBLIC   Pergamon Press GmbH, 6242 Kronberg/Taunus,
OF GERMANY   Pferdstrasse 1, Federal Republic of Germany

The views expressed in this publication are those of the author and do
not necessarily reflect those of the Overseas Development Council, its
directors, officers, or staff.

Library of Congress Cataloging in Publication Data

Morris, Morris David.
    Measuring the condition of the world's poor.

    (Pergamon policy studies)
    Bibliography: p.
    Includes index.
    1. Underdeveloped areas–Poor. 2. Under-
developed areas–Economic indicators.
3. Underdeveloped areas–Social indicators.
I. Overseas Development Council. II. Title.
III. Title: Physical quality of life index.
HC59.7.M592 1979   330.9'172'4   79-16613
ISBN 0-08-023890-4
ISBN 0-08-023889-0 pbk.

Printed in the United States of America

To the memory of Dr. Birenda Nath Ganguli
(1902 - 1978)

Contents

List of Figures and Tables   ix

Foreword—*James P. Grant*   xi

Acknowledgments   xiii

1. Introduction: The Need for a New Indicator   1

2. GNP: What It Does and Does Not Measure   7
    Limitations of GNP   8
    Problems of International Comparison   10

3. Other Composite Indicators: Their Advantages and Disadvantages   15
    Measures of Development   16
    Measures of Welfare   17
    Normative Models   18

4. The PQLI Components: Why These?   20
    Criteria for a Composite Indicator   21
    Need for Unethnocentric Measures   22
    The Uni-Evolutionary Bias   22
    The Value Bias   25
    Need to Measure Results   28
    Need to Reflect Distribution   29
    Need for Simplicity   29
    Need for International Comparability   30
    Three Indicators Meet the Criteria   30
    What Do the Three Indicators Show?   34
    Indicators Not Chosen   38
    Death Rate   38
    Birth Rate   39
    Morbidity Rate   39
    Structural Measures   39
    Subjective Measures   39

5. The Technical Problems of Creating a Composite Index   41
       Indexing the Indicators   42
       The Impact of Weighting   47
       The Scaling Problem   49
       The Relationship among PQLI, Its Component
       Indicators, and GNP   52

6. What Does the PQLI Show?   57
       Data Limitations   57
       "Money Is Not Everything"   60
       Low GNP Countries Don't All Have Low PQLIs   63
       Country Clusters   66
       Distribution of Benefits   71
       Special Purpose PQLIs   72
          Historical PQLIs   74
          Ethnic Distinctions   78
          Regional PQLIs   80
          Female and Male PQLIs   82
          Rural and Urban PQLIs   87

7. Conclusions and Implications for Further Work   93
       What the PQLI Does Not Do   94
       Potential Uses of the PQLI   96
          A Measure of Performance   96
          A Criterion for International Decision Making   97
          A Tool for Targeting and Measuring Progress   99
          A Stimulus for Research   103

Notes   106

Appendix A. Population, Per Capita GNP, PQLI, and Component
Indicators (Actual Data and Index Numbers) for 150 Countries,
by Income Groups, early 1970s   125

Appendix B. 150 Countries Ranked by Increasing Per Capita GNP
(Table 1) and by Increasing PQLI (Table 2)   137

Appendix C. PQLI and Component Indicators for 74 Countries,
by Sex   147

Appendix D. United States: Historical Data by Race (Table 1)
and by State (Table 2)   161

Appendix E. Taiwan: Historical PQLI and Component
Indicators, 1950-1976   167

Index   169

About the Overseas Development Council and the Author   175

List of Figures and Tables

Figure 1. PQLI Map of the World   58

Figure 2. Scatter Diagram Showing PQLI and
           Per Capita GNP Distribution   65

Table 1. Two Estimates of Relative Incomes in
         Ten Countries, 1950 and 1975   11

Table 2. Senescent Deaths as a Percentage of Total Deaths,
         1841-1960/62   44

Table 3. Life Expectancy at Age One, Infant Mortality, and Literacy,
         Actual Data and Index Numbers, early 1970s   45

Table 4. Correlation of Component Indicators by Income Groups   54

Table 5. Correlation of Component Indicators with PQLI
         and with Per Capita GNP   55

Table 6. Correlation of PQLI with Per Capita GNP and with
         Repriced Per Capita GNP (114 Countries)   55

Table 7. Average Per Capita GNP and PQLI for 150 Countries,
         by Income Groups, early 1970s   61

Table 8. Five High-Income Countries with Low PQLIs, early 1970s   61

Table 9. Six Countries with Per Capita GNPs under $700 and
         PQLIs of 77 or More, early 1970s   63

Table 10. Eight Countries with Per Capita GNPs under $700 and
         PQLIs of 68 to 76, early 1970s   64

Table 11. Average Per Capita GNP, PQLI, and Component Indicators
         for 150 Countries, by Region, early 1970s   68

Table 12. Income Inequality, PQLI, and Per Capita GNP,
         Selected Countries, Various Years   73

Table 13. PQLI Performance and Per Capita GNP Growth Rates for
     Various Countries, circa 1950, 1960, and 1970   75

Table 14. Performance of Sri Lanka   76

Table 15. Historical PQLI Performance of the United States,
     by Race, 1900-1974   79

Table 16. Historical PQLI Performance of the United States,
     by State, 1940-1970   80

Table 17. Countries in Which Female PQLI is Lower than Male PQLI by
     More than Three Points, Various Years   84

Table 18. Female and Male PQLIs for Selected Countries, circa 1950 and
     circa 1970   88

Table 19. Female and Male PQLIs in India, by State, 1961   90

Table 20. Rural and Urban PQLIs for Three Countries, early 1970s   91

Table 21. Three Ways of Measuring the Amsterdam Declaration Goal of
     "Halving the Disparity" in Twenty Years   101

Table 22. PQLI Performance, DRR, and Average Annual
     Rate of Improvement for Selected Countries,
     circa 1950 to circa 1970   102

Table 23. DRRs Needed to Reach Year 2000 PQLI Targets,
     Selected Countries   103

Foreword

The aim of development strategies has shifted in recent years toward assuring the more effective address of essential human needs while increasing the output of goods. As a result, there have been a growing number of efforts to devise indicators that measure progress in physical well-being more effectively than is readily possible with gross national product and other monetary indicators. The Physical Quality of Life Index (PQLI) was developed at the Overseas Development Council (ODC) under the direction of Dr. Morris D. Morris in response to this widely felt need for an indicator that would measure the level of physical well-being and that could be used either by itself or in conjunction with per capita income indicators.

In the two years since the PQLI was first presented in summary and still preliminary form in ODC's annual assessment, *The United States and World Development: Agenda 1977,* wide public discussion has shown the PQLI to be a sturdy innovation requiring only minor modification. The analysis in this volume, the preparation of which was partially supported by a grant from the U.S. Agency for International Development, has benefited from the international discussion that followed after the PQLI was first introduced.

The growing number of national and international entities, both public and private, that already have adopted the PQLI as a useful measurement tool is a satisfying indication both of the PQLI's responsiveness to an urgent need for a more satisfactory measuring device and of its future potential. Yet the full range of uses to which the PQLI can be applied still awaits exploration. Further work clearly is needed on how it can be employed most usefully as well as on its limitations. In addition, substantial work is required to identify the impact of policy and program interventions on the PQLI. Planners today are still far more confident of their ability to predict output results from given inputs with respect to improvements in GNP than with respect to improvements in social indicators—including life expectancy, infant mortality, and literacy, the three components of the PQLI. Nothing comparable to the "production function"—the tool used by economists to correlate GNP input-output relationships—has yet been developed for programming social progress. Comments both on the concepts underlying the PQLI and on means for further increasing its already demonstrated utility are welcomed.

James P. Grant
President
Overseas Development Council

Acknowledgments

In 1974-75, I spent a fruitful year at the Indian Institute of Management, Ahmedabad. My colleagues, particularly Dwijendra Tripathi and V.S. Vyas, as well as P.B. Buch, Director of Statistics, Government of Gujarat, provided the stimulus that first caused me to consider a group of issues I had not before confronted and that ultimately led me to the subject of this book. Leroy Wehrle and John McQuown, two splendid colleagues on the National Academy of Science's World Food and Nutrition Study in 1976 and 1977, forced me to ask more direct questions about the quality of life and how it might be measured.

More immediate to this study, I received very generous advice (not always followed) and assistance from Mahinder Chaudhry, William Douglas, B.N. Ganguli, Stanley Heginbotham, Irving Hoch, Simon Kuznets, Mancur Olson, Jr., Richard Parke, and David Seidman. Data were easier to find and technical problems were more quickly resolved because of the cooperation I received from Robert McPheeters and his staff at the World Bank; from Samuel Baum, Head of the International Division, U.S. Bureau of the Census, and his colleagues; and from the staff of the Population Reference Bureau. My colleagues at the School for International Studies at the University of Washington, most particularly those in South Asian studies, were generous with their help. Joan Conlon and Frank Conlon provided unstinting support at many turns when my work became particularly demanding. In the background, always available to give assistance in a variety of ways, has been my long-time friend, P.R. Mehendiratta, Officiating Director, American Institute of Indian Studies, New Delhi.

The Overseas Development Council is a superbly collegial institution and I drew remorselessly on the knowledge, and tested the patience, of people throughout the organization. At one or another stage, the following colleagues were of particular assistance: Christine Fry, Davidson Gwatkin, Nina Halpern, Florizelle Liser, Angela LoRé, William Meyer, Michael O'Hare, and John Sewell. Drew Reynolds doggedly gathered data and provided statistical assistance under conditions that must not always have been easy, and Rosemarie Philips was a patient editor. Above all, I owe the opportunity to formulate the Physical Quality of

Life Index and the insistent pressure that I finish the manuscript much more rapidly than is my normal practice to James P. Grant, President of the Overseas Development Council. He is a friend of long standing whose unquenchable optimism and insatiable enthusiasm for public service is reinforced by formidable intelligence. To him and to Ethel Grant, who continues to provide a secure haven in Washington, my *namastes*.

Michelle McAlpin, whose great common sense is most uncommon, served as statistical advisor, general critic, and complete companion.

But after all is said and done, the manuscript is as I judged it must be. None of these people should be held liable for how I did or did not take their advice.

Morris David Morris
Department of Economics
University of Washington
Seattle, Washington

Measuring the
Condition of the
World's Poor
(Pergamon Policy Studies-42)

To measure is the first step to improve

Sir William Petty
(1623-1687)

1 Introduction: The Need for a New Indicator

Administrators more often than not effect results other than the ones they intend.

—Melvin Moses Knight

In response to disappointment with the perceived results of the growth-oriented strategies of the past quarter century, both rich and poor countries are exhibiting a renewed interest in the possibility of meeting the minimum human needs of the world's poorest people on a greatly accelerated timetable. The United Nations and its various agencies (particularly the International Labour Office), the World Bank, the Club of Rome, and the U.S. Congress all have expressed frustration. There is presently widespread and active exploration for alternative development strategies that place at least as much emphasis on equity as on growth. Such strategies are receiving growing attention from scholars at the Institute of Development Studies at the University of Sussex; in the activities of Mahbub ul Haq, Hollis Chenery, and others at the World Bank; and in the recent writings of Irma Adelman and Cynthia Taft Morris, among others.[1]

The changing orientation represents a return to older economic ideas that emphasize relative factor prices, the economizing of scarce resources, and the greater use of those resources that are relatively plentiful. This approach in turn creates the need to search for more relevant technologies. For poor countries, this typically means technologies that make greater use of unskilled and semi-skilled labor per unit of capital than are commonly employed in developed countries. The new strategies often incorporate a stronger preoccupation with popular participation and a greater reliance on local institutions and indigenous conceptual systems. The increasing "poorest-of-the-poor, labor-intensive, self-help" emphasis—the implications of which are not yet fully worked out—is seen as good in its own right. Some see equity as a desirable objective to be achieved even at the cost of some growth. Others recognize it as a necessary, but not sufficient, component of any humane growth strategy.[2]

The new approaches—whether called growth-with-equity or basic human needs or minimum human needs—are development policy coming full circle. The slogans "rural development," "integrated development," and "participation" all have been heard before.[3] It is not important how these ideas have emerged or resurfaced. It is not even important whether there is a coherent conception of the objectives or the mechanisms. What does matter is the recognition that equity and the satisfaction of basic or minimum human needs have an exceedingly high priority. A strategy that does not give at least lip service to these objectives (however defined) will have legitimacy neither in the councils of resource controllers nor in the international arena nor within individual poor countries.

Whether the strategies are real or a fad, whether their objectives are serious targets or slogans, they pose as never before the need to measure not only total economic output and the composition of that output, but also how output is distributed. There never has been an easy way to measure this type of performance. Gross national product (GNP) is the most widely accepted measure of progress. However, while per capita GNP measures general economic performance within and among countries, it is unable to show how output is distributed among people in poor (or even in rich) countries.[4] To the extent that development planners within poor countries and aid dispensers in donor countries now focus more directly on projects that emphasize distribution of benefits, they need not only new planning strategies but also additional measurement systems.

The issue of measurement surfaced at the Overseas Development Council not because of an interest in the abstract limitations of GNP but as a response to two policy problems with which the Council was concerned in 1976. Based on some early work on the implications of alternative development strategies, it became obvious that, no matter how rapidly poor countries grew, economic growth could not provide any dramatic increases in their absolute levels of per capita income. Estimates indicate that low-income countries (in this case, those with per capita incomes of $250 or less in constant 1975 dollars) under the most favorable circumstances can only look forward to raising their real per capita incomes from an average of $150 to $327 between 1975 and the year 2000.[5] This does not augur well for the world's ability to improve the life chances of its very poorest, who constitute at least one quarter of its population.

At the same time that this lesson was first being learned, two members of the Overseas Development Council—James P. Grant, its President, and I, at the time a Visiting Fellow—were involved in the National Academy of Sciences World Food and Nutrition Study, which was charged by President Ford with the task of determining how the United States could help lessen "the grim prospect that future generations of people around the world will be confronted with chronic shortages of food and with the debilitating effects of malnutrition."[6] Study

Team 12, which reported on "New Approaches to the Alleviation of Hunger," concluded that nutritional success—defined as enabling people to enjoy longer, healthier, and more satisfying lives—could not be achieved simply by increasing food supply, calorie intake, or even per capita income. It became apparent that improvements in physical well-being are the consequences of a complex interplay of physiological, psychological, nutritional, medical, social, cultural, and environmental relationships about which almost nothing is known.[7]

The Study Team data showed that, while there is some general correlation between levels of per capita income and longevity, health, literacy, etc., the relationships in specific countries are not obvious. Moreover, there are striking exceptions. Some countries with relatively high average per capita incomes perform poorly. Others with quite low average per capita incomes have relatively high literacy rates, long life expectancies, low infant mortalities, and low death rates. Countries have achieved these different qualities of life for their populations at almost any level of income and calorie consumption.[8] There appear to be both more efficient and less efficient ways of achieving desired results. The low-income examples were particularly intriguing to the Study Team because they suggested that the right mix of development strategies might make it possible to improve conditions in other very poor countries much more rapidly than historical experience or statistical correlation have suggested.

The Overseas Development Council set out to find answers to the questions raised by this possibility. The first step was to search for a measure that would help to identify such "success" stories. It had to be a measure that would work despite cultural and structural differences among countries. There had been many previous efforts—for example, by the United Nations, the U.N. Research Institute for Social Development (UNRISD), the Organisation for Economic Co-operation and Development (OECD), and the World Bank, as well as by a number of private organizations and individuals. None had produced a measure that conveniently could identify the extent to which poor people benefit from development progress. Excessive complexity had caused them to founder.

As a result of lessons learned from other efforts, we decided not to try to capture everything about the development process in a single measure. Instead, we identified certain conditions that had to be satisfied if a development policy was to be deemed successful in addressing the needs of the very poorest people. Not all of these lent themselves to measurement, particularly across national boundaries. We finally settled on three apparently universal concerns. We assumed that people generally prefer to have few deaths among the infants born to them and that under almost all circumstances people prefer to live longer rather than shorter lives. We also decided that—even if the desire for literacy *per se* is not as widely shared—literacy could serve as a surrogate for (although it does not guarantee) individual capacity for effective social participation. On the basis of these assumptions, three indicators—infant mortality, life expectancy at age one, and basic literacy—ultimately were selected as the components of the composite measure, the Physical Quality of Life Index (PQLI). Each of these indicators met six criteria for a composite indicator that had been established at the outset.

The PQLI has very limited objectives. It does not try to measure all "development"; nor does it measure freedom, justice, security, or other intangible goods. It does, however, attempt to measure how well societies satisfy certain specific life-serving social characteristics. Precisely because of the limits within which it operates, the PQLI seems to have considerable promise. It not only can measure change at the national level, it also can make comparisons between women and men and among other distinctive social, ethnic, regional, or sectoral groupings. It can measure change over time.

The usefulness of this—or any other—index depends on the accuracy and availability of data. One advantage of the PQLI is that it uses data that even countries that have not yet developed a complex bureaucratic infrastructure are likely to need for basic administrative purposes.

The PQLI is still in its early developmental stages. The concern thus far has been to determine whether or not the concept is promising. Thus we used existing, often imperfect data rather than wait for improvements in the collection of data. This is also why no attempt is made in this study to grapple with the underlying problems of theoretical coherence and causality. Only now that we are convinced that the PQLI approach has substance and utility does it appear worthwhile to advance to the second stage, to confront the formidable practical and conceptual issues that so far either have been ignored by analysts or have eluded resolution.

The surfacing of a measuring instrument without an underlying theory will seem to some to be at odds with prescribed scientific method, in which the stimulus for an instrument comes from an already existing theory. This issue will be discussed later; however, two points are worth making here. First, even without an elaborate, explicit theoretical foundation, the PQLI helps policymakers see certain things more clearly than they might otherwise. Second, while it is true that, in the absence of a theory, policy prescriptions cannot be made with certainty, this is not a defect from which the PQLI alone suffers. After all, the index was developed precisely because the level and/or rates of change of per capita GNP were not very good predictors of what benefits actually appeared in developing countries or who got them.

The fact that an established theory is an inadequate guide to action does not guarantee that another theory already exists to replace it. One usually is left to search for a more helpful formulation based on a more sophisticated reading of the evidence. The PQLI, while not itself a theory, points out the lines along which analysis almost certainly must proceed. It points to the possibility of getting better life-quality results of specific kinds at much lower levels of economic performance than policymakers and theorists generally have considered possible. (The index also shows that some countries have much poorer life-quality results at quite high per capita incomes than often is assumed.) The

PQLI sums the complex interrelationships among policies that affect infant mortality, life expectancy, and literacy rates. It implies that efficient results cannot be achieved by concentrating on individual components. The best results are achieved by a mix of policies that react on and reinforce one another. The problem is that we do not yet know what these interrelations are, even though we have some beginning insights and hypotheses; exploring these inter-relations constitutes the major task ahead.

Why did we not undertake this as part of our initial effort? The task is a formidable one that will require the work of many groups and individuals over a substantial period. The PQLI results pose a general equilibrium problem involv-ing nutrition, health, education, degree of social participation, employment levels, and income-earning capacity, etc., that is so complex that scholars long have sought to evade it. As long as it could be assumed that there was a system-atic correlation between rising GNP and improved life chances—in other words, that "trickle down" policies worked—there was no need to tackle the problem of how all these things interrelate. But now two matters have become clear. First, a very large proportion of the human race is going to live with distressingly low per capita incomes for decades to come. Second, there is no automatic and necessary connection between income and the life-quality results that can be attained. The implications of these facts must now be confronted directly.

We are satisfied that the PQLI can stimulate promising and exciting lines of analysis, not only for poor countries (for which it was mainly designed) but for rich countries as well. The composite nature of the PQLI not only encourages us to think along novel lines but also serves as a constant reminder of the crucial interrelatedness that seems to be at the core of the analytic task we face. The development of a solid set of theorems of use to policymakers will require large, diverse, and long-sustained efforts. In the meantime, however, it seems sensible to put this still somewhat crude product into the intellectual marketplace, where it can be subjected to sharp and creative development and modification by interested persons or groups.

The initial version of the PQLI was published early in 1977, with only minimal description of its intellectual underpinnings.[9] We hoped to elicit comments, and we were not disappointed. There were favorable reactions and there were harshly critical ones. We learned from the latter and were encouraged by the former. This much more detailed discussion of the PQLI is the result. The chapters that follow lay out the assumptions on which the PQLI is based. They examine the technical problems of constructing any such index, the in-sights that can be gained from the PQLI, the uses to which the index might be put, and the further work that will be needed to increase its usefulness as a welfare-focused development tool.

Human beings have a fascination with taxonomy and those concerned with development problems seem to have a special attraction to ranking and classifica-tion. The initial description of the PQLI may have attracted attention in part because it permitted this; one critic condemned the index as "nothing more than a parlor game." However, classification was not its prime purpose then, nor is it the PQLI's purpose now. The object of the PQLI is to help focus the search for strategies that might yield quicker improvements in the condition of the very poorest than can be expected if we wait for benefits to flow "naturally" from increases in national income. Much of the attention the index already has received has recognized this. There nevertheless may continue to be some who—despite our efforts to satisfy objections—will find the PQLI concept unacceptable. We hope that this study will stimulate them to renewed effort along other lines.

Readers interested only in the results of this study can turn to Chapter 4, which discusses the criteria used in selecting the component indicators; Chapter 6, which discusses the application of the index; and Chapter 7, which presents conclusions based on the current state of work as well as suggestions for further research.

2 GNP: What It Does and Does Not Measure

It is well known that, thus far, the problem of finding a social benefit or welfare function is unsolved.

—Oskar Morgenstern
On the Accuracy of Economic Observations

The system of national accounts and its components (as they are summarized in the gross national product—money value of all goods and services produced in a country in the course of a year) is probably the single most successful social science tool ever developed. It combines sophisticated theoretical characteristics and practical usefulness in a way that no other measure comes close to doing. It is a powerful instrument of social diagnosis that lends itself to cross-national comparison as well as to use within a country. When adjusted for population size, GNP has been widely used to measure the performance of individual countries over time and to compare performances among countries.

As a measuring instrument, GNP is not free of flaws and internal contradictions. Readers of introductory economics textbooks learn something about the limitations of GNP as a measure of performance and welfare. Those who investigate problems of economic development learn even more about its limitations as an instrument for comparing economic performance among countries, particularly for making comparisons between rich and poor countries. Some who use GNP may be excessively enthusiastic about its powers, but those who have been most actively involved in its development are most aware of its general defects and most sophisticated about its limitations.[10]

While there are continuing efforts to remedy defects, it is clear that GNP does not and cannot capture all features of social behavior. For certain purposes, particularly for measuring performance and aspects of welfare in less developed countries, GNP must be supplemented by other indicators. As long ago as 1947, the distinguished economist Simon Kuznets remarked:

> It does seem to me, however, that as customary national income estimates and analysis are extended, and as their coverage includes more and more countries that differ markedly in their industrial structure and form of social organization, investigators interested in quantitative comparisons will have to take greater cognizance of the aspects of economic and social life that do not now enter national income measurement; and that national income concepts will have to be either modified or partly abandoned, in favor of more inclusive measures, less dependent upon the appraisals of the market system.

He went so far as to suggest:

> The eventual solution would obviously lie in devising a single yardstick that could then be applied to both types of economies—a yardstick that would perhaps lie outside the different economic and social institutions and be grounded in experimental science (of nutrition, warmth, health, shelter, etc.).[11]

Limitations of GNP

Even in a modern, monetized economy, GNP is not a measure of total welfare. It measures goods and services that are valued in money terms. Many productive activities are excluded; the work of housewives and increasingly the "do-it-yourself" activities engaged in around the home are standard examples. Moreover, GNP encompasses some activities that many economists believe should not be included (e.g., police protection in urban areas), because they can be viewed as a cost of urban life, a "regrettable necessity."

GNP does not measure subjective elements—how much happiness, justice, security, freedom, or leisure a society provides. Given what it sets out to measure, there is no reason why GNP should be a satisfactory measure of these. Similarly, GNP does not measure a society's physical qualities of life—as represented, for example, by its life expectancy; its birth, death, and morbidity characteristics; and its literacy. There is no automatic and direct connection between any level of GNP or any rate of GNP growth and the performances such indicators measure. A nation's economic output—as measured in the national accounts—can be allocated in a variety of ways, both among sectors of activity and among social groups. A nation's policies may emphasize the growth of its military power and of certain areas of its economy that do not contribute in any obvious or direct way to the improvement of the population's health and well-being.

Nor does the growth of disposable personal income over time necessarily occur in ways that improve well-being. The very poorest groups of a society may not benefit much or at all from rising incomes; some groups may even suffer declines in real income. Even if rising incomes are shared with the poorest groups, there is no guarantee that those incomes are spent in ways that change calorie intake or improve the general welfare or the physical well-being of the population; for example, in some societies rising incomes have been accompanied by adverse dietary changes, and virtually all urbanized and industrialized countries have had to pay the price of various environmental pollutions.

On the other hand, a country can be made better off by any number of changes—improvements in security, social harmony, opportunity, length of life, or mortality rates—even without an increase in GNP. Kuznets explicitly notes that " . . . from the standpoint of basic wants or needs, the system of valuation in national income measures may lead to an underestimate of the extent of economic progress or of the extent of economic superiority across space in satisfying primary wants."[12]

Economists have not ignored the difficulties associated with GNP. William Nordhaus and James Tobin, for example, have made a heroic effort to transform GNP into a measure of economic welfare.

An obvious shortcoming of GNP is that it is an index of production, not consumption. The goal of economic activity, after all, is consumption. Although this is the central premise of economics, the profession has been slow to develop, either conceptually or statistically, a measure of economic performance oriented to consumption, broadly defined and carefully calculated. We have constructed a primitive and experimental 'measure of economic welfare' (MEW), in which we attempt to allow for the more obvious discrepancies between GNP and economic welfare. [13]

In constructing the MEW, Nordhaus and Tobin modified the existing system of national accounts in three major ways: 1) they reclassified expenditures; 2) they imputed values for the services of consumer capital, household activities, and leisure; and 3) they adjusted for some of the disamenities of industrialization and urbanization.

The proposal has produced considerable controversy. Some of its major critics fear that such modifications will dilute the usefulness of GNP as a measure of production while misleading the public into supposing that GNP measures social welfare.[14] Whatever the fate of the Nordhaus-Tobin proposal, it is widely agreed that GNP in its current form is not a satisfactory measure of welfare.[15] Furthermore, GNP is a particularly recalcitrant measure of welfare over time. Moses Abramovitz, in a widely cited essay, concluded that, while GNP certainly is the best measure of output yet devised, "we must be highly skeptical of the view that long-term changes in the rate of growth of welfare can be gauged even roughly from changes in the rate of growth of output."[16]

Dan Usher has noted a particularly perverse feature of GNP. The present way of calculating economic activity suggests that when per capita income falls because of an increase in population relative to GNP, there is a decline in welfare. However, if the increase in population occurred because of a decline in the death rate, individuals presumably would feel better off just because they and their children could expect to live longer. For example, in Canada the infant death rate per thousand live births fell from approximately 100 to 20 between 1926 and 1968 and the death rate of children aged one to four declined from 10 per 1,000 to 1 per 1,000. By assigning a value to the resulting increase in life expectancy, Usher showed that the annual rate of growth in real income in Canada from 1926 to 1968 was 22 percent greater than is conventionally estimated; it was 2.8 percent rather than 2.3 percent.[17]

Problems of International Comparison

The formidable issues that make GNP a less than perfect measure of the performance of a single country are greatly compounded when comparison of the performance of two or more countries is attempted.[18] How to value the output of different countries in a common measure poses a major problem. The most widely used method, adopted by the World Bank, converts local prices into U.S. dollars at official exchange rates. This method has a host of difficulties, not the least of which is the variability of exchange rates. One example, not at all exceptional, suggests what exchange rate shifts can do to income expressed in U.S. dollars. The officially estimated per capita income in Argentina in 1955 was 6,437 pesos. During most of that year, the official exchange rate was 7.5 pesos per U.S. dollar, implying a per capita income of $858. Late in 1955, the peso was officially devalued to 18 pesos per U.S. dollar. Thus per capita income fell to $358 without any obvious change in Argentina's level of economic activity. At the same time, the widely used black market rate of 30 pesos per U.S. dollar implied a per capita income of $215, and the completely free market rate of about 40 pesos per U.S. dollar indicated a per capita income of $161.[19] Because such variability is not constant, either among countries or over time, meaningful international comparisons are extremely difficult to make.

Even if the exchange rate issue could be resolved, the problem of what method of GNP comparison to use would remain. In addition to the exchange rate method, there are at least three other, equally legitimate methods of comparing income, each of which yields quite different results.[20] Table 1 compares the income relationship of the United States and nine other countries in two years, 1970 and 1975, using two methods: the purchasing power parity formula of the U.N. International Comparison Project and the official exchange rate method used by the World Bank.[21] The two methods yield not only different income levels for individual countries, but also different relationships among countries.

For example, in actual dollar figures, U.S. per capita income in 1975 was $7,120. Based on the official exchange rate method, India's real per capita income was reported by the World Bank to be $140. But when calculated according to the purchasing power parity formula, India's real per capita income in 1975 amounted to about $490, or three-and-one-half times as much, changing the ratio of per capita income between the United States and India from 50 to 1

Table 1. Two Estimates of Relative Incomes in Ten Countries, 1970 and 1975 (United States = 100)

	(1)	(2)	(3)	(4)	(5)	(6)
		1970			1975	
	Purchasing Power Parity Method	Official Exchange Rate Method	Ratio of Col. 1 to Col. 2	Purchasing Power Parity Method	Official Exchange Rate Method	Ratio of Col. 4 to Col. 5
United States	100.00	100.00	1.00	100.00	100.00	1.00
France	75.00	76.32	0.98	77.50	83.59	0.93
Germany, Fed. Rep.	74.70	91.92	0.81	76.52	93.73	0.81
Japan	61.50	54.68	1.12	66.85	62.47	1.07
United Kingdom	60.30	52.03	1.16	63.13	53.15	1.19
Italy	45.80	39.66	1.15	46.68	39.42	1.18
Hungary	40.30	27.53	1.46	52.65	30.25	1.74
Colombia	15.90	7.21	2.21	18.46	8.12	2.27
India	7.12	2.02	3.52	6.93	1.99	3.48
Kenya	5.72	2.98	1.92	5.72	3.12	1.83

SOURCE: *World Bank Atlas, 1977*, p. 31.

to 14 to 1. The change is not the product of a trivial statistical trick; it derives from formidable technical problems for which there is no perfect or even entirely obvious solution.

It is accepted widely that the exchange rate method has a bias that exaggerates the differences between more and less developed countries and that it can change country rankings. For example, on the basis of official exchange rates, Kenya has a per capita GNP of $220 compared with India's $140. However, the purchasing power parity formula results in a per capita GNP of only $407 for Kenya, compared with India's per capita GNP of $490. It is also generally believed that, "For purposes of international comparison, gross national product (GNP) estimates in U.S. dollars or some other numeraire should be calculated, ideally, on the basis of purchasing power parities or through direct real product comparisons."[22] Yet the World Bank, the United Nations, and other agencies and individuals continue to use the exchange rate method because of the time-consuming effort and great cost involved in establishing the basis of information needed for the purchasing power parity method.[23]

The relative levels and rates of change in per capita national income are used nationally and internationally in making a wide range of decisions. They play an important role in almost every theory of economic growth and change. Decision makers depend on these measures for the intellectual underpinnings to their policies. The large differences resulting from the accidents of methodological choice thus merit a greater degree of self-conscious caution than is contained in most economic analyses and policy prescriptions.

The World Bank cautions that its extensively used data, based on the exchange rate method, "provide only an approximate measure of economic conditions and trends . . . They are merely rough indicators of the absolute state of poverty in the developing world . . . "[24] Unfortunately, analysis and policy too often assume that the data correctly reflect relationships among countries and trends over time in any particular country. Little if any attention has been devoted to testing the accuracy of what appears to be a quite dubious assumption.[25]

Because of the complexity of the repricing procedures, there is some question whether the purchasing power parity method ever can become the basis of systematic international comparisons. Moreover, even if the technical problems were solved, great conceptual limitations to the international comparability of national income estimates for welfare purposes would remain. Kuznets pointed out long ago—and the work of Kravis and his associates reinforces—the fact that, however serious poverty in the developing world may be, there is something suspicious about estimates showing that the 957 million citizens of countries with 1970-75 per capita incomes of less than $200 have an average income of $132, while the citizens of the United States live with fifty-three times that much.[26] If this $132 figure indicates that people are living on the quantity of goods and services that could be bought in the United States for 36 cents per day, it poses a substantial puzzle. At that level of real income, a large proportion of these people would quickly die; yet the populations of these countries are growing very rapidly and, in general, life expectancy is increasing at the same time. But if the data do not mean that these nearly billion people live on what can be bought in the United States for 36 cents per day, it is not at all clear what they do mean.

The failure to examine the implications of the exchange rate paradox can lead to substantial misperceptions of the scale of the basic poverty problem in the world. For example, it has become common to define the world's "absolute poor" as those who live below two admittedly arbitrary poverty lines that are equivalent to annual per capita incomes of U.S. $50 and U.S. $75 (in 1971 prices). On the basis of data for countries representing about 60 percent of the total population in the developing world (that is, excluding the People's Republic of China), Ahluwalia estimated that some 370 million people live with annual incomes of less than $50, and 578 million live with annual incomes of less than $75.[27]

These numbers are extremely sensitive to the exchange rate method of comparing GNP. For example, Ahluwalia calculated that in India alone, 239 million people exist below the $50 annual per capita income line and 359 million people survive below the $75 poverty line. A conservative estimate suggests that recomputation of Indian per capita income according to the purchasing power parity method would move at least 50 percent of the Indian population (about 180 million people) currently below the $75 poverty line above it.[28] This alone would reduce the number of the whole world's absolute poor by about 30 percent, from 578 to 400 million people. Purchasing power parity adjustments for other countries would further reduce the number of those defined as being "absolutely poor." This is not a game in which the world's poverty problem is solved by reclassification. It is important to note, however, how substantially the dimensions of the problem are affected by the nature of the assumptions underlying GNP comparisons.[29]

However poor some societies are, the difference between developed and less developed countries is invariably exaggerated by this one-dimensional effort to capture the phenomenon. Kuznets, in fact, suggested that, "the ordinary impressions of the vast relative difference between the economic performance of industrial and pre-industrial societies may well be colored by vague thoughts concerning differences in national power, rather than in supplying goods for the satisfaction of consumer wants."[30] For a variety of reasons, it is probable that the less developed a society is—i.e., the smaller the proportion of goods and services that are produced for and exchanged in the market—the more difficult it is to make legitimate comparisons of economic performance. Kuznets referred to comparisons between developed and developing countries as "a compromise of compromises."[31]

When the objective is to determine the extent to which less developed countries provide benefits to the very poorest groups of their populations, the problems associated with GNP measurement are compounded. The difficulties are not resolved by the various attempts that have been made to estimate the distribution of income within countries, because the poorest countries and the poorest groups within countries are precisely the ones that most effectively escape the net of monetary measurement. Moreover, often the structure of productive activities in .poor countries cannot be captured by standard GNP categories. In effect, GNP is an appropriate measure of output, but not a very satisfactory measure of welfare. Even as a measure of output, it suffers from greater defects when used to measure developing than developed countries. As a measure of welfare, GNP is fundamentally flawed.[32]

The difficulties are not simply "errors of measurement" that can be resolved by technical ingenuity. Rather, they derive from the complex and varied social and economic structures within which people live. Thus one cannot arrive at a "true" solution but can only choose among a set of alternatives, selecting in order to minimize inconvenience. That GNP and the entire system of national accounts work is not so much a tribute to logical coherence as a reflection of the social urgencies that have induced analysts to agree to abide by the many conventions on which the system depends. Where agreement on appropriate conventions cannot be reached (as has been the case in the question of how to deal with centrally planned versus market economies), international comparison is a very treacherous business, indeed.[33]

This is not reason to discard GNP, as some non-economists are tempted to urge. The problem would not be avoided even if performance were measured in some "real" way, for example, with an energy indicator.[34] Rather, there is need for a measure to supplement (not replace) GNP. To cite Kuznets once again:

The refusal to extend discussion in these directions—of fuller coverage of consumption levels, of levels of living, and of experimentally established functional equivalents—is not due to the possibly low yield of such explorations. On the contrary, they promise results of great value. They might explain, more satisfactorily than can be done otherwise, the basic differences between industrial and pre-industrial economies, and the conditions on which of the latter can be industrialized. As already suggested, they might provide a more effective basis for comparison and help overcome the difficulties imposed by differences in the goods composition of national product. Studies of nutrition indicate unmistakably that pre-industrial economies manage to obtain the basic vitamin supply at much lower economic costs, and hence at much lower prices, than a price comparison of *identical commodities* would indicate.

That we have paid little attention to these aspects of the comparison is due largely to a feeling that study has not advanced sufficiently to permit abandonment of the more traditional approach.[35]

Thirty years have passed since Kuznets wrote these lines. What attempts have been made to grapple with the issues since then? What promise is there in another attempt?

3 Other Composite Indicators: Their Advantages and Disadvantages

Here is Edward Bear, coming downstairs now, bump, bump, bump, bump, on the back of his head, behind Christopher Robin. It is, as far as he knows, the only way of coming downstairs, but sometimes he feels that there really is another way if only he could stop bumping for a moment and think of it. And then he feels that perhaps there isn't.

—A.A. Milne
Winnie-the-Pooh

The entire system of national accounts, including GNP, was developed in the 1930s and 1940s, primarily in Britain and the United States, to deal with resource-mobilization and -allocation problems of depression, unemployment, and war. The system of national accounts is an excellent arsenal of diagnostic tools suited to the short-run problems of highly developed economies. Even though it is used to analyze poor countries' long-run development problems, there are many matters to which the system cannot address itself well or at all.

As noted in Chapter 2, numerous attempts have been made to broaden the scope of GNP to incorporate welfare considerations. While such efforts have the virtue of elegance in seeking to incorporate all social accounts into a single coherent system, they have a fundamental difficulty that has been well described by Arthur Okun:

What you can and do measure as national income statisticians is the output resulting from market-oriented activity. The key to market-oriented activity is the presence of price tags—the essential ingredient is an objective standard of measurement. Price tags enable you to sum up physicians' prescriptions and phonograph records and pounds of steaks and packages of beans, or all the things that money can buy. But if you were to be seduced by your critics into inventing price tags that neither exist nor can be reasonably approximated for things that money can't buy, you would have sacrificed the objective yardstick.[36]

On balance, it appears that those who oppose the expansion of the accounts have the superior case.

The present transactions-based Accounts are extraordinarily useful, have historical consistency, and in general should not be much tampered with in an attempt to improve their usefulness for other purposes than the ones for which they were designed.[37]

Those who have been concerned with welfare-oriented issues, particularly in relation to developing countries, have had to experiment with other kinds of measures.[38]

The system of national accounts was designed for a specific set of problems and therefore has a certain focus and advantages as well as certain conceptual and technical limitations. Similarly, other efforts have been designed to cope with specific kinds of issues and reflect those interests. The following discussion reviews some of the types of alternative indicators and the problems they were intended to address.

Measures of Development

One group of efforts consists of those that focus on creating a "development measure," that is, a composite indicator of the "normal" or "optimal" pattern of socio-economic change. Efforts of this type are based on the fact that if societies are to improve their abilities to increase per capita incomes (in the broadest sense), they typically must undergo substantial structural transformations that are not limited to narrow technical or economic matters. Major economic changes imply complementary social and political changes. While GNP can measure the quantitative aspects of economic growth, it is not a good measure—in fact, it may not be a measure at all—of the rate or the level of the combined social, political, and economic process on which sustained development depends.

The U.N. Research Institute for Social Development has long been preoccupied with such an effort and the 1972 study by McGranahan et al. is the most recent published summary of the work being done by UNRISD. Studies by Adelman and Morris, and by Chenery and Syrquin, are other major efforts. The three studies differ from one another in various ways, but they are similar not only in their effort to measure development (change) but also in the assumption —fundamental to their approaches—that economic development implies a "normal" or "optimal" pattern of interaction among social, economic, and (in the Adelman-Morris study) political factors.[39]

The assumption that there is some desirable or optimal pattern that can be described implies that planners can use the development measure as a diagnostic procedure for identifying impediments to progress and therefore as a tool for policy prescription.

> The correspondence system approach can serve to indicate to countries not only what their pattern of development is, compared with that of other countries at about the same general level of development, but also what pattern of development is normal at the next higher step of development—and therefore, in a sense, feasible, although typological and idiosyncratic features of the individual country must be taken into account . . . In other words, correspondence analysis provides background facts that may be usefully considered in planning and projections, along with other facts about current needs, stresses and strains, bottlenecks, etc.[40]

This type of measure is concerned primarily with development, not welfare. "The general index is not a measure of the level . . . of human welfare or happiness, or of a 'better life.' [41] This concern with development determines the methods of calculation and the range of component indicators selected.

Measures of Welfare

A second group of measurement efforts consists of those concerned with measuring what is happening to people relatively independent of national or social development.[42] There are two general types of such "welfare indicators." One type involves the use of subjective measures—measures of how people feel about economic growth. Are they happier? Do they feel more secure? There have been many such attitudinal investigations. The study by Campbell et al. is a recent example. A particularly imaginative study by Easterlin attempted to survey "human happiness" in nineteen developed and less developed countries since the end of World War II.[43]

The second type of welfare indicator attempts to measure welfare objectively rather than subjectively. The Physical Quality of Life Index falls into this group (although it includes far fewer components than most such welfare measures). Efforts to measure performance objectively go back a long time, but in their modern guise—with the possible exceptions of essays by Joseph S. Davis and M. K. Bennett—they have their beginnings with a report submitted by a U.N. Committee of Experts in 1954.[44] The Committee was instructed:

> . . . to prepare a report on the most satisfactory methods of defining and measuring standards of living and changes therein in the various countries, having regard to the possibility of international comparison. . . .

After exploring the problem very intensively, the Committee concluded that:

> . . . there is no single index of the level of living as a whole that can be applied internationally. . . . It was agreed that the problem of levels of living must be approached in a pluralistic manner by analysis of various components . . . and by the use of various statistical indicators. . . .

17

It was also agreed that, conceptually,

> . . . "non-material" as well as "material" factors should be included in the definition of levels of living; but that, in practice, comparative measurement of levels of living with regard to many "non-material" aspects, as in the case of those associated with differing cultural values, could not be meaningfully carried out.[45]

Efforts to find a composite index have foundered on a variety of difficulties: How to determine an adequate measure of welfare, how to quantify some of the components, how to establish international comparability, and so forth. Instead of continuing the research for a composite index, a group of international organizations in 1961 jointly prepared an interim guide identifying nine basic indicators of the level of living—health, food consumption and nutrition, education, employment and conditions of work, housing, social security, clothing, recreation, and human freedoms. It went no further than to ask countries to collect data describing these conditions.[46]

A decade later, the Organisation for Economic Co-operation and Development (OECD) established a Working Party on Social Indicators, which also has been unable to find a way to reflect the changing well-being of its member countries in a composite index incorporating the twenty-four common social concerns it identified. In fact, its 1976 progress report gloomily reported that "a single unitary 'social well-being' index serving the same summarization purpose as GNP with regard to a certain range of economic activities . . . has been ruled out as giving almost no information whatsoever."[47] Currently, OECD's activities are devoted to monitoring changes in the individual indicators. But the report went on to suggest that if a more modest and limited measure were sought, "a single-weighted indicator should not be ruled out prior to careful assessment."[48]

The U.N. Research Institute for Social Development has explored the possibilities of of creating two somewhat different composite measures. One would be a "level of living" index that would seek to measure the flow of goods and services affecting welfare, that is, it would be a measure of inputs. The other would be a "level of welfare" index that would measure the output of these activities, that is, the condition of the population. Jan Drewnowski has analyzed the accumulated experience of these efforts and has carefully explicated a great many of the problems facing those who seek to design a composite index.[49] The work on the PQLI has been conducted in the hope of avoiding the most treacherous pitfalls of which he and the UNRISD study warn.[50]

Normative Models

A third group of measurement efforts consists of "normative models." These establish minimal or basic human needs standards and then attempt to estimate what resources would be required to bring the world population to them within a specific period of time. Perhaps the most influential of these "world models" is that designed by the Fundacion Bariloche of Argentina. Another sophisticated effort is that formulated by Wassily Leontief and his associates. These normative models are not primarily concerned with measures of specific status or overall progress, although this could ultimately emerge from their efforts.[51]

4 The PQLI Components: Why These?

"Would you tell me, please, which way I ought to go from here?" said Alice. "That depends a good deal on where you want to get to," said the Cheshire Cat.

—Lewis Carroll
Alice in Wonderland

As noted in Chapter 1, there has been a growing awareness of the urgency of meeting basic needs. This concern has introduced added elements into development considerations. An important statement about the basic needs approach —although only one of many statements that have been made in national and international forums—was that made at the 1976 World Employment Conference. The "Declaration of Principles and Programme of Action" adopted at that Conference stated that:

Strategies and national development plans and policies should include explicitly as a priority objective the promotion of employment and the satisfaction of the basic needs of each country's population.

Basic needs, as understood in this Programme of Action, include two elements. First, they include certain minimum requirements of a family for private consumption: adequate food, shelter and clothing, as well as certain household equipment and furniture. Second, they include essential services provided by and for the community at large, such as safe drinking water, sanitation, public transport and health, educational and cultural facilities.

A basic-needs-oriented policy implies the participation of the people in making the decisions which affect them through organizations of their own choice.

In all countries freely chosen employment enters into a basic needs policy both as a means and as an end. Employment yields an output. It provides an income to the employed, and gives the individual a feeling of self-respect, dignity and of being a worthy member of society.

It is important to recognize that the concept of basic needs is a country-specific and dynamic concept. The concept of basic needs should be placed within a context of a nation's over-all economic and social development. In no circumstances should it be taken to mean merely the minimum necessary for subsistence; it should be placed within a context of national independence, the dignity of individuals and people and their freedom to chart their destiny without hindrance.[52]

Once development strategies incorporate more than GNP targets, the problem becomes one of measuring the extent to which progress is being made in moving toward those additional goals. It is intuitively obvious that no single quantitative measure can capture the complexity and subtlety of the basic needs concept even for a single country, much less for the diversity of countries in the international community. But can the measurable elements of the basic human needs concept be captured? The quarter century of effort by various U.N. agencies, by the Organisation for Economic Co-operation and Development, by the U.N. Research Institute for Social Development, and other groups and individuals testifies to the difficulty of creating any index of "measurable welfare" in the broad sense. Despite this disheartening experience, it is still possible that a somewhat less ambitious objective—a measure that does not try to incorporate everything of "measurable welfare"—may be attainable, particularly if the primary concern is to measure the performance of the poorest countries.

Previous efforts have tried to incorporate into a single measure a large number of indicators applicable to all countries, rich and poor. The sheer number of indicators has proved to be an intractable obstacle, while the effort to incorporate the welfare performance of high-income as well as low-income countries has made it difficult to think about reducing the number of indicators. In contrast, the focus here on the poorest countries and people makes emphasizing some of the most immediate aspects of "welfare" possible.[53]

Criteria for a Composite Indicator

Six criteria that a composite measure of international socio-economic performance should meet were established at the outset of this effort.

1. It should not assume that there is only one pattern of development.
2. It should avoid standards that reflect the values of specific societies.
3. It should measure results, not inputs.
4. It should be able to reflect the distribution of social results.
5. It should be simple to construct and easy to comprehend.
6. It should lend itself to international comparison.

Need for Unethnocentric Measures

In order for a composite measure to be unethnocentric, each of the component indicators must allow for differences in cultural experience and social institutions; they must be as pan-human as possible. Yet discussions about development easily fall into two general ethnocentric fallacies: 1) the assumption that the paths and consequences of development will be the same for today's developing countries as they were for the countries that industrialized in the late nineteenth and early twentieth centuries; and 2) the assumption that "basic human needs" are defined by all societies in the same way.

The Uni-Evolutionary Bias. The poor countries not only are vastly different from "developed" countries, but also are enormously diverse among themselves. Yet there is a tendency to minimize that diversity and to assume that countries that are economically less developed are merely underdeveloped versions of industrialized countries. Marx's famous statement that the "country that is more developed industrially only shows, to the less developed, the image of its own future" is widely assumed to be true.[54] A classic modern version of this sentiment is found in Rostow's *Stages of Economic Growth* and pervades the work of Adelman and Morris as well as that of McGranahan et al.[55] According to this formulation, whatever the differences among countries, the development process requires certain preconditions and generates certain inevitable consequences. This assumption of comparability motivates many policy judgments.

> Such comparisons also are useful for policy purposes at the international and national levels. . . . Without internationally comparable income, output, and expenditure indicators, it is difficult to use the experience of wealthier countries to anticipate the time pattern of the changes that may be expected to occur in the development of the poorer ones. . . . One evidence of the widespread feeling of need for international comparisons of the kind offered here is the fact that so many organizations concerned with international economic problems have attempted to produce their own estimates of per capita income relationships between countries.[56]

How much like Marx's comment:

> One nation can and should learn from others. And even when a society has got upon the right track for the discovery of the natural laws of its movement . . . it can neither clear by bold leaps, nor remove by legal enactments, the obstacles offered by the successive phases of its normal development. But it can shorten and lessen the birth-pangs.[57]

In the search for alternative strategies, it is important to stress the differentness, the diversity, among developing countries because the diversity of experiences can lead to new theories about development evolution and about the measurement of welfare performance. At this stage, it is sufficient to distinguish three major types of developing countries—one with essentially modern economic structures, another with institutions mainly derived from village economies, and another historically rooted in tribal systems.

The first type consists of those developing countries whose historical involvement in urban and international economic activities in the nineteenth and twentieth centuries has been sufficiently pervasive to produce essentially modern economic structures throughout much of their societies. The bulk of their productive activity is carried on through the market. These countries have modern public and private institutions, including highly integrated urban links with the countryside, that can mobilize resources for development purposes. Some sectors within these countries are quite efficient by world standards. There is deep poverty but it is largely confined to specific groups, often ethnically, culturally, and/or geographically distinct. They have had periods (not necessarily recently) when per capita GNP grew rapidly, but the benefits of this growth seem to have been fairly narrowly shared. One might call this the "Latin American model," because many Latin American countries fit this pattern—e.g., Argentina, Brazil, Chile, Mexico. But other countries also fit the model; among them are South Africa, Lebanon (before the current conflicts), and possibly Turkey. Although it is the structure of the economies and not the level of per capita income that is the distinguishing criterion, the 1970-75 per capita incomes of these countries were more than $300, typically ranging between $500 and $2,000 (see Appendix B, Table 1, for a ranking of countries according to per capita GNP). For the most part, policies that would solve the problems of poor minorities in rich countries should be appropriate for these developing countries, even though the difficulties of getting them adopted might be greater because of the extremely sharp socio-political differences within them.[58]

The second and third types of developing countries both fall into the so-called "Fourth World" category of countries. They are not just slow starters in the economic growth race. They tend to have very low incomes and to be poor in a way that was not true of today's rich countries in their early development stages. The 1.2 billion people living in the forty-two countries with 1970-75 per capita incomes under $300 had an average per capita income of $155. This is well below the present value of per capita income in Great Britain and the United States two hundred years ago.[59]

Within the Fourth World, there seem to be two distinctive types of countries. On the one hand, there are countries, mainly in South and Southeast Asia but also in North Africa, which historically have been organized to facilitate the bureaucratic extraction of social surpluses from relatively densely settled village systems and therefore typically have long-sustained urban traditions. This social structure depended for its working on groups of literate people. While the proportion of literates in the total population may have been small, their roles were crucial to these societies' functioning. On the other hand, there are countries—largely in sub-Saharan Africa but also including Afghanistan and many Arab Middle East countries—that historically were tribally organized. Complex urban organizations and literate bureaucratic infrastructures were not decisive to the functioning of such societies.

These vastly different historical experiences have contemporary significance. The modern development potentials of the two types of Fourth World countries are defined by vastly different sets of institutional capacities and characteristics and, of necessity, call for quite distinctive solutions. The differences among developing countries make it necessary to exercise considerable caution in selecting indicators, for these need to be appropriate to the enormously diverse conditions.

Not only do the poor countries begin with different backgrounds and institutions, they also will not necessarily follow either the development path of today's rich countries or the path of those developing countries already somewhat more advanced—today's "Third World." The developing countries' evolution certainly will be significantly influenced by modern energy, transport, and communications technologies very different from those that were available in the nineteenth and early twentieth centuries and that shaped the economic characteristics and patterns of now-developed countries. Moreover, the long-run implications of these influences will be intensified to the extent that the newly emerging labor-intensive strategies shape strategic development choices.

With different histories and factor proportions and different available technologies, it is likely that economic and social organization will be quite different in newly developing countries than in those already developed. For example, *rates* of urbanization may increase much more slowly and then level off with a smaller proportion of the population urbanized than is the case in most presently developed countries. Whether or not such a pattern emerges, the possibility alone cautions against selecting indicators based on the assumption that developing countries necessarily will develop along the same evolutionary path as rich countries. Measures linked to specific levels or rates of urbanization or to specific patterns of large-scale industrialization—that is, all transport, communication, energy consumption, and production measures—are inappropriate.

This implies, for example, that Latin America is probably not an appropriate region from which to derive development lessons of value for African and Asian countries. Latin America has been linked to the North Atlantic industrial nucleus for centuries and its current pattern of economic characteristics was shaped by that connection over many generations. Thus the fact that Latin America is now about 60 percent urban is not proof that Asian and African countries are destined to move to the same end in the foreseeable future. It is true that urban areas in Fourth World countries are growing absolutely, but only because population in general is also growing. Relatively, these countries are not becoming urban at a rapid pace. For example, as late as 1977, African countries on average still were only 24 percent urban and the sub-Saharan countries were less than 20 percent urbanized. The countries of South and Southeast Asia were only slightly more than 20 percent urban.[60] This is not to suggest that developing systems necessarily will remain entirely agricultural but that more labor-intensive policies may leave industry relatively more rural than was historically true in developed countries.

The Value Bias. The second ethnocentric fallacy into which those concerned with development frequently fall is to set up standards of performance that represent only the value choices of their own systems. To distinguish characteristics that are physiologically necessary, that are truly basic and minimum needs, from those merely valued by one's culture, is extremely difficult. Even the most sensitive observers or standard-setters are capable of gaucheries. For example, Gunnar Myrdal, bewailing the poverty of the region, wrote:

> Large numbers of South Asians have only one set of clothing which is seldom washed, except in bathing. Typically, the same clothes are worn day and night since pyjamas and even underwear are luxuries a great many people can ill afford. The hygienic consequences are easy to imagine.[61]

The distinguished Indian anthropologist T.N. Madan, reflecting on this statement, commented:

> Nobody is likely to dispute the poverty of Asia or the inadequacy of clothing and other necessities of life in these countries. But why do South Asians have to wear *pyjama* suits and underwear? Are these European-style garments a relevant yardstick for tropical Asia? Cannot an Indian sleep in his *kurta* and *dhoti*—his working clothes—and yet be *clean* and *comfortable?* It is indeed a pity that one who pleads for the institutional approach and draws attention to the "unique properties" of Asian economies and social systems, should disregard one of the elementary maxims of comparative sociology, namely, that which warns against ethnocentrism. Myrdal's not infrequent failure to practice the excellent principles that he proclaims should make the reader ponder over the over-whelming nature of the attempted task.[62]

Myrdal also exhibited his ethnocentricity when he wrote:

> Few people, particularly in the poorer classes, have shoes or even sandals. Children up to the age of seven or so often wear practically nothing when at home; beyond this age many wear only a piece of cloth covering the hips and thighs.[63]

It is true that the Old Testament refers to the sin of going naked before one's Lord and that Winston Churchill expressed his strong sense of what is appropriate human choice in matters of dress when he sneered at Gandhi as a "half-naked Fakir." Yet it is as much a matter of culture as poverty that leads many South Asians, rich as well as poor, to go without shoes or sandals or to have young children running about with "practically nothing" on.[64]

How does one select indicators that reflect the extent to which basic human desires are truly being met without being ethnocentric? Clothing standards are certainly not alone in reflecting specific values so pervasive as to make it impossible to characterize a basic human requirement. Housing patterns, too, are likely to reflect specific cultural standards—the amount of space required, the uses to which space is put, the facilities found within the house, even the material of which the house is made. The attempt to measure the presence of specific features like space, number of rooms, or their use is not likely to yield satisfactory indicators of basic well-being in developing countries. The fact that urban elites in many developing countries value housing facilities similar to our own does not say anthing about whether these are needed to achieve reasonable standards of living; it merely proves how westernized these elites are. Some have become accustomed to air-conditioning, even though traditional housing designed and constructed according to indigenous standards can be at least as satisfactory on all counts except the amount of capital equipment installed.

Another problem with international dwelling standards is that they almost invariably specify permanence of construction. Such standards frequently appear to have been selected primarily for definitional convenience, and they also ignore the fact that in flood- or earthquake-prone poor countries lightly constructed shelters may be much more rational and appropriate solutions.[65]

Similar ethnocentricity is exhibited in health and nutrition standards. The substantial death rate declines in the nineteenth and twentieth centuries resulted mainly from general environmental improvements and from extension of basic public health facilities. The major declines in the death rate since World War II— certainly in developing countries and possibly in developed countries—seem to have come in similar ways and to have had little to do with improvements in medical training or hospital facilities. While the United States has chosen to distribute health services through elaborate urban medical facilities and highly trained doctors, most of the gains in life expectancy and health did not require such a costly solution. The adoption by poor countries of the current U.S. pattern of medical organization will lead, because of distorted resource use, to less, rather than more, general health improvement in both urban and rural areas.

Poor countries could get substantial reductions in mortality and improvements in health with simple arrangements that do not require highly trained medical personnel and elaborate institutions for delivery of services. The experience of many areas has shown that health improvements can result largely from the development of efficient administrative capacity. The concern with results rather than inputs makes the extent to which favorable results can be achieved more efficiently, with fewer inputs, a positive feature. It makes indicators that measure the number of hospital beds, physicians per thousand population, or expenditures on health services totally unsatisfactory ways of determining the health record of a poor country.[66]

Nutritional standards also tend to be highly ethnocentric. One finds this in the calorie standards that are set as "minimum" or "optimum," the diet composition defined as necessary for "good health," and the physical evidences considered to manifest good health. While it is often said that "calorie requirement standards can be determined with fair precision," in fact, authorities are not agreed on what calorie requirements are. Moreover, figures are defined as "required," "optimal," "minimum necessary," or in some other, equally vague way. It is never clear what any particular level of calories maximizes: life expectancy, physical vigor or size, intellectual and/or emotional capacities. Moreover, it is not obvious that the same calorie intakes or the same dietary compositions maximize each of these desired ends.

Whatever figure is given for daily calorie requirements in developing countries–2,450, 2,250, 2,000, or some other number–the implication frequently is that at that level of intake and above (allowing for proteins, etc.) one is healthy and below that level one is dying. Except for the fact that we are all dying from the day we are born, this assertion is clearly unrealistic. Unless the figure given is intended as an absolutely basic minimum survival boundry (whatever that may mean), one is really dealing with a spectrum; in setting nutritional standards, this should be kept in mind. The problem takes on a complicated character, even at an abstract level. Any single body weight may have a range of potential requirements. Moreover, in the short-run and particularly in the long-run, body weights seem to adjust to available calories in a variety of ways. There appears to be a series of complex adaptations of weight, calorie intake, and performance that are consistent with what might be considered "reasonable functioning."[67]

Current standards of calorie requirement still seem to be quite ethnocentric, despite recent attempts to make adjustments. In the past, standards were based on values held in Europe and North America. Recently they have been adjusted somewhat for sex, size, age, and climate. But it appears that a "Western" model continues to lurk in the background, serving as the implicit standard for levels of energy intake, types of diet, and timing of energy intake and output. Expected rates of physical growth and ultimate size almost never take the significance of genetic differences into consideration. And whether they do or do not, measures tend to place great stress on speed of growth and on attaining large (i.e., Western) body size. Yet there is no obvious reason why people should be considered healthier or better off just because they grow faster as children or end up bigger as adults. Small can be beautiful! There is no evidence that smallness of size is necessarily a disadvantage for effective living. In fact, small size may be a favorable element that contributes to longer life.

Ethnocentricity exhibits itself in a variety of other ways. For example, nutritional standards generally still contain the implication that meat proteins are preferable to vegetable proteins, which tend to be considered less satisfactory even though there is no worthwhile evidence of this.[68] Such nutritional ethnocentricity is found not only in views of what is appropriate to eat, but also in how it should be eaten. Put crudely, official standards tend to emphasize the necessity of three square meals per day and a three-period, eight-hour work, recreation, and rest pattern. They tend to ignore the great adaptability of the human body and to confuse cultural behavior with physiological necessity.

Need to Measure Results

The discussion of nutrition raises an important methodological point: Indicators should measure results not inputs. After all, some poor economies have been able to get fairly impressive "welfare" results from relatively low per capita expenditures. Like per capita GNP, other input measures simply are not adequate measures of distributive performance.

For some purposes, information about inputs is essential. But if the aim is to learn about the effectiveness of an expenditure, it is important to know how much mortality or morbidity were reduced or literacy was increased. If, for example, death rates are reduced very dramatically through the introduction of inexpensive "barefoot doctors," medical care should not be considered inadequate because there are no swollen budgets for health or costly hospitals and medical facilities.[69]

This seems like an obvious proposition about which there would be no question; yet one of the major defects of "basic needs" and "welfare" measures has been the tendency to mix indicators that reflect input and results. The use of calories available or consumed is a prevalent case in point, since it is probably the most popular and widely used non-monetary indicator of well-being. Its use has been based on the assumption that there is a close relationship between calorie intake and health and other characteristics of well-being. In fact, however, per capita calorie consumption in various countries does not correlate well either with average per capita GNP or with other, more direct physical measures of well-being at any moment in time.[70] Moreover, there is little evidence that the number of calories consumed in any one country changes significantly over time or that, when it does change, it does so in systematic relation to changes in either income or life expectancy. For example, total calorie consumption in Japan appears to have remained low and surprisingly stable during much of the post-Tokugawa era, despite the steady rise in per capita income.[71] On the other hand, some widely accepted evidence suggests that per capita food grain availability in India declined steadily between World War I and 1947, while life expectancy rose steadily during that same period.[72] While the accuracy of the evidence that shows declining per capita food grain availability in India is subject to question, this does raise a provocative point that strengthens the argument against using nutrition intake as an indicator.

Suppose ways could be developed to make people longer-lived and healthier with lower calorie intakes; would this be treated as success or failure? Obviously, it would be a success if the objective is to make people healthier and longer-lived. It would not be a success if eating is considered a good thing in its own right. Some might suggest that improving life expectancy and health, while reducing calorie intake, is only possible among people like Americans, who consume 3,300-3,400 calories per day, and that it would not be possible to achieve favorable life quality results among people who consume less than 2,400 calories a day. Yet evidence shows that Indian life expectancy, for example, is rising, while average daily per capita calorie consumption remains relatively stable at about 1,900 to 2,100 calories. Sri Lanka clearly has reduced its mortality and morbidity rates in the past thirty years, and its population continues to consume an average of only 1,900 to 2,200 calories a day.[73]

This is not intended to suggest that all societies can reduce calorie consumption to that level—the relation of nutrition to all other components of social existence is far too complex for that—but it does suggest that calorie consumption is not a very good indicator of well-being. In addition to the issues already noted, there are awesome data problems, including considerable understatement of the diets of the very poor, distortions of intra-family distributions, and a neglect of inventories. Measuring the actual results is likely to be a more useful approach.[74]

Need to Reflect Distribution

Not only must indicators designed to measure the extent to which the world's benefits are flowing to the very poorest groups in very poor countries be relatively unethnocentric and reflect results, they also must be sensitive to distribution effects. As noted in Chapter 1, this has become a major policy concern of development planners. Two different distributional concerns have to be kept in mind: the distribution of benefits within countries and the distribution of benefits among countries.

GNP does not capture distributional features very well. Per capita GNP is merely an arithmetic average that does not provide information about the actual distribution of the product among groups. Intra-country GNP analysis is encumbered by many difficulties, of which the major ones are the questions of whether to measure wealth, income (current or permanent), or consumption, and whether the appropriate unit of measurement is the individual, the family, or the household. International comparisons are further afflicted by the standard problems of price comparison and the probably insoluble difficulties posed by social and economic structural differences among countries.[75]

Need for Simplicity

Another criterion for measures of international socio-economic performance is that of simplicity. A composite indicator should be relatively simple to construct and simple to comprehend. Simplicity of construction implies 1) that the data required for the individual indicators must be relatively easy to collect and process, 2) that the data represent information that all societies need to collect if they are even to pretend to be modern states, and 3) that the composite measure not require more precision than the components already being used by governments for administrative purposes.

There is no point to a composite index that is difficult to understand; comprehensibility is its main justification. A variety of individual indicators that provide information about social performance already exist; however, change in the individual measures takes place at different rates, thus making it difficult for policymakers to measure the total effectiveness of their efforts. A composite index offers, as does GNP, a measure that summarizes many aspects of performance. But it must be presented in a form that is not difficult to grasp and that allows changes to have some easily understood meaning.

Need for International Comparability

The final requirement for indicators used to measure socio-economic performance is that they lend themselves to international comparison. International comparability is important for a number of purposes. It permits international aid-givers to set general standards for concessional assistance as well as to set targets for performance. Moreover, comparability makes it possible to identify countries with different performance rates and to study the possibility of transferring techniques from good to slow performers. If the measures are not ethnocentric, they usually meet this criterion.

Three Indicators Meet the Criteria

Improving the well-being of the very poorest people and the very poorest countries cannot be achieved in any reasonable period merely by increasing GNP. Even among the twenty-two fastest growing developing countries—those with populations of one million or more whose growth rate in per capita income exceeded that of the OECD countries during the period 1960 to 1975—only eight could close the gap between themselves and the average of the OECD countries in less than one hundred years and only sixteen could close it within one thousand years![76]

While these numbers may be deceptive for a number of reasons, it nevertheless is obvious that a strategy designed to maximize economic growth as currently measured will not provide poor people in poor countries with great benefits in the foreseeable future. However, there do seem to be strategies with which it is possible to provide many of the basic elements of a decent existence before incomes have risen very much.

In their various attempts to measure development and/or welfare, the U.N. committees, the U.N. Research Institute for Social Development, Adelman and Morris, and the Organisation for Economic Co-operation and Development have made use of well over one hundred indicators.[77] Excluding those that are solely measures of political or economic development leaves only a small number. Of these, only three—infant mortality, life expectancy, and basic literacy—meet the criteria set out above; these are the components of the composite Physical Quality of Life Index. Let us consider these as well as others that were rejected.

1. *None of the three measures assumes any particular pattern of development or depends in any way on a particular organization of the economy.* A system can be non-market, non-urban, non-industrial, and still generate a high PQLI rating. Moreover, the measures bypass the very formidable problems of

valuation that make GNP comparisons between centrally planned and market economies so difficult.

2. *The three indicators are probably as unethnocentric as it is possible to get in an imperfect world.* The infant mortality measure assumes that, generally speaking, people everywhere would prefer that newborn children not die. The life expectancy measure assumes that people prefer to live longer rather than shorter lives. While there are some subtle issues about the ideology of choices that are bypassed—"A short life but a merry one"; "better to die on one's feet as a free person than to live on one's knees as a slave"; "the good die young"— these seem to raise difficulties only at very high levels of abstraction. One can reasonably conclude that such epigramatic summations would reflect less well-being than the following variants: "A long life *and* a merry one"; "better to live on one's feet as a free person than to live on one's knees as a slave"; "the good die young—whenever they die."

Some suggest that longer life expectancy may be accompanied by more frequent and more debilitating illnesses. Even if this were true, however, it probably would not diminish the general preference of humans to take their chances with life rather than death. Moreover, what little evidence there is does not support the view that a reduction of the death rate merely increases the morbidity rate because the weak are preserved.[78]

Some societies have had biases against universal literacy; the ability to read and write historically has been the monopoly of privileged groups. This is a bias that seems to be dwindling swiftly in the case of males, but there are still many societies in which the feelings against female literacy remain fairly strong. While it can be said that lower infant mortality and higher life expectancy are objectives generally regarded as good by societies everywhere, this still cannot be said of literacy. Nevertheless, literacy is now an objective to which every national society has committed itself in principle. If it is not really a universally accepted value, it comes close.[79]

But literacy as an indicator of well-being poses another difficulty. Is it an end in itself or is it a means by which all other ends are satisfied? There is no obvious answer. To accept literacy as an end requires a somewhat arbitrary choice, but one that has a reasonable justification if the aim is to measure benefits going to the very poorest groups. To the extent that social participation and control over one's environment represent desirable goods in themselves, widespread basic literacy can be seen as a measure (and expression) of expanded power and improved status, which are probably desired by increasing numbers of poor people.[80]

Of course, it can be argued that literacy may serve as a subtle instrument that enables the powerful to dominate the lower orders with a minimum of physical coercion. One can push such conundrums to the point of total relativism that would make all international (and interpersonal) comparisons, including GNP comparisons, impossible. This is not the place to explore such a fundamental issue; it is enough to recognize that living is a dangerous affair, carrying the possibility of enslavement as well as freedom. But comparisons *are* made and the three indicators—literacy, infant mortality, and life expectancy—raise fewer difficulties of international and inter-cultural comparison than others.

3. *Each of the three indicators measures results, not inputs.* By focussing on what really happens, national policymakers may be given greater stimulus to innovate along lines that are more consistent with indigenous capacities and therefore more efficient at meeting the basic needs of the very poorest groups.

4. *Each of the measures is fairly sensitive to distribution effects.* Per capita GNP is an arithmetic mean that says nothing about the actual distribution of income in a country; a country's income could be distributed quite equally or be concentrated among a small number of people. For example, an average per capita income of $1,000 could be distributed in either of the ways shown below:

	Country A	*Country B*
Richest 20%	96%	20%
Second 20%	1%	20%
Third 20%	1%	20%
Fourth 20%	1%	20%
Poorest 20%	1%	20%

Moreover, any increase in per capita income could also be distributed in a variety of ways.[81]

While the three indicators do not in themselves explicitly identify how the benefits they reflect are distributed among social groups at any moment, an improvement in these indicators means that the *proportion* of the people sharing the benefit almost certainly has risen. This is quite obvious with infant mortality and literacy. Individuals cannot accumulate what is measured by either of these indicators. Each is an "either-or" measure. An infant either lives or dies; a person either does or does not meet the basic literacy standard. An improvement in either of the indicators means that the benefit that indicator reflects has become more widespread and thus the distribution more equal.

Life expectancy is a different kind of indicator. It is the estimated average number of years a person of a given age—age one in this case—can be expected to live, using the current schedule of age-specific mortality. (The PQLI uses life expectancy at age one in order to avoid double counting the infant mortality rate.) Social equality does not necessarily mean that everyone has the same life span; rather, everyone has equal life chances and there are no socio-economic differences in the *proportion* of people who die at each age. In other words, if 10 percent of the population dies between ages 26 and 30, equality requires that 10 percent of the rich and 10 percent of the poor die. An example of inequality in life expectancy would be a country with a population of ten people, where the 80 percent who are poor die at the age of twenty-five while the 20 percent who are rich die at the age of one hundred. Average life expectancy in such a situation would be forty years.[82] While it may be conceivable for improvements in life expectancy to be captured entirely by the rich, there are at least three reasons (two arithmetic and one substantive) why this is not very likely.

(a) There is a realistic upper limit to average life expectancy. If the rich people already have attained it there is no way for them to add more years to their lives. The only way to increase life expectancy is for the 80 percent who are poor to live longer.

(b) Even if the rich in developing countries also have relatively low life expectancies (lower than have been achieved elsewhere) and therefore have the possibility of increasing life expectancy (by buying a superior social infra-structure for themselves), the rich constitute so small a group that an increase in their life expectancy is not likely to have a very great effect on the overall average. In the example above, where the rich constitute 20 percent of the population, a five-year increase in their life expectancy raises the society's average by one year, while an equivalent increase in the life expectancy of the poor raises the society's average life expectancy by four years.

(c) The major declines in mortality in the last two centuries have come mainly via declines in the impact of infectious diseases. The evidence suggests that these improvements have not come from developments that were very income elastic within societies. The improvements either have been innovations that have been almost equally accessible to rich and poor (smallpox vaccination) or they have depended on societal efforts—e.g., providing clean water or spraying DDT to eliminate malaria-carrying mosquitoes—from which it was hard to exclude the poor. Major reductions in mortality seem to result not from individual choice but from a social process. Even today the rich cannot really buy themselves enough isolation—as many Americans living in countries with high death rates have discovered to their dismay—to free themselves from the social relations that effectively determine their society's life expectancy rate.[83]

The three indicators can be thought of as measuring one form of *human* capital or another. This discussion implicitly has emphasized the distribution of these characteristics within a single generation. Ahluwalia stresses another important distributional aspect, the intergenerational significance of any improvement in such indicators.

> There is a limit beyond which human capital cannot be accumulated in a single person, and at any rate it cannot be bequeathed across generations in the same manner as physical capital. Both factors . . . combine to generate strong pressures toward equality in income distribution as the human resource endowment expands. . . . [84]

While one need not accept Ahluwalia's strong statement of the significance of the limitations on intergenerational transfers of human capital, his point reinforces the view that the three component indicators of the PQLI do capture distributive features in the social process.

5. *The three indicators fit the requirements of simplicity and comprehensibility quite well.* No social data are truly simple to comprehend, but these indicators are more straightforward than most others. They probably are less ambiguous than almost any other available indicators. This means that the components individually are fairly easy to understand and suggests that the composite index is also likely to be relatively easy to understand.

Equally important, the indicators are based on information which all governments must gather if they even pretend to apply any self-conscious economic or social policy whatsoever. Gathering these data therefore does not impose novel or extraordinary burdens on poor countries. The overriding problem is that poor countries do not have facilities to collect any data very well, but is is no more difficult—in fact, probably easier—to collect data on infant mortality, life expectancy, and literacy than, for example, on many of the components from which GNP is constructed. The fact that GNP data seem to be available in greater profusion and with higher levels of apparent precision is not proof that they are easier to come by; during the past quarter century there has been a formidable international effort to collect them. This collection effort has been complemented by a sustained search for agreement on conventions by which inferior data are to be used. A similar effort to get mortality, life expectancy, and literacy data should produce results at least as satisfactory.[85]

6. *The individual indicators lend themselves to international comparison.* Infant mortality and life expectancy involve technical definitions of life and death that can be applied to all humans without regard to culture. Literacy is different in that it reflects personal control over an individual skill in a particular culture. However, the literacy standards established by individual countries in cooperation with such organizations as the U.N. Educational, Scientific, and Cultural Organization (UNESCO) produce ratios comparable among countries.[86]

What Do the Three Indicators Show?

As noted, the prime objective of this effort is to measure the performance of the world's poorest countries in meeting the most basic needs of people. The PQLI is not concerned with the methods by which results are achieved but only with the results themselves. If improved performance is attained without any increase in GNP, this is not of immediate concern. If better results can be obtained without any improvement in diet or increase in calorie availability, this, too, is not of immediate concern. On the other hand, if the index shows that for any given level of per capita income or calorie intake, various national policies yield different PQLI results, this is of interest.

It is important to stress the fact that the PQLI is deliberately designed not to give weight to inputs, to effort, or to good intentions. By focussing on results, the index can identify countries that have used simple and inexpensive means of obtaining welfare improvements. This may encourage those who think about development to think more radically about alternative strategies. This does not imply that the PQLI is fully satisfactory as it stands. Further research may suggest refinements, other indicators, or ways to link the PQLI with such existing measures as GNP. But until that research is done, the index should be left to measure changes in elemental welfare; no attempt should be made to incorporate inputs or to measure "development."

The Physical Quality of Life Index is a limited measure. It makes no attempt to incorporate the many other social and psychological characteristics suggested by the term "quality of life"—security, justice, freedom of choice, human rights, employment, satisfaction, etc. Thus it is labelled a *physical* quality of life index, even though there is some question about calling literacy (and what it represents) a physical feature of existence. The name helps to indicate the narrowness of the target.

But why were these particular indicators picked? What does the PQLI measure? Life expectancy at age one and infant mortality appear to be very good indicators of the results of the total social process. They sum up the combined effects of social relations, nutritional status, public health, and family environment. To the extent that income and calorie intake do result in life and death changes, they show up in infant mortality and life expectancy rates. It can even be argued that these two indicators also reflect such subjective features as social order, personal satisfaction, etc.

While infant mortality rates and life expectancy data may appear to measure the same thing—i.e., "health"—they in fact reflect quite different aspects of social performance. The specific factors that seem to account for changes in life expectancy after age one apparently are not the same as those that affect infant mortality. The historical performance of the two indicators has been quite different. For example, while mortality rates of people over age one generally were declining in many Western countries during the second half of the nineteenth century, infant mortality rates remained notoriously resistent to improvement. The rapid decline of infant death rates generally was a separate and later process. The pattern differed among countries and even among regions within the same country. Whatever the sources of improvement in survival capacity—the environment, nutrition, education, medicine, or income—they did not affect every age group in the same way or at the same rate.[87] Today life expectancy and infant mortality performances continue to vary widely. As the data in Appendix A show, countries that have similar life expectancies do not always have the same infant mortality rates and vice versa.[88]

Mortality is greatest in all countries at the extremes of age. Risks of death are greatest during the early years of life and then begin to fall very rapidly. They reach their lowest from about age five until mid-forties and then start to rise rapidly. There has been very little success in reducing the causes of death that occur in old age. This means that the death-rate differences among countries are due mainly to differences in mortality rates before age forty-five. Variations in infant mortality rates typically are a major cause of the difference. For example, although European countries differ widely among themselves, they generally have infant mortalities of less than 30 deaths per thousand live births. Developing countries, on the other hand, tend to have rates ranging between 100 and 200 deaths per thousand live births. Countries with low death rates have virtually eliminated infectious, parasitic, and respiratory diseases that were great killers of people in young and middle age. However, not all developing countries have the same pattern of very high infant mortalities with sharply declining death rates thereafter. For example, tropical countries, particularly in Africa, show higher expectation of death among children aged one to five than among infants.[89]

But even among countries with more or less similar death rates, the pattern of deaths may vary quite considerably. For example, northern European countries have infant mortalities ranging from a low of 8 deaths per thousand live births for Sweden to 17 for Ireland. The United Kingdom and the United States have rates of 16 deaths per thousand live births. In the United States, this relatively high infant mortality rate is not caused entirely by high rates among blacks and other minorities; the mortality rate of white infants in the United States is at least 50 percent higher than the infant mortality rate of Sweden.[90]

Each society apparently kills its people differently, with particular diseases having different impacts in each system.[91] Improvements and innovations have not reduced average death rates equally for all age groups. For example, a large part of the great declines in mortality have come from the suppression of smallpox, cholera, malaria, typhoid, and plague. Each has its own age-group and sex-specific impact.[92]

Death patterns differ not only among age, ethnic, and racial groupings within a society, but also among regions. In the early nineteenth century, cities were apparently extra harsh killers of people. In our day, it is, even in many developing countries, probably healthier to live in cities than in the countryside.

Mortality patterns also vary by sex. For example, in most parts of the world, females have a longer life expectancy than males; the death rate of females also is lower than that of males at most, if not all, ages. In South Asia and in some other parts of the world, however, this is not true. While this exception frequently is attributed to childbearing practices, the age-specific evidence does not completely support this conclusion. In South Asia, being female generally entails considerable risk.[93] That this is probably due to the ways societies function at particular times rather than to physiological characteristics is suggested not only by differences elsewhere in our own day, but also by changes over time. For example, the higher female death rate in adolescence and early adulthood in England and Wales before 1890 resulted mainly from the higher incidence of tuberculosis in girls than in boys.[94]

Knowledge of the causes of death and of declining death rates is, to put the matter moderately, less than satisfactory.

When the experts search for an explanation of *how* the conquest of group 1 (infectious, parasitic and respiratory) diseases was brought about, it turns out to be a highly complex and intricate problem. The quick and easy answer would be, of course, "improved public health and medical care," but some of the facts fail to support this as a complete explanation. The more carefully one studies the situation, the more one realizes that almost every major accomplishment of "industrialization" helps to bring about a reduction in mortality.[95]

Despite the uncertainty surrounding the precise social characteristics of death rates, some conclusions are suggested by the evidence. Mortality during the first year tends to be set off from other periods not only because it is so important in determining a society's total mortality pattern, but because infant mortality tends to be "due to a peculiar set of diseases and conditions to which the adult population is less exposed and less vulnerable."[96] Broadly speaking, infant mortality is a combination of two types of causes: 1) the genetic, biological, and other factors that operate upon the infant mainly before, during, and in the weeks just after birth, and 2) the factors that affect the infant in the weeks and months thereafter. The former—what Bourgeois-Pichat has called endogenic causes[97]—are not the result of narrowly defined genetic elements but reflect to a very large extent what is happening to the mother while the child is *in utero*. During infancy, patterns that affect feeding and rearing, specifically those reflected in maternal and family practices, are extremely important. This suggests that infant mortality is a reflection of specific environmental influences and family characteristics, a great part of which are affected by the role and position of women. Beyond infancy, life expectancy at age one is an indicator of the much broader and all-embracing environmental impact on life and death chances.[98]

It has been suggested that the death rate of children up to five years of age, rather than the infant mortality rate, should be used as one of the PQLI components. This would combine infant mortality and the worst period of child mortality in a single indicator. It would, however, blur the specific social causes that distinguish infant deaths from other deaths.

Studies have shown that infant mortality is not a more adequate predictor of overall mortality conditions than are other age-specific measures or is life expectancy itself. The widespread impression that infant mortality is a satisfactory measure of a population's total mortality (or vice versa) derives in large part from the homogenizing effects of two widely employed techniques. The model life tables developed by the United Nations and by Coale-Demeny both impose highly structured relationships between infant and other age-group mortalities despite the fact that these relationships vary widely among countries.[99] Moreover, estimates of mortality rates are built on the assumption that the experience of the developing countries will resemble that of the already developed. This assumption reinforces the standardizing effects of the model life tables.[100]

The literacy indicator provides information about the potential for development and the extent to which poor groups can share the possibilities and advantages of development activity. A very large proportion of people (including whole societies) existed without literacy for a great part of the world's history. But a world that depends on increasing productivity to raise levels of well-being requires increasing specialization and division of labor, albeit not necessarily of the sort that emerged in the North Atlantic world after 1750. Increased specialization requires increased literacy. Whatever specific form economic organization takes, those in a position to help shape the form of that organization as well as to make a claim on increased productivity must be literate. Of course, those who get the greatest shares must be more than merely literate. But among the poorest of the poor in developing countries, the achievement of even basic literacy is itself a step that increases the potential for participation.

In fact, while literacy typically is defined as the capacity to read *and* write, the potential power of the poor initially rests on the ability to read. Writing is obviously important, but professional scribes can always be hired. The skill of a scribe does not establish a monopoly over comprehension and thus over opportunity. But whatever definition of literacy is used, literacy is a more useful measure than enrollment or numbers of classrooms or teachers. Such indicators often either do not provide information about results or simply reflect the benefits (secondary or higher education) that are going primarily to elite groups. In contrast, a basic literacy indicator not only records gains going to the very poor but is able to mark literacy gains made via informal mechanisms as well as those resulting from formal schooling.

Indicators Not Chosen

A number of other measures were considered to be potential Physical Quality of Life Index components before being discarded for a variety of reasons.

Death Rate. Death rate figures are almost always gross rates. Unless they are adjusted for the age composition of the population, use of the death rate as an indicator of a society's well-being can produce some rather odd results. Developing countries can sometimes appear to have achieved levels equal to or better than many developed countries, not because they in fact have done so, but because developed countries generally have much higher average ages than less developed countries do—e.g., Sri Lanka has a lower death rate (eight per thousand) than the United States (nine per thousand) or Sweden (eleven per thousand). Life expectancy data, in contrast, are corrected for age structure and give more meaningful results. For example, U.S. life expectancy at age one is two years longer, and Sweden's four years longer, than that of Sri Lanka.[101]

Other death rate measures have similar problems. As noted above, use of a combined mortality rate for infants and children to age five blurs what seems to be the rather significant distinction between the causes of infant mortality and the causes of death at all other ages. An indicator measuring deaths at age fifty and over suffers from the same defects when used as a substitute for total deaths.[102]

Birth Rate. The use of birth rates poses the same age-composition difficulties as does the use of death rates. Moreover, it is not clear what direction of movement should be called an improvement. Despite current enthusiasm for reducing the birth rates of other countries, a low level of births is not in itself a measure of well-being. It is a cultural preference. Similarly, a declining rate of births is not necessarily proof that people are increasingly better off.[103]

Morbidity Rate. Life expectancy is a measure of length of life. It has been suggested that people can live longer but be sicker and thus worse off, and that therefore a composite index should include a measure of illness. The factual point is probably not supportable. In any case, the problems of defining illness are so formidable as to defy solution.[104]

The fact that no acceptable index of illness has been produced is not as disastrous as it might seem on first glance. The call for a morbidity measure seems to have a strong touch of ethnocentricity. One reason mortality indexes have been popular as measures of health is that, in the past, changes in mortality really have reflected changes in other aspects of health; life expectancy reflected the historic fact that sick people died quickly. In developed countries, however, illness now has become an issue because death on average comes so late in life. Not mortal disease, but chronic illness—disease that prolongs disability, reduces productivity, and increases the need for care—has become a vital issue. But these are the problems of rich and long-lived societies. In poor countries, increasing the length of life is not likely to mean a more miserable life in a physical sense.[105]

Structural Measures. Dependency rates and other measures of population structure—that is, whether workers are predominantly in agriculture or in industry, whether people live mainly on farms or in towns—do not provide information about individual well-being, even though they may tell us something about the changing productive capacity of a society. This is also true of land tenure and unemployment measures. Neither ownership of a piece of land nor the holding of an income-generating activity is necessarily correlated with personal well-being. Moreover, such measures are relevant only to some societies and, even for these, formidable conceptual problems make cross-national comparisons virtually impossible. For example, the definition of unemployment as used in developed countries—based on the question: "Are you looking for work and unable to find it?"—is not particularly relevant in less developed countries. Much activity is unpaid family labor and is affected by how time and tasks are allocated within the household. It is not merely that there is no sharp division between work and leisure. For example, an older child while at home may be contributing to the basic skills and acculturation (the formation of human capital) of younger siblings, may be improving his or her own work skills via on-the-job training obtained by helping parents, or may make it possible for other members of the family to undertake income-earning activities.

Subjective Measures. A great many attempts to measure quality of life in rich countries are focused on happiness, satisfaction, etc. This type of indicator involves many subtle (and not so subtle) assumptions. Historical experience suggests that a good case can be made for the proposition that economic growth, economic development, and long-term progress may not actually increase "happiness" in the human race. These developments probably merely increase our ability to make self-conscious choices and to increase the number of groups to which we are sensitive. In effect, "progress" increases our ability to bear responsibility.[106] This old testamental view of the human career on earth bears on the various attempts to formulate subjective quality of life indicators, but this is not the place to examine that problem. The reader is reminded once again that the PQLI is designed not to represent all there is to measure but to reflect important elements of what must be included in a humane existence.[107]

5 The Technical Problems of Creating a Composite Index

For so it is, o Lord my God, I measure it; but
what is it that I measure?

—St. Augustine
Confessions

How can the three different measures—life expectancy at age one, infant mortality, and literacy—be combined into a single measure? "Apples and oranges" are combined in GNP via the numeraire of price. Because commodities are valued by a common unit—money—all things that are sold or given a monetary value by imputation can be combined. A society may produce an automobile that sells for $5,000, a shirt that sells for $10, an apple that sells for $1, and a visit to a doctor that sells for $50, making the total value of its gross output $5,061. But there is no price by which infant mortality, life expectancy, and literacy can be valued.[108] Nor is it possible to use any one of the indicators as a standard against which the others can be converted.

The PQLI is based on a simple indexing system. For each indicator, the performance of individual countries is placed on a scale of 0 to 100, where 0 represents an explicitly defined "worst" performance and 100 represents an explicit "best" performance. Once performance for each indicator is scaled to this common measure, a composite index can be calculated by averaging the three indicators, giving equal weight to each of them. The resulting Physical Quality of Life Index thus is scaled automatically on an index of 0 to 100.[109]

Because the index should be able to show change in performance over time— not only change between past and present but also change that might occur in the future—it is constructed to allow for improvement even by those countries with the best current performance without going beyond the number 100 and to show deterioration even by poor performers without using negative numbers. There is, in effect, a fixed range of "worst" to "best" within which past, present, and future performance can be incorporated. Remaining within the 0 to 100 range is primarily a matter of convenience, but it also increases comprehensibility.

A scale with a fixed bottom and a fixed top implies that countries can be expected gradually to close the gap between their current levels of performance (in either the composite index or the individual indicators) and the explicitly defined and fixed upper limit. This is different from a measure like per capita GNP, which may show the gap between countries to be increasing whether or not absolute progress is being made. In the following situation (which is not untypical) the fact that the relative difference between countries A and B has narrowed is hidden because the absolute difference has grown so substantially.

	Per Capita GNP	
	Period I	*Period II*
Country A	$ 1,000	$ 1,500
Country B	$ 100	$ 200
Absolute difference in per capita income	$ 900	$ 1,300
Ratio of Country A to Country B	10:1	7.5:1

For each indicator, the 0 to 100 scale was constructed on the basis of reasonable assumptions about best and worst performance. It was designed to provide as much spread as possible. The composite index shows to what extent individual countries actually do make specific aspects of well-being available to their populations.

Some countries have data that go back a very long time. Sweden and Britain, for example, have demographic material that goes back many generations. On the other hand, for many countries, the data still are totally unsatisfactory. Comparative data on a worldwide scale only began to become available in the 1950s, after the formation of the United Nations. The PQLI was developed on the basis of these post-1950 data. The bottom and top limits for each indicator are based on post-1950 experience. If future work suggests that the range should be adjusted, recomputation will be relatively simple.

Indexing the Indicators

The task of placing historical experience on a scale of 0 to 100 is different for each indicator. Basic *literacy*, of course, poses no problem. Data are reported as a percentage of the population fifteen years and older who are literate; the percentage figures correspond to the index numbers.

The scaling of the other two indicators is not quite as simple. One might assume that *infant mortality* could lend itself to a solution similar to that for literacy, in that it is expressed as the number of infant deaths per thousand live births; the worst conceivable situation would be one in which every child died within the first year (that is, an infant mortality rate of 1,000 deaths per thousand live births); the best situation would be one in which no person died within the first year (an infant mortality rate of 0 deaths per thousand live births). This would allow for easy conversion to a scale of 0 to 100.

While these extremes are intellectually conceivable, however, they are not at all probable. Some demographers claim that infant mortality rates of 250 deaths per thousand live births are fairly common in the worst urban slums of very poor countries and that, in a few places where health and medical care are particularly bad, the infant mortality rate can rise as high as 500 deaths per thousand live births.[110] However, rates of 500 deaths per thousand are very rare and even rates of 250 occur only among relatively small groups in the total population of any country. Gabon's infant mortality rate of 229 deaths per thousand live births is the worst recorded by the United Nations for any country since 1950. The next worst rates are all below 210 deaths per thousand.[111]

If the full range of possible infant mortalities (1,000 deaths per thousand to 0 deaths per thousand) were indexed, only half the scale would be used, even in the most extreme circumstances. All 150 countries for which there are data would be clustered in the upper quarter of the scale. The clustering would in fact be more extreme, not only because the majority of countries have infant mortalities well below 200, but also because the lowest infant mortality (in Sweden) is not 0 but 8 per thousand.

Scaling that leads to the concentration of all examples within a very narrow part of the 0 to 100 range will not show the rank, spread, and cluster effects that it is desirable to emphasize. It makes sense to exclude from the index that portion of the range that is not needed to express current, recent, or probable rates. Thus the worst infant mortality recorded since 1950 for a country (229 per thousand) is assigned the value of 0 on the 0 to 100 scale.

The best infant mortality achieved to date has been 8 per thousand, in Sweden. Medical authorities doubt that any nation can achieve much better performance in its infant mortality than this in the foreseeable future, certainly no better than 7 deaths per thousand by the year 2000; thus 7 deaths per thousand is the high (100) end of the index. Using a range of 229 to 7 deaths per thousand means that a 2.22-point change in the infant mortality rate will show up as a 1-point change in the infant mortality index. If a country were engulfed by a great social catastrophe that raised its infant mortality above 229, the index would have to show the result as a negative number. This does not seem likely for more than a few, relatively small countries. The advantage of a scale that fairly effectively spreads infant mortality across the 0 to 100 range is worth the outside chance of an occasional negative number. Because each indicator is equally weighted, only a disastrous infant mortality experience could produce a negative PQLI.

To determine appropriate lower and upper limits of *life expectancy at age one* requires the application of even greater intuition than is required to determine the range for infant mortality. How was the range that runs from a low of 38 years to a high of 77 years established?

With data for life expectancy at birth and for infant mortality, it is possible to calculate life expectancy at age one.[112] Based on such calculations, the lowest reported life expectancy at age one for the entire post-World War II period is 38 years for Vietnam in 1950. This figure is used as the low (0) end of the life expectancy index—even though this poses the possibility of encountering a negative number for this indicator sometime in the future—in order to get the benefit of greater spread among countries.[113]

The upper limit of the average life expectancy at age one index was determined on the basis of the best available estimates of what average life expectancy at age one is likely to be at the end of the century. However, the examination of life expectancy estimates revealed that there is not even full agreement on precisely what needs to be measured. Actuaries have experimented with a number of concepts. The Registrar General of Great Britain, using a "normal span of life" concept—that is, what might be expected but for the early "accident" of death—has determined life expectancy to be 85 years.[114]

Another method of determining life expectancy is based on the assumption that humans are endowed genetically with a fairly fixed term of life, after which they more or less fall apart. This is based on evidence that on the whole people have not increased their potential length of life, even though larger proportions of people born are surviving to that age of senescence that marks the "natural lifespan." For example, in England and Wales the modal lifespan—"peak age" in Table 2—has only increased about three years for men and seven years for women in the last 120 years, but the proportion of deaths occurring within the senescent period has increased from 40 to over 70 percent of the population. (Senescent deaths, according to the hypothesis, are those which occur because

Table 2. Senescent Deaths as a Percentage of Total Deaths, 1841-1960/62

	Males		Females	
	Peak Age	Senescent Deaths as a Proportion of Total Deaths	Peak Age	Senescent Deaths as a Proportion of Total Deaths
	(years)	*(%)*	*(years)*	*(%)*
1841	72.0	39.9	73.5	41.0
1910/12	73.5	51.5	76.0	55.3
1950/52	75.7	69.4	80.3	70.3
1960/62	74.8	74.5	80.6	72.3

SOURCE: Bernard Benjamin and H. W. Haycocks, *The Analysis of Mortality and Other Actuarial Statistics* (Cambridge: Cambridge University Press, 1970), p. 26.

the term of the lifespan has run out. The "peak age" is the center of a distribution of senescent deaths.)[115] If life expectancy is taken to be an average of male and female peak ages, it would be 77.7, or approximately 78 years.

One does not have to depend on such formulations. Another way to make an estimate is to look directly at the possibilities of saving lives at various ages, as these might bear on increasing average life expectancy. In countries that already have long life expectancies, the big source of improvement that comes from eliminating the impact of infant and child mortality already has been substantially obtained. Further major decreases that will affect the average must come from lowering mortality from chronic noninfective diseases and from deaths by accidents and other violent forms. It is widely agreed that large improvements in longevity will only occur if there is a general breakthrough in the study of geriatrics.[116] On the basis of a survey of scientific expectations, it is reasonable to set the upper limit of achievable life expectancy at age one at 77 years, two years above the current best (Sweden, with 75 years).[117] This means that a change in life expectancy of .39 years will result in a one-point change in the index.

Thus the range for each index was based on an examination of historical experience, modified where appropriate by expectations of possible change. The life expectancy at age one index ranges from 38 to 77 years; the infant mortality index ranges from 229 to 7 per thousand live births; the literacy index ranges from 0 literacy to 100 percent literacy. Table 3 shows for three countries how the indicators were changed to index numbers and then averaged (equally weighted) to form the PQLI.[118]

Table 3. Life Expectancy at Age One, Infant Mortality, and Literacy, Actual Data and Index Numbers, early 1970s

	Life Expectancy at Age One[1]		Infant Mortality[2]		Literacy[3]		PQLI[4]
	(years)	Index Number	(per 1,000 live births)	Index Number	(%)	Index Number	
Nigeria	49	28	180	22	25	25	25
India	56	46	122	48	34	34	43
United States	72	88	16	96	99	99	94

[1]Years of life expectancy are converted to an index number according to the formula:
$$\frac{\text{life expectancy at age one} - 38}{.39}$$

[2]The infant mortality rate is converted to an index number according to the formula:
$$\frac{229 - \text{infant mortality rate per thousand}}{2.22}$$

[3]Literacy index numbers correspond to the actual data.

[4]Average of life expectancy at age one, infant mortality, and literacy indexes (equally weighted).

SOURCE: Appendix A

While it would be possible to work only with individual indicators, Chapter 6 will show that the PQLI offers interesting information precisely because it is a composite indicator. The fact that it is a composite encourages movement from the current policy preoccupation with raising the values of individual indicators toward creative thinking about the interrelationship of the processes that yield the PQLI results. It has become increasingly obvious from both historical evidence and recent development experience that synergistic characteristics are extremely important in defining the rates at which individual indicators change. Not very much is known about these connections. If the condition of the world's poorest people is to be improved, the interrelationships must be understood; the PQLI can help focus analysis on those interrelationships.

Because it sets fixed lower and upper limits, the PQLI measures only movement in relation to those fixed limits. Unlike per capita GNP, it does not have the same capacity to tempt planners and policymakers into establishing unrealistic targets or cause them to fail to recognize improved performance.[119] But its advantages are also its limitations and these should be recognized. Unlike per capita GNP, the PQLI seeks to measure only a very specific type of performance for which there is an upper limit of achievement. As country performance moves close to the top of the index, there is less to measure. For example, Sweden (with a PQLI of 97) is the best provider and Guinea-Bissau (with a PQLI of 12) the poorest provider of the social results measured by the PQLI. There is only slight range for improvement in Sweden. Literacy is virtually universal, infant mortality is extremely low, and life expectancy is long and close to a society's attainable maximum. In effect, Sweden and a number of other developed countries—there are eight countries with PQLIs of 95 or more—have been able to cope with most of the specific problems which the PQLI measures. Their current social tasks are different. The PQLI cannot measure their progress in solving the particular problems that face them.[120]

Countries with low PQLIs will improve their literacy, infant mortality, and life expectancy performance. The gap between where countries are and what is possible will narrow. As these specific social objectives are realized, the PQLI will be "used up." The fact that the PQLI has a limited life span would constitute a serious defect only if all countries moved into the high PQLI range in a shorter time than it will take to put the index into use. This is a situation much to be desired. Unfortunately, however, it is probable that a number of generations will pass before the majority of the world's people will be living in countries where the PQLI level is such as to render it useless. Over 3.6 billion people live in countries where the PQLI is below 95; only 167 million people (about 4 percent of the world's people) live in countries having PQLIs of 95 or above.

This discussion about the use and limitations of the PQLI is not intended to imply that the only objectives with which poor countries should concern themselves are those measured by the PQLI. While the PQLI measures elements that are very important to the world's poor people, poor people and poor countries have other, equally important concerns. For the more general and diverse objectives, GNP and the system of national accounts (however modified and improved) must remain the major effective measure of performance. The Physical Quality of Life Index, however, does promise to be a very useful measure for determining the extent to which societies distribute certain important social benefits among their populations. Yet the PQLI is not without difficulties and these—particularly problems of weighting and scaling—must be addressed.

The Impact of Weighting

Every composite measure explicitly or implicitly assigns weights to its components. Weighting is a troublesome issue that cannot be ignored. Yet it is not unique to the PQLI. There is no solution that can be applied automatically; there is no solution that cannot be challenged. The PQLI is comprised of three indicators that have no obvious relationship. Each provides important information about the social process. Each was selected because it met the established criteria. Because there is no reason to treat any one indicator as more important than another, equal weight was assigned to each of the components of the composite index. This somewhat arbitrary judgment is based on the fact that the results measured by the PQLI are the summation of complex social interrelationships for which there is as yet no theoretical explanation that imposes (or even suggests) any other set of weights.

The World Bank also has recognized that, in seeking to measure the results of development policy by the benefits that policy yields to different socio-economic groups, it is necessary to apply some system of weights that is arbitrary—arbitrary in that the weights are not set by the market but by the distributional emphasis that one wishes to assign to growth at each income level. The Bank offers two alternatives to the "income weighted" measure of growth that is normally used. One involves the equal weighting of income going to each quintile or decile of income receivers; the other involves the application of "poverty weights," which assign more value to the income growth of the poorer segments of the population. One version of the poverty weights system assigns a 10 percent weight to the upper 20 percent of income recipients, a 30 percent weight to the middle 40 percent, and a 60 percent weight to the poorest 40 percent. Such an altered method of weighting, of course, changes aggregate growth rates.[121]

The component indicators of the PQLI could be weighted in a number of ways and need not necessarily be weighted equally. A different method of weighting would produce differences in PQLI rankings at any one point and would affect rates of change over time, primarily because the spread of the three indicators is not likely to be the same even among countries that have the same PQLI. In the example below, equal weighting of the three indicators results in a PQLI of 40 for both Country A and Country B.

	Literacy	Life Expectancy	Infant Mortality	PQLI
		(index numbers)		
Country A	40	40	40	40
Country B	50	40	30	40

However, if literacy were weighted at 50 percent, while infant mortality and life expectancy were each valued at 25 percent, Country A would have a PQLI of 40 and Country B would have a PQLI of 43. If infant mortality were weighted at 50 percent and each of the other indicators at 25 percent, Country B would have a PQLI of 38, while Country A's PQLI would remain 40.

The country data in Appendix A show that the spread of the three indicators does vary; thus changed weights would change values for individual countries' PQLIs somewhat. But Spearman rank correlation coefficients based on various combinations of 50 percent, 25 percent, and 25 percent weights for the three indicators indicate that different weights would change relative country rankings very little. The Spearman rank correlation coefficients (r) showed the following results when compared with equal weighting of the three indicators:

50 percent weight to life expectancy at age one	$r = 0.997$
50 percent weight to infant mortality	$r = 0.996$
50 percent weight to literacy	$r = 0.984$

Although it is useful to know that the PQLI is sturdy in the face of changed weights, the more important requirement is that the weights used are made explicit. As long as the chosen system of weights remains constant, the index remains unimpaired. Determining some absolutely true ranking of countries is not the point of the index; moreover, the index is not measuring a race in which there is some importance to the particular placing of individual countries in relation to one another. Rather the index shows where a country is placed in relation to the ultimate objective (that is, a PQLI of 100) as well as how well a country is making progress toward that end. Equal weighting has the advantage that it limits the influence of any indicator. No indicator can affect the PQLI by more than thirty-three points. The effect of any independent change in one indicator thus is dampened. As a result, the stability of the PQLI tends to be greater than the stability of the individual components.

Some have suggested that the PQLI actually gives double weight to "health" because it includes both infant mortality and life expectancy at age one. As noted in Chapter 4, however, infant mortality and life expectancy measure different results and different social processes. The fact that infants typically die for quite different reasons than do those over age one means that "health" is not a simple condition, but the result of a complex mix of differing social characteristics. Health results are produced by interrelated physiological, nutritional, environmental, social, and cultural contributions; yet to include all these variations within the rubric of "health" is purely nominal. The social policies and family practices that affect mortality of infants do not necessarily affect the life chances of young children and adults.

The feeling that infant mortality and life expectancy at age one both represent "health" possibly derives in part from the unspoken assumption that both are improved by the same devices—medicines and doctors—and that what improves one improves the other. Once the evidence is accepted that improvements in infant mortality and life expectancy generally result from different social activities, this conceptual difficulty should disappear.

However, even if both infant mortality and life expectancy were "health" measures, this does not seem to be a significant issue. The criticism rests on the assumption that a composite measure should be a "balanced" measure. Yet it is not clear what a balanced measure would be. If it is meant that a composite measure should describe all aspects of reality, it need only be noted that attempts to develop an instrument that can measure general social performance have so far been unsuccessful. One major virtue of the PQLI is that it is a modest proposal. As long as it is recognized that infant mortality and life expectancy at age one measure different things (which they do), it does not matter that both are included. Both are useful measures of different conditions of the very poor, and the improvement of each represents a desirable and important objective.

The Scaling Problem

Construction of a composite index involves not only explicit but also implicit weighting problems. These derive from the way the individual indicators are scaled and how the calibrations affect the composite index. As with explicit weights, the scaling issue is not as crucial for the PQLI as it has been for other attempts to measure welfare or development.

Let us review how each of the indexes is constructed and what the scaling implications are in each case:

a) in the infant mortality index (which is based on a range of 229 to 7 deaths per thousand live births), each 2.22-point change in infant mortality results in a 1-point change in the index;

b) in the life expectancy at age one index (which is based on a range of 38 to 77 years), each 0.39-year change in life expectancy at age one results in a 1-point change in the index;

c) in the literacy index (which assumes that populations aged fifteen and over range from completely illiterate to completely literate), each one percentage point change in literacy results in a 1-point change in the index.

The extremes that define each index affect the placing of countries on that particular index as well as on the composite index. For example, if the infant mortality index were based on an assumed range of 500 to 7 infant deaths per thousand live births, India's infant mortality of 122 would appear as 76.7 on the 0 to 100 scale, rather than (as it presently does) as 48.2. This would not affect the infant mortality ranking of countries because all countries would be changed in the same way, but it would change the weight of infant mortality in the composite PQLI. India's PQLI is 43; if its infant mortality were 76.7, its PQLI would show as 52 (assuming that the other two indicators remain scaled as they now are and the indicators remain equally weighted). In other words, the changed scaling of infant mortality would automatically weight infant mortality more heavily in the composite index.

Another aspect of the scaling problem affects rates of change. The larger the range chosen for an indicator, the more movement is needed to produce a change in the index for that indicator. For example, a 500 to 7 range for infant mortality would mean that a change of 4.93 deaths per thousand live births would be needed in the actual infant mortality rate to produce a 1-point change in the index. In effect, the use of the 229 to 7 range gives more weight to a change in infant mortality than would the 500 to 7 range.

These two examples show that the choice of scale affects the "weight" of the indicator in opposite ways. Using the larger (500 to 7) range for infant mortality would give greater "weight" to infant mortality in the PQLI at any moment but would reduce the impact on the PQLI of any change in infant mortality. Conversely, the use of the narrower (229 to 7) range reduces the initial weight of infant mortality in the PQLI but increases the impact on the PQLI of any change in infant mortality.

Clearly, there is no obviously correct range that expresses an indicator's inherent or real properties. Nor is there an objective basis for determining whether the scale should give more weight to one or another indicator in the PQLI at a particular time or over time. Finally, there is no obvious interrelationship among the three indicators that enables one to establish a "proper" rate of transformation among them. In other words, in no circumstances can it be said in a logically or historically irrefutable way that a one percent change in literacy is necessarily the equivalent of a 0.39-year change in life expectancy or a 2.22 per thousand change in infant mortality.[122]

It is often suggested that GNP is a superior composite index because it employs a neutral system of weights, namely the prices of goods and services. But GNP does not, in fact, avoid the value-laden issue of choosing weights. Prices in an economy (and therefore the values given) are a function of the existing distribution of income. Any change in income distribution produces a different structure of prices as well as a change in the composition and value of national output. As Meier noted, "a judgment regarding economic welfare will also involve a value judgment on the desirability of a particular distribution of income."[123] Hollis Chenery and others at the World Bank have recognized this.

. . . if one is interested in the welfare of individuals and not merely in the growth of GNP, what measure does one use to evaluate human-oriented projects, or social programs, or the performance of the economy as a whole? Though GNP is a simple and convenient index, it has obvious deficiencies as a welfare measure. Since the (highest) 20 percent typically receives more than 50 percent of total income, GNP weights the income of the rich much more heavily than that of the poor. If the objective is to alleviate poverty, one must allow for the fact that an additional dollar of income would make far more difference to the welfare of a poor family than to that of a rich family. This approach yields different answers as to what is a profitable, sound, or efficient project. . . . How the incomes of different groups should be weighted is still a matter of experiment in Bank work. . . . [124]

Thus the Bank has found it necessary to experiment with arbitrary equal weight and "poverty weight" systems that are no different in principle from those implied in the Physical Quality of Life Index.

Are these issues of implicit weighting significant? Any change in scale would produce some changes in country rankings. But the evidence is that rankings would not change very much; Spearman rank correlation coefficients based on two infant mortality ranges (500 to 7 and 229 to 7) equalled 0.994. More important, even with changed weights, the composite PQLI would depict how individual countries stand in relation to the absolute targets that have been specified and how they make progress toward those targets. As long as there are no changes in scaling between one period and another, one cannot talk of "distortions."[125]

Another question is whether the scale says anything about the ease or difficulty of movement along the index. On the infant mortality scale as constructed, a rate of 111 deaths per thousand is the midpoint (50) of the index. If the lower end of the index (0) had been defined as 500 infant deaths per thousand, then an infant mortality of 247 would represent the midpoint of the index. Neither of these possible indexes provides information about the ease or difficulty of improving infant mortality.

It also has been suggested that it is easier for a poor country to move, for example, from 0 to 10 on the infant mortality index (that is, from 229 to 207 deaths per thousand live births) than from 90 to 100 on the index (that is, from 29 to 7 deaths per thousand live births). It is argued that there are many easy gains to be made at the lower end of the index, while improvements at the upper end are hard to come by, and that the scales ought to be adjusted to reflect this fact. Yet the available evidence provides no basis for drawing this conclusion. It is as reasonable to argue that when societies are very poor and structurally unprepared, improvements in infant mortality, life expectancy, and literacy—which ultimately depend on social organization—are extremely difficult to obtain and sustain, and that once an organizational structure is put in place— for this is the most difficult part of the process—social gains come rather quickly. With what degree of difficulty change takes place at the uppermost end of the scale is not clear. Given the lack of evidence one way or another, it is not possible to say anything about this aspect of the scaling problem.[126]

Some may be troubled by this somewhat cavalier attitude toward the problems of weighting and scaling. However, as long as the rules are clear and are not changed, users will have no great problem with the PQLI. The concept is simple and the basic components are easily disaggregated, thereby minimizing the danger of confusion.

A major concern of critics seems to be that the choice of weights and scales—the explicit and implicit weighting—will affect the ranking of countries. As noted, experimentation with the index suggests that it is fairly resistant to changes in weights and scales. The fact of equal weighting contributes to the inability of improvement in any one component to "swamp" the PQLI. It should be clear by now, however, that the precise ranking of countries is not a prime objective. No effort is being made to measure a race in which there is a winner or to establish some absolute truth in ranking. Just as GNP is useful even though it does not capture social reality in its entirety, the PQLI also is intended as a useful tool to help analysts and policymakers focus on other aspects of that reality.

The Relationship among PQLI, Its Component Indicators, and GNP

The focus of the PQLI is to identify the position of countries in relation to the best performance that nations can expect to achieve during the foreseeable future. If there is a general, even if not inevitable, tendency toward improvement, countries will be converging in a slow or rapid way toward the levels now nearly achieved by the most advanced countries. This makes the PQLI a different kind of measure from GNP, which, because of the lack of any upper limit, may show the gap between rich and poor countries to be growing absolutely and relatively—even as poor countries are, in fact, increasing the real goods and services available per citizen.

This is not to deny the importance of the study of comparative rates of change. Information about different rates of change (particularly for countries with low PQLIs) might increase knowledge about alternative and more creative development strategies. Moreover, once there is a better understanding of causal interrelations, it may be possible to use the percentage rate of PQLI change as a target—as the social goal for a generation or a decade—in the same way that an annual rate of per capita GNP change was the goal of the First and Second U.N. Development Decades.[127] At a much later stage of work on this subject, it may be possible to establish clear functional interrelationships among the three components of the PQLI and GNP and other development indicators. At that time, it will become necessary to search for a natural scheme of weighting. Until then, any weighting scheme will have to be arbitrary.

The ultimate test of the usefulness of the World Bank approach (which continues to depend on per capita income but which weights changes in income arbitrarily—arbitrarily in the sense that the weights are chosen to reflect specific policy objectives) in comparison with the usefulness of the PQLI is not to be decided by the system of weights. The test should be one of efficiency and simplicity. To the extent that the instruments seek to measure the same thing—

distribution of benefits—the PQLI appears to be more elegant. The World Bank approach has the advantage of working with familiar GNP categories, but the results have no more welfare meaning than GNP data currently do and tell nothing about what sort of benefits have been distributed. But a change in a country's PQLI expresses a change in the distribution of specific social results. For example, between 1963 and 1971, Sri Lanka's performance in PQLI, as well as in its component indicators, improved in the following way:

	PQLI	Literacy	Life Expectancy at Age One	Infant Mortality
		(index numbers)		
1963	73	72	69	78
1971	79	78	75	84

Does the PQLI show anything not revealed by per capita GNP or by any one of the component indicators of the PQLI? That is, do the two measures move together in a way that allows GNP to serve as a surrogate for the PQLI? Similarly, does any one component of the PQLI correlate so perfectly with the PQLI as to be an adequate substitute for the composite measure? In effect, is there any need for the PQLI?

The PQLI emerged as a device to identify outliers, deviant performers—particularly those countries with low per capita GNP and high PQLI performance—whose experience might yield some insight into novel ways of improving life-quality results more rapidly than could be expected on the basis of typical assumptions about the relationship between PQLI and GNP. For this purpose, high correlation between per capita GNP and PQLI would not be enough to justify dropping the PQLI. Only a perfect correlation would warrant not using the PQLI. In fact, however, the correlation between the log of 1970-75 per capita GNP and PQLI for all 150 countries implies that GNP "explains" only slightly more than half the life-quality results countries have been able to achieve, leaving the rest to be "explained" by other—institutional, historical, and structural —factors. The correlation, not all that strong overall, varies among groups of countries:

All Countries (N=150)	$r = 0.729$
Countries with per capita GNP under $300 (N=42)	$r = 0.202$
Countries with per capita GNP $300-$699 (N=38)	$r = 0.126$
Countries with per capita GNP $700-$1,999 (N=32)	$r = 0.404$
Countries with per capita GNP $2,000 and over (N=38)	$r = -0.116$

In effect, per capita GNP is not a very good predictor of PQLI performance and cannot serve as a surrogate for it.[128]

The other question is whether any one component is sensitive enough to reflect the behavior of the composite PQLI. The correlation coefficients of individual components with one another are shown in Table 4 and with PQLI and GNP in Table 5. Table 4 shows that the correlation among the three indicators is high for all 150 countries as a group. Within income classes, however, this is true only in the group of countries having per capita incomes of $2,000 or more. The data do not suggest that using only one of the indicators would adequately represent the others. Furthermore, the figures also support the point already made that the correlations between infant mortality and life expectancy at age one are not close in poor countries.

Table 5 shows that the correlations between the individual indicators and the PQLI for all 150 countries together are high but that they are somewhat lower for each of the income groups separately (except the high-income group). Thus for the developing countries, at any rate, the PQLI does provide additional information. Moreover, the relationships between PQLI and the individual indicators do not change in the same way for all countries; it is important to explain these variations, which are dampened by averaging.[129] The performance of individual countries should be analyzed with a particular eye to the likelihood

Table 4. Correlation of Component Indicators by Income Groups

	Infant Mortality	Life Expectancy at Age One
Low-Income Countries (N=42) **(per capita GNP under $300)**		
Life Expectancy at Age One	−0.586	—
Literacy	−0.684	0.587
Lower Middle-Income Countries (N=38) **(per capita GNP $300-$699)**		
Life Expectancy at Age One	−0.819	—
Literacy	−0.779	0.776
Upper Middle-Income Countries (N=32) **(per capita GNP $700-$1,999)**		
Life Expectancy at Age One	−0.768	—
Literacy	−0.798	0.707
High-Income Countries (N=38) **(per capita GNP $2,000 and over)**		
Life Expectancy at Age One	−0.964	—
Literacy	−0.963	0.930
All Countries (N=150)		
Life Expectancy at Age One	−0.919	—
Literacy	−0.919	0.897

SOURCE: Based on Appendix A data.

Table 5. Correlation of Component Indicators with PQLI and with Per Capita GNP

| | Physical Quality of Life Index | | | | | Per Capita GNP |
	Low-Income (N=42)	Lower Middle-Income (N=38)	Upper Middle-Income (N=32)	High-Income (N=38)	All Countries (N=150)	All Countries (N=150)
Life Expectancy at Age One	0.818	0.921	0.854	0.974	0.962	0.754
Infant Mortality	−0.866	−0.944	−0.928	−0.991	−0.975	−0.714
Literacy	0.889	0.906	0.941	0.986	0.968	0.680

SOURCE: Based on Appendix A data.

that the interrelationships among the three components are decisive in determining the progress of human well-being.

A final question is whether the work of Kravis et al. that seeks to eliminate exchange rate distortions and to re-price countries' economic activity more realistically—the so-called purchasing power parity approach—closes the gap between what GNP and the PQLI tell us. While the comparison is quite rough, Table 6 shows that the adjustment for purchasing power parities does result in a higher correlation between GNP and PQLI for all but the anomalous lower middle-income countries. Yet there still remain substantial differences between GNP and PQLI that even re-priced GNP does not explain. When more precise

Table 6. Correlation of PQLI with Per Capita GNP and with Repriced Per Capita GNP (114 Countries)

	Per capita GNP, 1970-75 average (logged)	Repriced Per capita GNP, 1970 (logged)
World (N=114)	0.79	0.84
Low-Income Countries (N=35)	0.17	0.46
Lower Middle-Income Countries (N=28)	0.24	0.10
Upper Middle-Income Countries (N=22)	0.45	0.71
High-Income Countries (N=29)	0.28	0.67

SOURCE: Per capita GNP data (1970-75 average) are from Appendix A. Repriced per capita data (1970) are from Irving B. Kravis, Alan W. Heston, and Robert Summers, "Real GDP Per Capita for More than One Hundred Countries." *The Economic Journal*, Vol. 88 (June 1978), Table 4, pp. 232-37. The 114 countries are those for which data are available in both sources. Countries are classified by income groups as in Appendix A.

income distribution data become available and can be applied to the re-priced GNP data, it will be worth examining whether and to what extent the additional correction would help reduce the remaining discrepancies between GNP and PQLI.[130]

The re-pricing technique is costly and time-consuming, even when shortcuts are employed. If comparative research suggests that some combination of re-pricing and income distribution analysis produces a high correlation between GNP and PQLI, it may be possible to use the PQLI as an inexpensive surrogate for adjusted GNP. A more likely possibility, however, is that some significant gap between the two measures will persist because they actually measure different things. In this case, the PQLI would remain what it even now promises to be, a measure that complements per capita GNP.

6 What Does the PQLI Show?

The analytic priority of purpose over indicators cannot provide an absolute or 'correct' solution to the problem of meaning, but it does keep the game honest.

—Eugene J. Meehan
"The Social Indicators Movement"
Frontiers of Economics

As a social science tool, the PQLI's major value is in the new information it provides and in the new lines of analysis it stimulates. This chapter explores the question of what can be learned by using the PQLI. It illustrates some of the ways PQLI can help characterize the performance of countries as well as the performance of regions and groups within countries. It also shows how PQLI can be examined over time.

As noted, PQLIs of countries vary widely. Many of these differences are discussed below. In the meantime, however, Figure 1 offers an overview of the PQLI relationships among countries, indicating that differences are not simply regional.

Data Limitations

While the best data available from the most reliable sources were used in the construction of the PQLI, these are clearly inadequate both in quantity and quality. However, at this stage in the PQLI's development—when the purpose is primarily to explore its potential—the data limitations are not unacceptably restricting (although they do affect the amount of intensive analysis that is methodologically appropriate and make whatever conclusions drawn from them very tentative). Because of the data limitations, composite PQLI numbers are always rounded and are presented as whole numbers. Moreover, 3- to 5-point

Figure 1. PQLI Map of the World

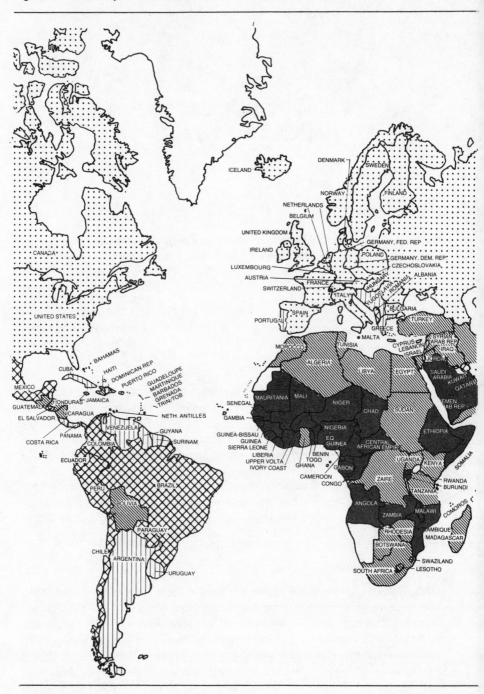

SOURCE: Appendix A.

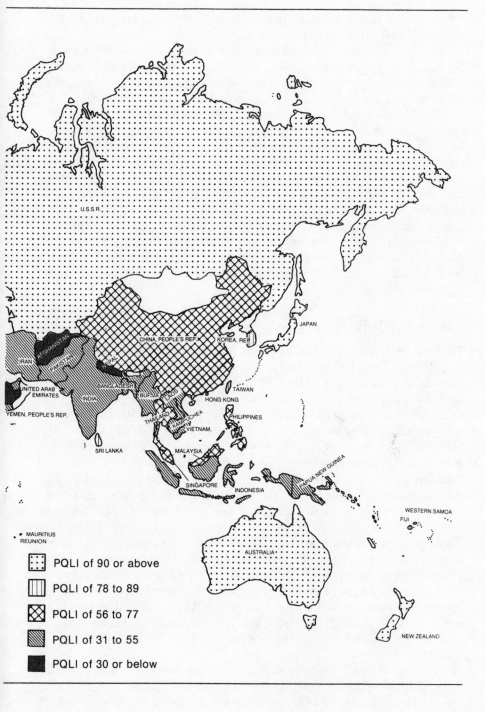

- ⣿ PQLI of 90 or above
- ⣿ PQLI of 78 to 89
- ⣿ PQLI of 56 to 77
- ⣿ PQLI of 31 to 55
- ⣿ PQLI of 30 or below

differences are treated as relatively insignificant. The only exception to this occurs in intra-United States comparisons.

Yet the weaknesses of the data are not inevitable. The task of generating the data needed to extend the use of the PQLI is far less formidable than the task of developing internationally comparable systems of national accounts was thirty years ago. Moreover, the PQLI requires only a few types of data.

The PQLI is a data-economizing device in yet another way. Early work suggests that it is not necessary for the individual components of the index to be absolutely comparable internationally. While it is not yet clear how much variation is tolerable, it appears that it is more important that the definition of the components be stable over time within a country rather than among countries. In any case, widespread adoption of the PQLI as an indicator for measuring social progress would set in motion a search for better, more frequently collected data and for more economical ways to obtain them. International conventions of use similar to those that have been developed for national income accounts also will need to be developed. But even with these limitations, the PQLI can provide much additional information. Some of the possibilities are discussed below.[131]

"Money Is Not Everything"

The variation among groups of countries—in terms of income and the physical quality of life measure—shown in Table 7 is not entirely surprising. Poor countries (those with low per capita GNPs) tend to have low PQLIs, while high-income countries tend to have high PQLIs. If this were all that is to be learned by using PQLI, there would be little justification for its use. In fact, however, the correlations between GNP and PQLI are not all that close (see Chapter 5). While the deviations exist at all levels of income, they are particularly evident at the upper and lower ends of the per capita income range. [132]

At one end of the spectrum, the oil producers of the Middle East—most particularly Saudi Arabia, Qatar, and the United Arab Emirates—and Libya, stand out with high per capita GNPs and low PQLIs (see Table 8). Of these high-income oil states, only Kuwait has a relatively high PQLI of 74. Four of the five countries have incomes equal to or above the average of all high-income countries; yet three have PQLIs below the average of the poorest countries— and Libya's PQLI is only marginally higher than that of the low-income countries.

Other gross deviations in which PQLI is quite low relative to GNP include Angola (where per capita GNP is $601 and PQLI is 16) and Gabon (where per capita GNP is $2,123 and PQLI is 21).[133] Although Iran has a per capita GNP ($1,260) more than nine times larger than India ($133), its PQLI is no higher.[134]

If nothing else, such examples show that "money is not everything." While this observation may not be surprising, policymakers and analysts have tended to ignore its implications. The fact that there is a distinction between the level of

**Table 7. Average Per Capita GNP and PQLI for 150 Countries,
by Income Groups, early 1970s
(weighted by population)**

	Total Population	Per Capita GNP	PQLI
	(millions)	($)	
Low-Income Countries (N=42) (per capita GNP under $300)	1,242	155	40
Lower Middle-Income Countries (N = 38) (per capita GNP $300-$699)	1,081	340	67
Upper Middle-Income Countries (N=32) (per capita GNP $700-$1,999)	417	1,047	68
High-Income Countries (N=38) (per capita GNP $2,000 and over)	1,040	4,404	92
All Countries (N=150)	3,781	1,476	65

SOURCE: Appendix A. In order to emphasize the number of people living at various income levels, averages weighted by population are used throughout the text in discussions about groups of countries.

Table 8. Five High-Income Countries with Low PQLIs, early 1970s

	Per Capita GNP	PQLI
	($)	
All High-Income Countries (N=38)	4,404	92
Kuwait	13,787	74
Libya	4,402	45
Qatar	11,779	31
Saudi Arabia	3,529	29
United Arab Emirates	14,368	34
All Low-Income Countries (N=42)	155	40

SOURCE: Appendix A.

per capita GNP and the presence or absence of the social infrastructure that determines a society's PQLI poses important policy questions. This is not to suggest that a society ought to choose to be "poor but happy." It is intended, however, to advance the all-too-frequently neglected proposition that a system can be quite rich in what the GNP measures and still give its population inferior life chances. Not only is there no automatic link between per capita GNP and even the barest elements of well-being, but it appears that it takes considerable time to build the institutional infrastructure that can generate and sustain a high PQLI even once a commitment to an improved quality of life is made. It also appears that poor countries can raise their PQLIs at lower cost than generally is assumed.

The data suggest that a PQLI of 90 or more—arbitrarily chosen to represent a fairly satisfactory level of life chance achievement—can be attained at GNP levels well below that of the United States ($7,024). Twenty-nine countries— total population 1,032 million—have a PQLI of 90 or more. All but Switzerland and Sweden have lower per capita GNPs than the United States. Of the twenty-six developed countries with lower per capita GNP, ten have a PQLI equal to or higher than that of the United States. For example, the United Kingdom, with the same PQLI, has a per capita income just over half that of the United States, and Ireland, only 1 PQLI point below the United States, has a per capita income only one third as large. As noted, small differences in PQLI are probably unimportant. On the other hand, roughly similar PQLIs—say, 3 or 4 points on either side of the United States—and rather large differences in per capita incomes are certainly significant.

However, these data offer very little comfort. Even if it were assumed that generally accepted growth-oriented policies could produce PQLIs of 90 with per capita GNPs as low as $2,500—Romania, Bulgaria, Hungary, Puerto Rico, Ireland, the U.S.S.R., and Spain all did so with per capita incomes of less than $2,500—nearly three quarters of the world's people currently live in countries with per capita incomes lower than this level. Even a very high per capita income growth rate of 5 percent for all countries during the next quarter century would only put those countries that already have a per capita income of at least $739 across the $2,500 threshold within twenty-five years. In effect, about 62 percent of the current world population would not reach that level of income.[135]

The Tinbergen-group report, *Reshaping the International Order* (RIO), suggested somewhat less ambitious "basic human needs" targets that are equivalent to achieving a PQLI of 77 by the end of the century.[136] At the present time, more than two thirds of the world's population is not at that standard. Policies that have been used in the past (as the "trickle-down" consequences of a growth-oriented strategy) on average will not result in a PQLI of 77 until per capita GNP has risen at least to $1,100.[137]

Even with an annual growth rate in per capita income of 5 percent, only countries with a current per capita income of at least $325 can achieve the

$1,100 level within twenty-five years. In other words, countries containing more than half of the current world population—2.1 billion people—would be likely not to reach even the RIO target within a quarter century if currently dominant economic growth strategies are practiced. Since 5 percent would be a very high rate of growth, this is a conservative estimate of the proportion of the world's people that still would not have attained the minimum level of human needs represented by a PQLI of 77.

Low GNP Countries Don't All Have Low PQLIs

Low-income countries also exhibit some significant deviations from the general pattern that countries with low per capita GNPs have low PQLIs. Six countries with per capita incomes still under $700 already have achieved the RIO targets equivalent to a PQLI of 77 (Table 9). Eight additional countries with per capita incomes below $700 have PQLI ratings of 68 or more (see Table 10). (A PQLI of 68 is equivalent to the weighted average PQLI of the thirty-two upper-middle income countries in Table 7, i.e., those countries having per capita incomes ranging between $700 and $1,999 and an average per capita income of $1,047.)

Tables 9 and 10 show that the results measured by the PQLI do not flow from development choices that are made only by a particular type of economic-political system. Cuba, the Republic of Korea, Sri Lanka, and (before their

Table 9. Six Countries with Per Capita GNPs under $700 and PQLIs of 77 or More, early 1970s

	Per Capita GNP	PQLI
	($)	
All Low-Income Countries (N = 42) (per capita GNP under $300)	155	40
Sri Lanka	179	82
All Lower Middle-Income Countries (N=38) (per capita GNP $300-$699)	340	67
Cuba	640	84
Grenada	465	77
Guyana	559	85
Korea, Republic of	464	82
Western Samoa	300	84

NOTE: Three additional countries—Costa Rica, Hong Kong, and Taiwan—presently with incomes higher than $700 achieved PQLIs of 77 or more in the early 1960s, when their per capita incomes were still below $700. (PQLI information from Appendix C; income information calculated from David Morawetz, *Twenty-Five Years of Economic Development, 1950-1975* (Washington, D.C.: World Bank, 1977), Table A-1).

SOURCE: Appendix A.

Table 10. Eight Countries with Per Capita GNPs under $700 and PQLIs of 68 to 76, early 1970s

	Per Capita GNP	PQLI
	($)	
Albania	530	75
China, People's Rep.	300	69
Colombia	526	71
Ecuador	505	68
Kerala State[1]	126	68
Mauritius	552	71
Paraguay	533	75
Philippines	342	71
Thailand	318	68

[1]While the Indian state of Kerala is not an independent country, it is included not only because fairly good data are available, but also because of its anomolously high PQLI (in comparison with the all-India average of 43) and low per capita income (India's per capita income is $133). Moreover, its population of 21 million makes it larger than many countries. Kerala's PQLI is based on an infant mortality rate of 58 deaths per thousand live births, a life expectancy at age one of 66.4 years, and a literacy rate of 60 per cent. The data are from "Study Team 12: New Approaches to the Alleviation of Hunger," *Supporting Papers: World Food and Nutrition Study*, Vol. 4, pp. 86-88. Kerala's per capita GNP is variously estimated to be between 75 and 95 per cent of India's; $126 is 95 per cent of the all-India average.

SOURCE: Appendix A.

rapid rises in per capita GNP) Costa Rica, Hong Kong, and Taiwan—with very different political systems—all achieved PQLIs in the mid-80s at per capita GNP levels below $700. Other countries with equally varied systems—Albania, China, the Philippines, Colombia, and others—have been able to attain PQLI levels that are only slightly less satisfactory. Sri Lanka and the Indian state of Kerala, where extremely low per capita GNPs are associated with quite high PQLI ratings, are the most striking examples.

At the moment, understanding of how and why these favorable aberrations have come about is limited. The policy implications of these deviations are looked at more closely in Chapter 7. For the moment, it is sufficient to say that some countries—whether by design, by force of circumstances, or by accident—have employed policies that have been atypical in their effects. The alternative strategies that have produced these results may offer insights on how to improve life chances more rapidly than has been possible with orthodox development policies. For example, if the PQLI of countries having per capita GNPs of $700 or more and PQLIs below 68 could be raised to 68, over 143 million people would be affected. If countries having per capita incomes of more than $179 and PQLIs of less than 82 could duplicate Sri Lanka's experience, 1.6 billion people would be affected. Clearly, these are experiences worth exploring.

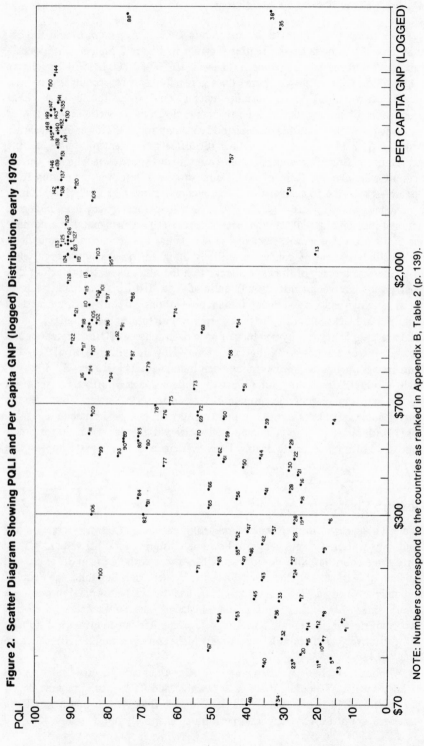

Figure 2. Scatter Diagram Showing PQLI and Per Capita GNP (logged) Distribution, early 1970s

NOTE: Numbers correspond to the countries as ranked in Appendix B, Table 2 (p. 139).

65

The ordering of countries by per capita GNP in Appendix B and the distribution of countries in the scatter diagram in Figure 2 indicate that, once a certain level of per capita income is achieved ($2,100-$2,200 in 1974-76 dollars), a high PQLI (one of 90 or more) does generally tend to accompany it. As average per capita GNP rises, absolute incomes tend to rise for all or very large proportions of the population even if income distribution becomes less equal at the same time. This, in turn, increases food consumption at the lower income levels which in itself probably produces favorable effects on infant mortality and life expectancy. Some expanded social overhead investment—of which a certain amount will take the form of added education and improved protection from disease—is required to sustain the rise in income. However socially inegalitarian a national leadership may be, there is a certain spillover effect from increased national income that will improve performance of those elements that enter into the PQLI. In other words, sustained growth in average per capita income yields benefits independent of policies specifically designed to reduce infant mortality or to increase literacy or life expectancy. (On the other hand, to the extent that poor groups are geographically and culturally isolated from the mainstream of social activity—as, for example, Indian populations in some Latin American countries or blacks in South Africa—the spillover effect may be minimal.)

It is clear that, as a by-product of growth in income, PQLI progress comes slowly. Rich oil states—with the exception of Kuwait (with a PQLI of 75)—still have ratings only equal to or even less than India, with its PQLI of 43. However, their low PQLI results do not necessarily reflect a lack of effort. In many of these countries, considerable revenue is devoted to social services. But even the force-feeding of social overhead improvements does not yield immediate results. Along with larger per capita incomes and social will, there is also need for time—time to design appropriate institutional systems and to integrate appropriate social and individual behaviors.[138]

Country Clusters

Table 11 suggests another set of interesting patterns. Countries are not just randomly scattered; there tends to be some clustering of PQLI values. Of the forty-three countries with the lowest PQLIs—those with PQLIs of 36 or less—all but ten are African. Of these ten, five—the Yemen Arab Republic, the People's Republic of Yemen, Saudi Arabia, Qatar, and the United Arab Emirates—are Arab; three—Afghanistan, Nepal, and Bangladesh—are South Asian; the other two countries are Haiti and Laos. On average, the African countries individually and collectively tend to rank substantially higher on a per capita GNP scale than on a PQLI scale.

Although emphasis is often put on Latin America's poverty and its gross maldistribution of income, the area as a whole and its particular regions clearly have reached a higher level of PQLI performance than African countries. Latin American countries generally also perform substantially better than South and

Southeast Asian countries. With the exception of Haiti (with a PQLI of 36), Bolivia (43), and Honduras (51), no Latin American country has a PQLI as low as the highest state in Africa (South Africa, 53). While no Latin American country has reached a PQLI of 90, the regional PQLIs (weighted by national populations) are all well above the African figures. In comparison with the world average PQLI weighted by national populations (65), Latin America as a whole (PQLI = 71) is substantially above the figure and Africa (32) is dramatically below it.

South Asia (with a PQLI of 41) seems to have its own pattern which, even though Afghanistan (18) and Nepal (25) are included, still is well above the PQLI level of black Africa but not of the other African nations. On the other hand, it is below the average for Southeast Asia (55). When disaggregated, Southeast Asia seems to have three groupings: Kampuchea and Laos, with very low PQLIs; Indonesia, Vietnam, and Burma, with PQLIs at or slightly below the average for the region; and Malaysia, Thailand, the Philippines, and Singapore, with PQLIs well above the average.

There are other visible clusterings; one of these is found in the Caribbean, with an average weighted PQLI of 73. With the exception of Haiti (36) and the Dominican Republic (64), the other Caribbean islands all have PQLIs in or near the 80s.

Development discussions often imply that all poverty is of much the same sort and can be confronted in much the same way. Differences in the nature and scope of poverty often are attributed to resource differences, technical differences, and narrowly defined economic differences. To the extent that differences are seen as something more general, they are defined by continent—there are African, Asian, and Latin American poverty problems. Some of this is, of course, a function of political groupings in the world, but much of it has an independent life in the minds of analysts. While the concentration of countries may appear to be fundamentally regional, geography is not the decisive element. The clustering seems to express similar forms of social organization and historical experience. The PQLI clusterings suggest that there may be other significant features that ought to be taken into account in designing the strategies for dealing with the most grievous aspects of world poverty.

Africa and South Asia are two of the poorest areas in the world. If any general distinction is to be made about these two areas, it would be that South Asia is much poorer and its problems appear to be more intractable. While a few African countries have per capita GNPs lower than any in South Asia, this is not typical (see Appendix B, Table 1). Table 11 shows that the poorest African region—the fifteen countries of Eastern Africa—has an average per capita income (weighted by population) about 60 percent higher than the South Asian per capita income. The per capita income of all Africa *excluding* Southern Africa averaged $314 during the period 1970-75, while the per capita income of South Asia averaged only $131. Nevertheless, the average South Asian PQLI (41) is meaningfully higher than the average for Africa *including* Southern Africa

Table 11. Average Per Capita GNP, PQLI, and Component Indicators for 150 Countries, by Region, early 1970s (weighted by population)

	Number of Countries	Total Population (millions)	Per Capita GNP ($)	PQLI	Life Expectancy at Age One (years)	Infant Mortality Rate (per 1,000 live births)	Literacy (%)
Africa	**49**	**375.4**	**368**	**32**	**53.1**	**152**	**23.7**
Northern Africa	6	91.8	486	41	59.1	128	23.5
Western Africa	16	108.5	292	24	49.3	175	19.6
Eastern Africa	15	107.0	211	31	52.2	152	20.8
Middle Africa	8	42.8	258	27	49.3	165	22.9
Southern Africa	4	25.3	1,121	52	57.5	117	56.1
Middle East	**15**	**111.9**	**1,351**	**49**	**60.2**	**120**	**40.7**
Asia	**20**	**2,025.2**	**455**	**58**	**60.7**	**87**	**52.6**
South Asia	6	757.7	131	41	55.8	124	31.2
Southeast Asia	9	302.6	252	55	57.2	115	65.3
East Asia	5	964.9	749	73	65.8	49	65.7
Latin America	**31**	**302.8**	**929**	**71**	**65.8**	**76**	**72.2**
Central America	7	72.7	898	70	65.0	69	69.8
Caribbean	12	25.4	847	73	66.9	63	69.3
Tropical South America	9	167.4	884	70	65.0	84	69.4
Temperate South America	3	37.4	1,245	83	70.3	63	91.5

Oceania	5	19.4	4,436	85	69.2	35	88.3
Europe	28	714.7	3,374	92	71.2	23	97.2
Northern Europe	7	80.9	4,401	95	72.5	14	99.0
Western Europe	7	150.3	6,050	94	71.9	16	98.0
Eastern Europe	7	353.5	2,400	91	70.3	27	99.5
Southern Europe	7	130.0	2,290	89	71.9	25	88.7
North America	2	231.3	6,980	94	72.3	16	99.0
World	150	3,780.7	1,476	65	63.1	77	62.5

NOTES: *Northern Africa*: Algeria, Egypt, Libya, Morocco, Sudan, and Tunisia.
Western Africa: Benin, Cape Verde, Gambia, Ghana, Guinea, Guinea-Bissau, Ivory Coast, Liberia, Mali, Mauritania, Niger, Nigeria, Senegal, Sierra Leone, Togo, and Upper Volta.
Eastern Africa: Burundi, Comoros, Ethiopia, Kenya, Madagascar, Malawi, Mauritius, Mozambique, Reunion, Rhodesia, Rwanda, Somalia, Tanzania, Uganda, and Zambia.
Middle Africa: Angola, Cameroon, Central African Empire, Chad, Congo, Equatorial Guinea, Gabon, and Zaire.
Southern Africa: Botswana, Lesotho, South Africa, and Swaziland.
Middle East: Bahrain, Cyprus, Iran, Iraq, Israel, Jordan, Kuwait, Lebanon, Qatar, Saudi Arabia, Syria, Turkey, United Arab Emirates, Yemen Arab Republic, and People's Republic of Yemen.
South Asia: Afghanistan, Bangladesh, India, Nepal, Pakistan, and Sri Lanka.
Southeast Asia: Burma, Kampuchea, Indonesia, Laos, Malaysia, Philippines, Singapore, Thailand, and Vietnam.
East Asia: People's Republic of China, Hong Kong, Japan, Republic of Korea, and Taiwan.
Central America: Costa Rica, El Salvador, Guatemala, Honduras, Mexico, Nicaragua, and Panama.
Caribbean: Bahamas, Barbados, Cuba, Dominican Republic, Grenada, Guadeloupe, Haiti, Jamaica, Martinique, Netherlands Antilles, Puerto Rico, and Trinidad and Tobago.
Tropical South America: Bolivia, Brazil, Colombia, Ecuador, Guyana, Paraguay, Peru, Surinam, and Venezuela.
Temperate South America: Argentina, Chile, and Uruguay.
Oceania: Australia, Fiji, New Zealand, Papua New Guinea, and Western Samoa.
Northern Europe: Denmark, Finland, Iceland, Ireland, Norway, Sweden, and United Kingdom.
Western Europe: Austria, Belgium, France, Federal Republic of Germany, Luxembourg, Netherlands, and Switzerland.
Eastern Europe: Bulgaria, Czechoslovakia, Democratic Republic of Germany, Hungary, Poland, Romania, and U.S.S.R.
Southern Europe: Albania, Greece, Italy, Malta, Portugal, Spain, and Yugoslavia.
North America: Canada and the United States.

SOURCE: Based on Appendix A.

(32). But such gross analysis seems only to point out the paradox; more detailed examination may point toward possible explanations.[139]

All the African and South Asian countries have colonial histories and all are relatively newly independent. This common experience of dependency may help explain the fact of low PQLIs, but it does not account for the regional differences.[140] The extremely low PQLI ratings of all black African countries suggest that something else is involved—perhaps that the traditional social organization makes delivery of the modern services that tend to produce high PQLIs more difficult and that alternative administrative structures have not yet emerged to provide channels through which those services can be effectively furnished. An alternate hypothesis is that these countries uniformly refuse to attempt to improve the living standards of their people. This, however, does not conform to recent experience.

In general, these new black African countries have pervasive tribal traditions characterized by the absence of extensive social division of labor and by quite limited specialization of function. Historically, these societies did not have elaborate hierarchies of command and subordination. There was thus relatively little sustained extraction and transfer of the social surplus from lower to higher administrative levels. These societies also tended to be non-literate, probably because of the absence of complex bureaucratic structures.[141]

By contrast, settled agricultural societies that were organized around villages generated concentrated social surpluses that could be mobilized. These surpluses were used to support substantial hierarchical organizations and permanent imperial centers. Sustaining such systems required different functional capacities than those needed in tribal societies. The much greater specialization and division of labor required bureaucratic relationships which (however high illiteracy was) depended not only on the presence of literate groups but also on institutional arrangements of the type needed to provide those services that contribute to a higher average PQLI.

This distinction between tribal and village systems would explain why Northern African countries (PQLI = 41) and such South Asian countries as India, Pakistan, and (despite its long period of social and political disruption) Bangladesh have quite similar PQLIs (South Asia = 41), while Afghanistan's rating (18) is similar to that of black Africa. It would also help to explain the low PQLIs of the oil countries of the Middle East, which are still essentially tribal, despite their high per capita incomes. Conversely, Latin American countries have the organizational capacity to deliver resources and services in ways that produce relatively high PQLIs. This may be the result of either or both long involvement in the North Atlantic system of complex social organization and the impact of powerful imperial systems on relatively small societies.[142]

It has been suggested that the low PQLIs of black Africa are due not to their tribal organization but to the relatively brief interval of formal imperialist control in this region—that the imperial powers did not have the time to acquaint themselves with, or to cope with, the specific health and medical problems of these tropical regions and that, as a result, the former colonies were left without usable techniques for improving the social conditions measured by the PQLI. But Europeans were in Africa as early and as aggressively as in South Asia. Why was effective control established so much later?

The differences between tribal and village structures suggest two possible explanations: 1) European imperialists found it very difficult to conquer and impose a surplus-generating organization on tribal societies, and 2) tribal systems did not generate surpluses that could be mobilized easily by Europeans and thus were not attractive to them.[143] In either case—and these are not necessarily contradictory explanations—their structure and functioning made tribal systems less easy to organize than village-based systems of the sort described above.

This interpretation clearly does not in itself provide an adequate hypothesis. However, the particular clustering of PQLI performances already suggests that the results derive not so much from the level of per capita GNP as from the total structure of inputs, including the different types of socially organized capacity. Detailed explanations are not possible without much more research and analysis; but it does seem apparent that the problems confronting black African states *as a group* (and probably also Afghanistan, some of the Arab states, and others) in trying to raise their PQLIs are probably quite different from those that confront South Asian, Southeast Asian, and North African countries as a group or Latin American countries as another group. Thus specific attention should be paid to these institutional differences and to their policy implications.

Distribution of Benefits

The PQLI's components express distributional characteristics. Changes in literacy, infant mortality, and life expectancy at age one reflect changes in the availability of these benefits to the whole population. Changes in PQLI reflect the aggregate effect of changes in the component indicators. Overall the PQLI is a much simpler measure of distribution than those that try to measure the distribution of national incomes.

Attempts to measure income distribution encounter at least three major problems.[144] First, how should the income-receiving unit be defined? Does one measure the income of a household, of a family, or of an individual, and does one allow for various phases of the life cycle? Second, should income be measured before or after taxes and transfers? This is an important consideration in developed countries having sophisticated systems of taxation and social benefits. But developing countries often provide subsidized goods and services to various groups and regions; the effects of these on the distribution of incomes can be quite substantial. Third, in addition to private-wealth holdings, should the flow of benefits from social facilities (public wealth) already in place—clean water, sanitation systems, public health organization, education, etc.—be measured?

The World Bank recently compared income distribution in sixty-six countries. The Bank ranked households ordinally by income and measured inequality by the share of income going to the poorest 40 percent of households. The smaller the share going to this group, the more unequal income distribution was said to be.[145] The Bank's income distribution measure and the PQLI do not appear to correlate well. Table 12 contains a list of seventeen countries taken from the larger World Bank study. The seventeen were selected to show the variety of PQLI results that can be obtained among countries with similar distributions of income and the variety of income distributions that are found with the same PQLI.

A comparison of Senegal, the Philippines, the Republic of Korea, and Taiwan might lead one to conclude that there is a positive correlation between income distribution and PQLI, particularly since these countries have nearly identical GNPs. However, in many cases, this relation does not hold. For example, Sri Lanka and Niger have simlar incomes and similar income distribution, but Niger's PQLI is less than one sixth that of Sri Lanka.[146] Because Sri Lanka is so often pointed out as an exceptionally good performer, it is worth noting that large PQLI differences (despite relatively similar income distributions) also are apparent between Burma and Chad and between India and Niger. The Philippines, Malaysia, Iran, and Zambia provide an example of this at somewhat higher income levels. A comparison of Jamaica and Yugoslavia also shows the lack of correlation between income distribution and PQLI; despite identical PQLIs, Jamaica has a much more unequal distribution of income.

Finally, there seems to be no correlation between income and PQLI even where income distribution is identical (for example, Honduras, Ecuador, and Peru, or Chad, Niger, and Korea). The PQLI captures the total effect of social and economic policy as well as of how private income is spent. The welfare results cannot be predicted from income distribution data.

Special Purpose PQLIs

Because literacy, infant mortality, and life expectancy data presently are not available by income groups within countries, it is not possible to construct a PQLI of this sort. There is, however, no conceptual bar to comparing the PQLIs of income classes; doing so should be an important long-run research objective. In the meantime, however, PQLIs can be constructed for other intra-country categories that, in turn, can yield significant information about the distribution process. PQLIs describing differences among ethnic groups (where this is relevant), among subnational geographical regions (where a county is large enough to make this important), between females and males, and between rural and urban sectors can be constructed.

The examples below of the various uses to which PQLI can be put use historical data whenever possible in order to highlight the ability of the PQLI to measure performance over time. Historical experience is one of the few laboratories available to the social scientist and the policymaker. A historical dimen-

**Table 12. Income Inequality, PQLI, and Per Capita GNP,
Selected Countries, Various Years
(ranked by degree of income inequality)**

	Income Going to Poorest 40% of Households	PQLI	Per Capita GNP
	(%)		*($)*
Honduras (1968)	6.5	51	265
Ecuador (1970)	6.5	68	277
Peru (1971)	6.5	62	480
Jamaica (1958)	8.2	84	510
Senegal (1960)	10.0	25	245
Philippines (1971)	11.6	71	239
Malaysia (1970)	11.6	66	330
Iran (1968)	12.5	43	332
Zambia (1959)	14.5	29	230
India (1964)	16.0	43	99
Burma (1958)	16.5	51	82
Sri Lanka (1969)	17.0	82	95
Chad (1958)	18.0	18	78
Niger (1960)	18.0	13	97
Korea (1970)	18.0	82	235
Yugoslavia (1968)	18.5	84	529
Taiwan (1964)	20.4	86	241

NOTE: The income data are in constant 1971 U.S. dollars and are for the years noted in parentheses. PQLI data are for 1970-75. Because income shares do not appear to change dramatically in the short run, it is reasonably safe to compare these income distribution data and PQLI results, even though they do not necessarily relate to the same years.

SOURCES: Per capita GNP and percent of income going to poorest households are from Hollis Chenery, Montek Ahluwalia, G.L.C. Bell, John H. Duloy, and Richard Jolly, *Redistribution with Growth* (London: Oxford University Press, 1974), pp. 8 and 9; PQLI data are from Appendix A of this volume.

sion enhances the usefulness of both national and subnational PQLIs by helping to test explanations of differential performances. Moreover, historical analysis can alleviate the defects of cross-sectional analysis.[147]

Constructing reasonably long series for some already developed countries—e.g., Britain, Sweden, France, Germany, and the United States—is easier than constructing them for developing countries, which do not have the same long history of data collecting. The United States is the only country for which a PQLI time series extending back to the beginning of this century has been constructed. The PQLI was not designed as a tool for analyzing countries that already have high physical quality of life characteristics, since these countries have by definition already come close to reaching the levels of life expectancy, infant mortality, and literacy assumed to be the maximum feasible. Nevertheless, the historical, ethnic, and state data for the United States show some characteristics that are interesting in themselves and that indicate how such data might be used for developing countries.

PQLIs have been constructed for a number of other countries for various years from about 1950 on. With effort and imagination, it will be possible to produce much longer time series for several other countries, including Sri Lanka and what are now India, Pakistan, and Bangladesh. In fact, for much of the Indian subcontinent it will be possible to construct female and male PQLIs as well as PQLIs for various provinces from census sources going back to the earliest decades of this century.[148]

The possible usefulness of these various kinds of data, for both comparative and historical analysis of the development process, is considerable. The data presently available permit illustrations of the various ways in which the PQLI can be used. It should be cautioned, however, that patterns do not in themselves provide causality and that the analysis of regional or group differences and of changes over time requires time-consuming research yet to be conducted. But the fact that the PQLI lends itself to state, provincial, and/or district divisions strengthens its usefulness as an instrument with which to study the impact of developmental processes. One advantage of subnational comparisons is that they minimize some, if not all, of the cultural, social, and political differences that are so troublesome in inter-country comparisons. For example, it is provocative to discover that the state of Kerala (with a lower per capita income than India as a whole) has a PQLI of 68, while the all-India PQLI (including Kerala) is 43. Such a gross difference begs for explanation, particularly when continous states do not stand out in the same way (see Table 19, p. 90).

The following sections provide examples of historical PQLIs, PQLIs of various ethnic groups and intra-country regions, and PQLIs differentiated by sex and by sector. But before examining these special purpose PQLIs, a brief word about the concept of the Disparity Reduction Rate (DRR), used below, is in order. The DRR is a tool developed at the Overseas Development Council. As employed here, it measures the rate at which the disparity between a country's PQLI performance and the best projected performance (100) decreased between two periods. Thus a high DRR indicates a rapid annual reduction, and a low DRR reflects a slow annual reduction, in the gap between current performance and a PQLI of 100. Unlike the normal percentage rate of change, the DRR permits meaningful comparisons of performance toward fixed goals to be made. Such comparisons are distorted by the ordinary percentage rate of change.[149]

Historical PQLIs

The few historical data available for developing countries should be looked at for whatever information they provide. Table 13 shows PQLI changes for thirty-four countries for three dates from *circa* 1950 through *circa* 1970. The basic data from which these PQLIs were constructed pose many problems and the results must be treated with extreme caution.[150]

Table 13. PQLI Performance and Per Capita GNP Growth Rates for Various Countries. circa 1950, 1960, and 1970 (ranked by "1950" PQLI)

	PQLI			Average Annual DRR, 1950s-70s[1]	Avg. Annual Per Capita GNP Growth Rate, 1950-70
	circa 1950	circa 1960	circa 1970		
				(%)	(%)
India	14	30	40	1.7	1.8
Turkey	30	42	55	2.1	3.5
Egypt	32	42	43[2]	0.8	1.2
Algeria	34	36	41	0.6	1.8
Nicaragua	42	53	54[2]	1.2	3.2
Malaysia	47	47	67	2.2	2.3
Colombia	47	66	71[2]	3.1	1.6
Ecuador	48	60	68[2]	2.7	2.0
Réunion	48	60	70	3.4	—
El Salvador	51	61	64[2]	1.5	2.0
Brazil	53	63	66	1.6	2.7
Mauritius	55	67	71[2]	2.4	−1.9
Mexico	55	65	71	2.3	3.1
Philippines	55	60	72	2.2	2.6
Thailand	55	58	70	1.7	3.8
Venezuela	58	69	79	3.2	3.0
Portugal	62	69	80[2]	3.2	—
Chile	62	65	77	2.8	1.5
Taiwan	63	77	87	5.1	5.3
Sri Lanka	65	75	80	3.4	1.9
Costa Rica	67	78	86	3.7	2.4
Jamaica	68	80	87	4.6	4.7
Panama	68	73	81	2.5	3.2
Trinidad	69	81	87	4.1	4.0
Martinique	72	78	86	4.2	—
Cyprus	72	82	85[2]	2.8	3.8
Bulgaria	74	79	89	5.6	—
Puerto Rico	74	83	91	5.2	—
Argentina	77	82	85	2.1	1.9
Hungary	80	87	90	3.2	—
Greece	82	84	88	2.4	5.8
Italy	80	87	92[2]	5.0	5.0
Israel	84	86	89[2]	1.9	4.7
United States	89	91	93	2.1	2.4

[1]Average annual DRRs are calculated for the actual number of years between "1950" and "1970" PQLIs. These vary for individual countries as noted in Appendix C.
[2]Data from Appendix A. Treated as if for 1970.

SOURCE: PQLI data from Appendix C, Table 1. GNP average annual growth rates calculated from Morawetz, *Twenty-Five Years of Economic Development*, Table A-1.

India, often referred to as "a basket case," exhibited slow but not insignificant improvement in its PQLI over a period of about twenty years, despite its slow growth in per capita income. Algeria, which had a rate of growth in income similar to India's but a level of income considerably higher, had considerably less PQLI improvement. Put in other terms, India's average annual Disparity Reduction Rate (1.7 percent) was three times that of Algeria (0.6 percent) during the period 1950 to 1970. The period was one of great turmoil in Algeria and the poor level of improvement may well be associated with the migration of French *colons* from the country. However, India was faced with the gross consequences of partition and subsequent instability. It is essential to examine each case individually in order to be able to interpret historical data.

Sri Lanka and Taiwan currently have relatively high PQLIs for their per capita incomes. While PQLI progress between 1950 and 1970 was substantial, both countries already had fairly high PQLI levels by 1950. In fact, fragmentary data suggest that by 1946, when its per capita income (in 1974 dollars) was probably less than $90, Sri Lanka already had attained a PQLI of 42 (similar to India's PQLI today).

The Sri Lanka data (see Table 14) suggest once again that substantial PQLI improvement depends on the presence of a solid social infrastructure and cannot be generated merely by some quick technological or medical innovation. This conclusion is not negated by its rapid PQLI improvement between 1946 and

Table 14. Historical Performance in Sri Lanka's Life Expectancy at Age One, Infant Mortality, Literacy, PQLI, and Per Capita GNP

	Life Expectancy at Age One	Infant Mortality	Literacy	PQLI	Average Annual DRR in PQLI	Per Capita GNP Growth Rate
	(years)	(per 1,000 live births)	(%)		(%)	(%)
1881	—	—	17.4	—	—	—
1891	—	—	21.7	—	—	—
1901	—	170	26.4	—	—	—
1911	—	218	31.0	—	—	—
1921	37.9	192	39.9	19	—	—
1946	48.5	141	57.8	42	1.3	—
1953	60.0	71	65.4	64	6.6	—
1963	64.8	56	71.6	73	2.8	0.3
1971	67.4	43	78.1	79	3.1	1.6
1921-1971	—	—	—	—	2.7	—

SOURCE: James P. Grant, *Disparity Reduction Rates: A Proposal for Measuring and Targeting Progress in Meeting Basic Needs.* Monograph No. 11 (Washington, D.C.: Overseas Development Council, 1978), p. 24.

1953, when the Disparity Reduction Rate was higher than during any other period anywhere for which data exist. Whatever the precise mix of factors accounting for Sri Lanka's progress, the malaria eradication campaign of that period certainly played a substantial part. But more important than this quick burst of improvement is that Sri Lanka's PQLI rose during the quarter century before 1946 and continued to rise, albeit not so dramatically, during the two decades after 1953. Without a sturdy social infrastructure on which to depend, Sri Lanka (or any other country) could perhaps have been provided with an external "technological fix," but it certainly could not have expanded or even sustained the gains from it.

The arithmetic of Sri Lanka's experience—from a PQLI of 42 to 79 in twenty-five years—might suggest that India, with a PQLI of 43, could reach a PQLI of 79 twenty-five years from now. How reasonable is this? One way to think about the matter is to look at the difference in performance in the component indicators of India today and of Sri Lanka when it had a PQLI of 42.[151]

	Infant Mortality (per 1,000 births)	Life Expectancy at Age One (years)	Literacy (%)	PQLI
Sri Lanka (1946)	141	48.5	57.8	42
India (early 1970s)	122	55.9	34.0	43

The differences in structure are interesting. India's infant mortality rate and its life expectancy at age one are much better than Sri Lanka's, but its literacy rate is far worse. The patterns are the result of specific kinds of social organization. At present, it is not known what caused these differences or whether and in what form they are likely to affect the prospect of future improvement. In seeking to explain specific current conditions and future possibilities, looking at the historical data can provide important clues to the nature of the social process.

The experience of Taiwan—whose PQLI increased from 63 in 1950 to 90 in 1976 (see Appendix E)—suggests that it is possible to achieve high rates of economic growth at the same time that life chances are improving. During the 1950-76 period, when Taiwan's per capita GNP was growing at a high average annual rate of over 5 percent, the average annual Disparity Reduction Rate in PQLI was 4.9 percent, quite high by comparison with other developing countries.

A comparison of the Taiwan and Sri Lanka cases is useful. In the period 1953-71, Taiwan's PQLI rose from 68 to 87, and Sri Lanka's from 64 to 79. Not only was Sri Lanka's Disparity Reduction Rate less rapid than Taiwan's (3.0 percent compared with 4.9 percent), but its per capita GNP growth rate also was slower (1.8 percent compared with 5.3 percent in the period 1950-70).[152] This sort of comparison clearly is worth pursuing. Taiwan's per capita income in 1950 was two-and-one-half times as large as Sri Lanka's ($224 compared with a mere $90). It is not known how important that advantage was. Nor is it known, for example, how their different experiences as colonies of Japan and Britain affected them.

The historical experience of the United States is also worth examining, if only because of the insights it may add to our understanding of the development process. Table 15 shows that the U.S. PQLI in 1900 was 56; this is a level already higher than the 1970-75 achievements of any African country or of the Middle East or South Asian regions. The 1974 U.S. PQLI level (94.0) was achieved relatively slowly, at a Disparity Reduction Rate that averaged 2.7 percent over seventy-four years and that never rose above 4.6 percent in any shorter period. It is also worth noting that the DRR for the shorter periods tended to be somewhat volatile; the low was 0.8 percent and the high was 4.6 percent. The causes of the average rate or the fluctuations in rate are not known. Further investigation is needed.

Ethnic Distinctions

Table 15 also shows that it is possible to measure the performance of different ethnic groups. The penalties of poverty and discrimination are clearly reflected in the U.S. data. In 1915, whites already had a PQLI of 70 while minorities (largely the black population) only had a PQLI of 39. Although the PQLI of non-whites had risen to 88.2 by 1974, minorities continue to have lower physical quality of life chances than do whites (95.0). U.S. minority populations have PQLIs similar to Taiwan, Malta, and Uruguay; their PQLIs are lower than the averages achieved by Greece, Israel, and Barbados, even though their average per capita income is considerably higher than average per capita income in these countries.

The historical record is not particularly inspiring. For the period 1915-74, the rate at which the PQLI gap decreased for minorities was marginally slower than the rate at which the gap decreased for whites. It is tempting to suggest that the fairly high average annual PQLI Disparity Reduction Rate in the period 1969-74 (4.6 percent) reflects increased political pressures from minorities. Yet whites had an even better DRR during the same period.

The one period in which the DRR was dramatically higher for minorities than for whites was between 1915 and 1920 (4.5 vs. 1.0 percent). One possible reason for this is the different impact the influenza epidemic of 1918-19 had on the two groups, perhaps resulting from the different regional distribution of the two races. Another (and potentially contradictory) hypothesis is that the high rate of black migration into northern cities during this period took blacks into environments in which the existing social infrastructure was significantly more favorable than in the southern rural systems from which they came. However segregated blacks may have been in urban ghettos, this urbanization process generated a faster rise in PQLI than per capita income improvements and other conditions might suggest. Blacks could have been

Table 15. Historical PQLI Performance of the United States, by Race, 1900-1974

	United States		Whites		Blacks and Other Races[1]	
	PQLI	DRR (%)	PQLI	DRR (%)	PQLI	DRR (%)
1900	56.1	—	—	—	—	—
1910	61.8	1.4	—	—	—	—
1915	68.9	4.0	70.3	—	38.8	—
1920	70.1	0.8	71.8	1.0	51.4	4.5
1930	77.8	2.9	80.2	3.5	59.5	1.8
1940	82.8	2.5	84.6	2.5	68.4	2.5
1947	87.6	4.6	88.8	4.4	77.1	4.5
1950	88.9	3.6	90.4	5.0	78.5	2.1
1952	89.6	3.2	90.9	2.6	79.0	1.2
1959	91.1	2.2	92.2	2.2	82.4	2.5
1969	92.4	1.6	93.5	1.8	85.1	1.7
1974	94.0	4.6	95.0	5.1	88.2	4.6
1900-1974		2.7		—		—
1915-1974		2.8		3.0		2.8

[1]This classification includes Native Americans, Orientals, and others who may have quite different performance patterns. It is likely that "Orientals" currently have a fairly high PQLI; if this is so, Blacks and/or Native Americans would have somewhat lower averages.

NOTE: Unlike other PQLI data, U.S. data are presented to one decimal place, partly because the data are better, partly so that differences, which are frequently minor, will show up.

SOURCE: Based on Appendix D, Table 2.

denied the benefits of urban social overhead only if they had been totally segregated in the South African manner.

Historical PQLI data provide a sharper focus for examining the development process, even if they do not explain different PQLI patterns within a country. The study of the white and black patterns within the United States, both current and historical, can provide some insight into the difficulties that other countries face in trying to raise their PQLIs.

While there are no easily available disaggregated black/white data for South Africa, which has a combined PQLI of 53, it is possible to speculate about the current situation. If it is assumed that whites in South Africa have PQLIs comparable to those of Western European populations (about 95), the PQLI for all other groups in South Africa (allowing for different-sized populations) is no higher than 40, about the same level as in the two black African countries of Kenya and Uganda, and lower than in India. On the other hand, if whites do not have a PQLI level comparable to most of Europe's despite their quite high per capita income, they may be paying the price for the racial policies they impose.

Regional PQLIs

To see how PQLIs can be used to look at performance in different regions of a country, it is useful to examine data for the states of the United States. Between 1940 and 1970, all the states exhibited steady PQLI improvement (see Table 16). Moreover, at least until 1960, the absolute difference between the lowest and the highest PQLI was narrowing.

	State with Lowest PQLI	*State with Highest PQLI*	*Absolute Difference*
1940	71.9 (N.M.)	89.0 (Minn.)	17.1
1950	82.9 (S.C.)	92.9 (Minn.)	10.0
1960	86.2 (S.C.)	93.7 (Ia./Neb.)	7.5
1970	87.5 (D.C.)	95.2 (Utah)	7.7

Table 16. Historical PQLI Performance of the United States, by State, 1940-1970

	PQLI				Average Annual DRR, 1940-70
	1940	**1950**	**1960**	**1970**	*(%)*
Alabama	80.1	84.5	88.3	90.9	2.6
Alaska	—	—	87.5	91.3	3.6[1]
Arizona	74.8	85.4	89.2	92.9	4.1
Arkansas	84.5	88.5	90.7	92.5	2.4
California	85.5	90.4	92.3	94.1	3.0
Colorado	82.8	89.7	92.1	94.3	3.6
Connecticut	86.2	91.3	92.5	94.3	2.9
Delaware	84.3	85.3	91.0	92.2	2.3
Florida	83.9	85.6	90.6	92.4	2.5
Georgia	81.8	83.6	87.9	90.3	2.1
Hawaii	—	88.8	91.9	95.1	4.0[2]
Idaho	86.5	91.4	92.9	94.1	2.7
Illinois	86.0	90.4	91.1	92.1	1.9
Indiana	85.4	90.4	92.0	93.0	2.4
Iowa	88.9	92.6	93.7	94.6	2.4
Kansas	88.6	92.4	93.6	94.6	2.5
Kentucky	82.3	84.4	90.4	92.0	2.6
Louisiana	79.1	83.4	87.7	92.5	3.4

Table 16 (continued)

	PQLI				Average Annual DRR, 1940-70
	1940	**1950**	**1960**	**1970**	
					(%)
Maine	84.3	89.9	91.6	93.1	2.7
Maryland	83.3	86.5	90.1	92.4	2.6
Massachusetts	85.3	90.3	92.1	93.6	2.7
Michigan	85.2	90.4	91.7	92.7	2.3
Minnesota	89.0	92.9	93.5	95.0	2.6
Mississippi	81.3	84.2	86.8	88.9	1.7
Missouri	85.8	90.2	91.7	92.8	2.2
Montana	85.1	90.2	91.2	92.6	2.3
Nebraska	88.9	92.5	93.7	94.7	2.4
Nevada	82.1	87.5	88.9	91.3	2.4
New Hampshire	86.3	90.5	92.0	93.4	2.4
New Jersey	85.4	90.2	91.2	92.9	2.4
New Mexico	71.9	84.6	89.5	91.8	4.0
New York	85.2	90.0	90.7	92.5	2.2
North Carolina	81.9	84.9	88.6	90.8	2.2
North Dakota	87.8	91.9	93.0	95.0	2.9
Ohio	85.4	91.2	91.7	93.0	2.4
Oklahoma	85.4	87.2	92.1	93.3	2.6
Oregon	88.3	91.8	92.6	94.3	2.4
Pennsylvania	83.8	89.1	90.9	92.5	2.5
Rhode Island	85.0	89.9	91.9	93.7	2.9
South Carolina	77.8	82.9	86.2	89.7	2.5
South Dakota	88.6	92.2	92.3	94.2	2.2
Tennessee	82.9	85.1	89.9	91.7	2.4
Texas	80.7	84.7	90.4	92.4	3.1
Utah	86.6	91.6	93.5	95.2	3.4
Vermont	85.2	90.6	92.0.	93.9	2.9
Virginia	80.9	84.2	89.4	91.9	2.8
Washington	87.1	91.4	92.7	93.9	2.5
West Virginia	82.5	85.4	90.6	91.3	2.3
Wisconsin	87.7	91.3	92.9	94.6	2.7
Wyoming	85.1	89.9	91.3	92.2	2.1
District of Columbia	85.1	86.0	87.9	87.5	0.6
United States	**82.4**	**89.0**	**90.9**	**92.8**	**2.9**
Puerto Rico	—	74.3	83.5	90.8	5.0[2]

[1]DRR is for 1960-70.   [2]DRR is for 1950-70.

SOURCE: Based on data in Appendix D, Table 2.

The general pattern suggests numerous questions. The most puzzling specific feature is the almost static performance of the District of Columbia, in spite of a very high level of per capita income. Washington's lack of PQLI improvement may be the result of the massive influx of blacks into the District from states where average PQLI or at least black PQLI was quite low.[153]

In some cases, in-migration appears to have affected the PQLI favorably. For example, in 1940, New Mexico and Arizona both had quite low PQLIs (71.9 and 74.8, respectively), because Native American and Mexican American minorities (which have low PQLIs) comprised large segments of their populations. The rapid rate of PQLI change in these two states between 1940 and 1970, as measured by the DRR, may partly reflect the large in-migration of whites from areas with relatively high PQLI—migrants who also may have had the wealth and political influence to generate speedily the needed infrastructure.

Once again, there seems to be no close correlation between per capita incomes and PQLI levels. The District of Columbia, with the highest 1970 per capita personal income in the country ($5,333) and the lowest PQLI (87.5) is not the only example of a gross divergence. Alaska, with a 1970 per capita income of $4,603, had a PQLI of only 91.3, even though Hawaii—with a per capita income nearly as high ($4,562)—had the second highest PQLI (95.1) in the United States. While the high cost of living frequently distorts income rankings, a more likely reason for Alaska's comparatively low PQLI is that its Eskimos and Native Americans—who comprise about one sixth of its total population—have low PQLIs that affected the state's total PQLI performance.

Nevada, with the same PQLI as Alaska (91.3) and a similar average per capita income ($4,452), does not have the same proportion of low-PQLI minorities, suggesting that even after adjustments are made for ethnic, rural-urban, and income differences, some of the PQLI variation among states may be associated with different types of social policy.[154]

Female and Male PQLIs

Many current development programs explicitly directed toward satisfying basic human needs are focused on women. Furthermore, the new alternative development strategies tend to incorporate a more vigorous role for the household as a production unit and thus to provide an explicit role for women. This makes the impact of policy on women an even more important concern. Numerous attempts have been made to measure this impact, but most of them are not particularly useful for international comparisons. They are unable to accommodate the varied ways women function in diverse social, cultural, and economic settings. They also do not lend themselves well to measuring change over time. The PQLI, on the other hand, can measure the condition of women in all settings as well as their changing status.

Appendix C contains data for separate male and female PQLIs for seventy-three countries. In the case of forty-three of these, there are data for two or even three time periods. At this stage, the data are not very good.

Of the seventy-three countries, there are twenty-eight in which the female PQLI was lower than the male PQLI in one or more years between 1949 and 1972. The eighteen countries that had differences of more than three points are listed in Table 17. In the case of six of these countries, there are PQLIs for two or three years. The list includes countries at various levels of income and PQLI. The countries do not seem to be concentrated in any culture area. This diversity suggests that explanations of the status of women are likely to be complex and varied. However, it is possible to examine the performance of the components that account for these lower PQLIs.

Female literacy rates are somewhat lower in sixty-six of the seventy-three countries listed in Appendix C. But in the eighteen countries noted in Table 17, the female literacy rates range from 17 to 49 points lower than the male literacy rates. (The one exception is Liberia, where both male and female rates are extremely low.)

Female performance in the other two indicators—infant mortality and life expectancy at age one—typically is better than male performance. However, of the eighteen countries in Table 17, seven had female infant mortality rates that were worse than male infant mortality rates, but in each case, for only one year.[155] Three countries had lower life expectancy rates for women than for men; each of these is in South Asia. Two other countries not on the list of eighteen—Afghanistan (unspecific date) and Guatemala (1950)—had lower life expectancies for women than for men. These also had lower PQLIs for women, but the differences were less than three points.

In Table 17, India (1970) is the only country for which all three indicators registered worse performance for women than for men. This does not mean that the PQLI of women has been worsening—between 1949 and 1970 it rose from 10 to 35—but that it has risen less rapidly than the PQLI of men. Among the individual components, female literacy improved very slowly and, between 1959 and 1970 at least, female infant mortality did not improve at all. On the other hand, life expectancy at age one improved rather dramatically, but so did male life expectancy.

In all countries, raising female literacy to the level of male literacy would of course, change female-male PQLI comparisons, but it would not change dramatically the level of the composite PQLI, since the individual indicators are equally weighted and any change in an indicator affects the total PQLI by only one third its absolute value. In the most extreme case, if female literacy in Burma (1955) increased by 49 points (to the male literacy level), the female PQLI would rise from 36 to 52. If there are equal numbers of men and women, the combined PQLI would rise about 9 points, from 41 to 50. Similarly, even if India's (1970) female literacy rate increased by 23 points, making it equal to the male rate, the female PQLI would only improve by approximately 8 points, bringing it to 43; India's combined PQLI would increase only from 40 to 44. In other words, if a country wants to raise its PQLI, improvements in female literacy will help some but not dramatically. Large changes in a

Table 17. Countries in Which Female PQLI is Lower than Male PQLI by More than Three Points, Various Years

		PQLI			Difference	Life Expectancy at Age One Index		Infant Mortality Index		Literacy Index	
	Date	Total	Female	Male	(Female -Male)	Female	Male	Female	Male	Female	Male
Algeria	1964	36	34	38	– 4	43	37	52	47	8	30
Burma	1955	41	36	47	–11	35	30	39	27	34	83
Cameroon	1962	45	40	49	– 9	37	31	44	37	40	80
	1965	24	20	28	– 8	8	5	45	48	7	31
Cyprus	1948	72	69	75	– 6	89	75	73	73	44	78
	1960	82	80	85	– 5	87	76	85	90	64	88
Egypt	1960	42	39	45	– 6	56	48	51	56	9	32
Greece	1955	82	79	85	– 6	89	81	86	86	61	88
	1961	84	82	86	– 4	91	83	86	84	70	92
Hong Kong	1960	76	74	79	– 5	83	63	86	83	52	90
India	1949	14	10	17	– 7	-2	3	24	18	8	29
	1959	30	25	34	– 9	21	27	41	34	13	42
	1970	40	35	45	–10	42	44	41	44	22	45
Indonesia	1971	49	47	51	– 4	42	37	50	44	49	71
Jordan	1961	54	48	61	–13	52	52	77	81	15	50
Liberia	scattered	26	21	31	–10	38	36	21	41	4	14

Malaysia	1949	47	42	51	− 9	38	33	71	63	16	56
	1970	67	65	69	− 4	59	51	87	82	50	72
Pakistan	1966	35	32	38	− 6	37	40	51	44	7	29
Peru	1961	58	55	62	− 7	53	51	64	60	48	74
Sri Lanka	1953	65	60	70	−10	52	60	74	69	53	81
	1963	75	72	78	− 6	72	73	81	77	64	86
	1969	80	78	82	− 4	79	75	84	80	72	89
Thailand	1949	55	52	59	− 7	44	36	76	72	36	69
Turkey	1971	55	52	59	− 7	70	63	51	43	34	69
Zambia	1969	33	30	37	− 7	20	11	37	38	35	61

NOTE: Occasional anomolies are due to rounding.

SOURCE: Based on Appendix C.

country's average PQLI probably require a broader array of programs. [156]

The issues involved in comparing the PQLIs of women and of men are not merely arithmetic. A case can be made that the potential PQLI performance of women is different from that of men and that, therefore, the female PQLI and the male PQLI should not be based on the same 0 to 100 scales. In the case of literacy, this is not an issue, since 100 percent literacy is the best level of achievement possible for both women and men. But for infant mortality and life expectancy, performance levels differ for males and females.

The evidence suggests that, both where infant mortality rates are very high and where they are extremely low, females generally have higher survival rates. Similarly, women seem to have longer average life spans and, as average life expectancy rises, the gap between females and males seems to widen. In countries with the longest average life expectancies, there currently is a difference of six to eight years between the life expectancies of men and those of women.

For the purpose of making most development policy, such differences may not matter, since the basic task is to raise the average PQLI for both sexes. However, if improvements in the status of women are sought directly through target programs rather than as a by-product of general development policies, the PQLI can be used to reflect more precisely the differences between men and women. Under these circumstances, some modification of the index may be necessary.

The reasons for the differences between male and female infant mortality and longevity are not clear. These differences seem to be due in part to genetic-biological characteristics and in part to social and cultural factors.[157] The latter frequently work counter to the former. The genetic-biological factors seem to be the cause of lower female than male infant mortality rates and of higher female than male life expectancies, and thus tend to contribute to *higher* female PQLIs. Socio-cultural factors, on the other hand, seem to reduce female life expectancies and to increase their infant mortality rates, contributing to *lower* female PQLIs. The combined PQLI, using life expectancy and infant mortality values whose end points are set on the basis of average performance (including both males and females), blurs these distinctions.

To distinguish social from biogenetic influences, upper end values could be set for infant mortality and life expectancy rates that reflect the different potentials of the two sexes. Further investigation is necessary to establish the appropriate differences. For example, a life expectancy index whose upper limit (100) was set at 80 years for women and at 73 years for men would appear to allow for genetic-biological differences as they are now known. This would enable comparisons to be made between men and women that are corrected for what may be fundamental physiological differences between the sexes. Such an adjustment would change the relative PQLI standing of females to males in all countries; it would show lower female PQLI performances than the current scale does.

Female and male PQLIs also can show changes over time. Table 18 shows Disparity Reduction Rates for twenty-two countries for the period 1950 through 1970. In all twenty two cases, total PQLIs rose between 1950 and 1970, as did the female and male PQLIs separately. With the exception of India and Guatemala, the Disparity Reduction Rate was higher for women than for men. There is no apparent relationship between GNP growth rates and PQLI Disparity Reduction Rates for either females or males. It is also not clear what adjusting the index ranges for genetic-biological differences would do to the rates of change.

Once again, India offers a useful case study because of its diversity and the potential availability of data. Table 19 provides 1961 data for the states of India. In each state—as for India as a whole—female life expectancy and literacy are worse than those for males, and the female infant mortality rate is better, or at least no worse. Among states, the levels of performance vary greatly for both men and women—although in all states men have higher PQLIs than women. In Kerala, women fare much better than either men or women in any other state, but not nearly as well as men in Kerala. Men in Kerala, despite the fact that combined PQLI performance tends to be comparatively better than in other states, have a lower life expectancy than men in Punjab.

The differences among states almost certainly reflect historical conditions and trends as well as post-independence national and state policies. Because its decennial censuses go back to 1872, India seems to provide an excellent opportunity for obtaining disaggregated data both by sex and by state for making intra-country comparisons.

Rural and Urban PQLIs

Rural-urban comparisons are difficult to make. Generating such data is a task that has long frustrated demographers. The demands of the PQLI are probably less stringent than they are for many other purposes, but extensive rural-urban PQLI comparisons still will require a major research effort to deal with some of the problems involved.[158] Thus far rural-urban PQLI data are available for only three developing countries (see Table 20).

On the basis of available information, it appears that in developed countries rural-urban differences are relatively small and possibly beginning to favor urban areas.[159] This is a reflection of the tendency for public services of all sorts to be superior, and for average real per capita incomes to be higher in urban than in rural areas. The gross superiority of urban PQLIs in the three developing countries is somewhat surprising. Development literature and policies have stressed the great influx of people into urban areas and the consequent strains on whatever frail social infrastructure might have existed. The high population densities, the gross poverty of large groups of people, and inadequate public facilities would lead one to expect worse conditions in the city than in the countryside. This certainly is the implication of the historical experience of nineteenth century urbanization in Britain and other North Atlantic countries.

Table 18. Female and Male PQLIs for Selected Countries, circa 1950 and circa 1970 (ranked by "1950" PQLI)

	PQLI, circa 1950			PQLI, circa 1970			Average Annual DRR[1]			Average Annual Per Capita GNP Growth Rate, 1950-70 (%)
	Total	Female	Male	Total	Female	Male	Total (%)	Female (%)	Male (%)	
India (1949, 1970)	14	10	17	40	35	45	1.7	1.5	1.9	1.8
Guatemala (1950, 1970)	36	36	38	52	50	53	1.4	1.2	1.4	1.8
Dominican Rep. (1951, 1968)	47	49	46	63	65	61	2.1	2.2	1.9	1.8
Malaysia (1949, 1970)	47	42	51	67	65	69	2.2	2.4	2.2	2.3
Réunion (1954, 1970)	48	52	44	70	74	66	3.4	3.8	3.1	—
Brazil (1950, 1970)	53	55	51	66	68	64	1.6	1.7	1.5	2.7
Mexico (1951, 1970)	55	56	54	71	73	70	2.3	2.5	2.2	3.1
Philippines (1950, 1971)	55	57	53	72	74	71	2.2	2.4	2.3	2.6
Thailand (1949, 1972)	55	52	59	70	71	69	1.7	2.2	1.2	3.8
Venezuela (1950, 1971)	58	59	58	79	80	78	3.2	3.4	3.0	3.0
Chile (1952, 1970)	62	64	60	77	79	75	2.8	3.0	2.6	1.5
Yugoslavia (1950, 1972)	64	63	65	84	84	84	3.6	3.7	3.5	4.4
Sri Lanka (1953, 1969)	65	60	70	80	78	82	3.4	3.7	3.1	1.9

Panama (1950, 1971)	68	69	67	81	82	80	—	2.5	2.6	2.4	3.2
Trinidad (1950, 1971)	69	69	68	87	88	85	—	4.1	4.4	3.5	4.0
Martinique (1954, 1970)	72	74	69	86	88	83	—	4.2	4.7	3.7	—
Bulgaria (1950, 1965)	74	73	75	89	89	89	—	5.6	5.8	5.3	—
Poland (1951, 1972)	76	79	73	92	95	88	—	5.1	6.6	3.8	—
Argentina (1950, 1970)	77	79	75	85	88	82	—	2.1	2.8	1.6	1.9
Hungary (1951, 1972)	80	82	78	90	93	87	—	3.2	4.4	2.5	—
Greece (1955, 1972)	82	79	85	88	88	89	—	2.4	3.2	1.8	5.8
United States (1950, 1971)	89	92	86	93	97	90	—	2.1	4.6	1.6	2.4

[1]Average annual DRRs are calculated for the actual number of years between "1950" and "1970" PQLI, as indicated within the parentheses.

SOURCES: PQLI data are from Appendix C. Per capita GNP growth rates are calculated from Morawetz, *Twenty-Five Years of Economic Development*.

Table 19. Female and Male PQLI Comparisons in India, by State, 1961

	PQLI			Life Expectancy at Age One (years)		Infant Mortality (per 1,000 live births)		Literacy (%)	
	Total	Female	Male	Female	Male	Female	Male	Female	Male
Andhra Pradesh	25	21	29	41.2	43.4	135	145	11.9	35.6
Assam	22	19	25	42.1	45.4	161	207	15.8	45.3
Bihar	22	18	26	43.1	44.4	151	170	6.7	35.6
Gujarat	32	27	37	44.5	45.8	132	136	19.8	49.8
Jammu and Kashmir	21	18	24	40.3	43.8	133	162	4.2	28.2
Karnatika (Mysore)	31	26	35	43.1	46.3	113	137	13.8	43.5
Kerala	50	46	55	53.2	54.0	110	110	44.0	70.4
Madhya Pradesh	19	18	21	45.4	48.3	166	182	6.4	14.8
Maharashtra	36	31	42	49.5	51.3	128	139	16.5	50.7
Orissa	27	20	33	46.5	47.9	159	159	7.9	41.9
Punjab	38	33	44	52.2	55.0	120	120	14.0	38.4
Rajasthan	33	28	38	48.8	53.1	115	120	5.9	27.4
Tamil Nadu (Madras)	32	25	38	42.7	45.6	124	135	16.8	51.9
Uttar Pradesh	21	16	25	44.7	47.7	175	190	7.3	32.2
West Bengal	38	32	44	48.8	49.8	120	120	19.4	51.3
All-India	**29**	**24**	**34**	**45.5**	**47.8**	**140**	**153**	**13.2**	**41.5**

SOURCES: Infant mortality and life expectancy at age one are from Krishan Lal Kohli, "Spatial Variations of Mortality in India, 1951-61" (Unpublished Ph.D. dissertation, University of Pennsylvania, 1971), pp. 74-75 and 104-11. Literacy data are from Mahinder Chaudhry and K. R. G. Nair, "Social Indicators and Regional Development in Developing Countries" (unpublished), Appendix Table A-2, p. 54. The literacy data were generously made available by Dr. Chaudhry.

What are the explanations for this seeming paradox? The data may be wrong. But in less developed countries urban data tend to be somewhat better than rural data and adverse mortality rates could be expected to show up. Nor is it likely that much better literacy performance has "swamped" the PQLI.[160] It is unlikely that average per capita incomes in urban areas are themselves a good explanation; the income differentials between rural and urban areas were probably at least as great in the nineteenth century in Britain and the United States, where life chances favored the countryside.

The adverse urban experience of early industrializers like Britain and the United States was a function of the unavailability of facilities capable of dealing with rapid urban growth, high densities, and the social disorganization that produced high infant and adult death rates in the nineteenth century. Density of population and gross poverty had decisive effects on infant mortality and the general quality of life. There were few public health facilities and scientific knowledge of epidemiological processes was virtually nonexistent. The quantity and quality of nutrition available to the urban population, certainly the very poor, was adversely affected by inadequate transport. Literacy rates may actually have been lower in many urban areas than in the countryside, where some facilities for basic education existed. Urban organization was often insufficient to provide education at a rate to match the influx of people.[161]

During the past century or so, innovations have made it easier to improve those urban life chances that the PQLI measures. Cast iron pipe and chlorination make it possible to improve water supply; simple chemotherapy and organizational techniques can control some epidemic threats. Improved transport makes possible better and more stable supplies of food to urban centers. Whatever medical and hospital resources are available in a poor country, the largest proportion of them typically are concentrated in towns. Because cities tend to be

Table 20. Rural and Urban PQLIs for Three Countries, early 1970s

	Rural	Urban	% Urban Superiority
Ghana	28	54	93
Indonesia	45	61	36
Liberia	27	42	56

SOURCES: Ghana life expectancy and infant mortality data are from *The Population of Ghana* (part of U.N. C.I.C.R.E.D. Monograph Series, 1974); literacy data are from B. Gil, R. T. deGraft-Johnson, and E. A. Colecraft, *1960 Population Canvas of Ghana*, Vol. 6 (Accra: Census Office, 1971).

Indonesia life expectancy and infant mortality data are from *The Population of Indonesia* (part of U.N. C.I.C.R.E.D. Monograph Series, 1974); literacy data are from *UNESCO Yearbook, 1973* and *UNESCO Yearbook, 1975*.

Liberia life expectancy and infant mortality data are from *The Population of Liberia* (part of U.N. C.I.C.R.E.D. Monograph Series, 1974); literacy data are from Department of Planning and Economic Affairs, *Selected Demographic Characteristics of the Population, 1970* (December 1970), Republic of Liberia, Doc. No. L.P.G.S. P-1.

the centers of political instability, governments seem to make efforts to dampen unrest by providing their populations with social resources through various systems of public distribution. Moreover, international assistance, whether intended to dampen the impact of specific crises or to make long-run development contributions, seems invariably to be more effective in urban areas than in the countryside.

These limited data suggest that—in spite of fairly widespread ideas about the horrors of urban existence in less developed countries—developing-country towns seem to be able to offer people better physical life chances of the kind measured by the PQLI than exist in the countryside.[162]

To the extent that life chances appear to be better in urban than rural areas, this may reinforce economic incentives for moving to towns and for remaining there. If it is desirable for economic or social reasons to reduce the growth of urban concentrations, the provision of facilities that will narrow rural-urban PQLI differentials may be helpful in stemming townward migration. Moreover, relatively crude and inexpensive facilities may be sufficient to accomplish this task, especially if policymakers (including many in less developed countries) are prepared to suspend rich-country notions of how things must be done. Much more research is needed to determine whether the urban areas of developing countries generally have higher PQLIs than the rural areas. If so, a possible line of analysis would be to link the PQLI to the Harris-Todaro model of migration, which suggests that people's decisions about migration are influenced by total benefits and not merely by the wage rate.[163]

7 Conclusions and Implications for Further Work

Observations and description are planned processes, in which the initial stimulus comes from some existing theory, however rudimentary it may be. . . . Many measurements, it is true, are initiated without much help from a formal theory, especially when a field is very new. It is, in general, difficult to decide in advance what new measurements the desired future theory will demand. But a theory is always the ultimate aim. . . .

—Oskar Morgenstern
On the Accuracy of Economic Observations

The Physical Quality of Life Index promises to serve as a creative complement to the GNP. By focusing on results rather than inputs, it records how widely certain basic characteristics are distributed within and among populations. It informs about the changing distribution of social benefits among countries and, within a country, between the sexes, among ethnic groups, and by region and sector.

By minimizing the developmental and cultural ethnocentricities that bedevil most other measures, the PQLI facilitates international and regional comparisons. Because it is bounded at the upper end, the PQLI can be used to set objectives that are achievable. As countries move slowly or less slowly toward closing the gap between their current performance and that presently considered to be the maximum attainable performance, the gap between "rich" and "poor" countries can be expected to narrow.[164]

The PQLI disparities among countries can be understood in a way that disparities in per capita GNP sometimes are not. Knowing that, in absolute terms, world poverty is so extreme that in 1969 about half the combined populations of Latin America, Africa, and Asia (excluding China) lived with average per capita incomes below $75 (in 1971 prices) is not very meaningful, especially when, in most of these countries, life expectancies are increasing and infant mortality rates are declining at the same time.

The numbers obviously do not mean that these people are living for a year on what a person in the United States could buy with $75. Yet if they are used merely to note that there are a great many poor in the world, they may in fact do more harm than good. Such well-intentioned but shrill and unqualified presentations tend to discourage, rather than to elicit, remedial action. The Secretary General of the United Nations commented that exaggeration of the income gap between rich and poor countries:

> ... tends to be a discouraging feature of the world economy rather than a challenge to remedial action.... Conventionally measured, no achievable rate of growth in the developing countries is likely to reduce that disparity: the developing countries are doomed to lag further and further behind in absolute terms of dollars of gross product per person.[165]

The PQLI, in contrast, does not create the picture of a hopeless race. In fact, it avoids the necessity of thinking about the problem as a race at all. It places a country on a meaningful scale in relation to specific and fixed objectives and records over time the performance toward meeting those objectives.

What the PQLI Does Not Do

Before examining the PQLI's potential, it is useful to be explicit about what the PQLI does *not* measure or do.

First, the PQLI does not measure economic growth. Whereas GNP measures the output of goods and services, PQLI is an expression of the results of combined public and private activity whether measured in the system of national accounts or not.

Second, the PQLI does not measure economic development. It does not describe the changing structure of economic and social organization, and it does not attempt to define some model of "normal" development. To the contrary, it assumes that specific PQLI results can be achieved with a variety (albeit not an infinite variety) of economic and social structures and levels of GNP. It highlights deviance, not "normality." In fact, its development was prompted by the search for explanations for the fact that some deviant societies—by most "development" standards they would be classified as underdeveloped—have been able to achieve relatively high PQLI levels.

Third, the PQLI does not measure total welfare. Just as it cannot be said that a country with a higher GNP is "better off" than a country with a lower GNP unless composition and distribution of output, level of employment, etc., are disregarded, so, too, it cannot be said that a country with a higher PQLI is "better off" than one with a lower PQLI—except in terms of what it measures, that is, some (but certainly not all) desired qualities of life.

Fourth, the PQLI does not measure effort, only results. This decision was made in response to the proven failures of large expenditures and enormous programs to meet the needs of the world's poorest people. Some have urged a more generous measure that would include allowance for effort. The PQLI takes seriously the principle that the road to hell is paved with good intentions. As long as people can satisfy themselves with the virtuousness of the efforts they are making, they will tend to avoid the truly hard rethinking that equity-oriented development strategies require.

Fifth, the PQLI does not identify the need for, or measure the results of, individual projects. It is an index of "macro" rather than "micro" performance.

With its limitations, is the PQLI worth the effort? Is it an appropriate instrument for measuring how well societies provide certain basic benefits to their populations? Those who have argued that it is not, have done so for one of two reasons: 1) a concern that composite indicators (including the PQLI) hide details, and 2) objection to the fact that the PQLI does not have a theoretical base.

Those who object to composite indexes because of a concern that the act of composition hides the important details of any situation fear that the PQLI blurs the often differing performances of the individual components. However, the PQLI does not deprive the user of specific detail. Appendix A makes clear that the individual indicators used to construct the PQLI can be monitored as readily as the PQLI. Because the PQLI is simply constructed, the component indicators are never lost to the user of the PQLI. More important, the composite index has an independent creative function. In the very act of summarizing complexity, the PQLI reveals certain relationships that are not obvious from observing the individual indicators. In effect, the PQLI is a way of not allowing the trees to get in the way of seeing the forest.[166] Moreover, putting the three individual indicators together highlights a potentially crucial synergistic interrelationship.

A second major criticism of the PQLI is that it lacks the support of an underlying theory. The system of national accounts and GNP measures are acceptable because they are founded on the assumptions of neoclassical economic theory. In effect, it is possible to justify the specific system of weights (the price relationships) that are applied to the components. The existence of the theory makes it possible to specify a model, that is, a series of behavioral relationships from which policy recommendations can be drawn.

It is correct that the PQLI does not have a sturdy theoretical base, but it is not clear that this should be a major reason for opposing it. One way of responding to the criticism would be to say that the PQLI does not require a theory, that it is merely a convenient way of summarizing the behavior of the separate indicators in which policy strategists are interested. As long as the users of the PQLI are clear about how the chosen weights might affect place on, and movement along, the scale, the limited claim for the PQLI is unassailable.

The history of the PQLI's development suggests another response to this criticism. The PQLI was developed to deal with several concerns: 1) economic growth theory has been unable to generate policies such that their benefits would "trickle down" at any acceptable pace (if at all) to the poorest groups in poor societies; 2) specific *ad hoc* "target" policies focused explicitly on the most disadvantaged have proved to be unsatisfactory; and 3) it has proven very difficult to reach the target groups and almost impossible to sustain what effect there has been at any reasonable cost. In effect, neither economic nor administrative theory has been able to tell policymakers how to get development with equity—a problem which has been compounded by the lack of an indicator that satisfactorily measures the distribution of benefits to the poor.

There is thus no theory that can advise on how to deal with the problems of the most poor. In this bankrupt condition, policymakers have had two choices: 1) to continue to blunder along with *ad hoc* and essentially wasteful solutions, hoping that something will work, or 2) to cling to the one last hope of the analysts, that if economies somehow can be made to grow fast enough for long enough, incomes ultimately will rise to levels high enough to spill over into reasonable benefits to the poor. There is enough evidence among countries in the upper-income range to suggest that this expectation is not entirely valid. But even if it were correct in principle, the observation would not constitute a theory.[167] Moreover, it offers a politically intolerable council of despair. It would take an inhumanly long wait for poor countries to get to the needed income levels.

The PQLI, on the other hand, identifies countries that have been able to achieve socially desirable results at levels of economic performance previously considered incapable of producing such results. It also identifies countries of high economic performance that have not achieved comparable social performance. The PQLI encourages a search for reasons—for explanations that might lead to a theory and then to a general guide to action.[168]

Potential Uses of the PQLI

The PQLI has a variety of potential uses and also suggests directions for future research.

A Measure of Performance

In a conveniently summarized form, the PQLI shows how successful a country is in providing certain specific social qualities to its population and how it performs over time. In its 1973 "New Directions" foreign assistance legislation, the U.S. Congress requested a measure that can be used in determining how successful U.S. development assistance is in contributing to the improvement of the condition of the very poor.[169] Because the PQLI provides information about a country's overall success in this area, it can assist the United States and other aid donors—other nations as well as international agencies—in their evaluations of their foreign assistance programs.

A Criterion for International Decision Making

Considerable attention has been devoted to identifying specific types of under-development and to developing ways of classifying countries that need various kinds of assistance.[170] Per capita GNP is the most widely used tool for identifying countries that are or are not eligible for specific types of grants and/or forms of concessional assistance. For example, countries which had per capita incomes below $375 in 1972 are able to obtain soft loans through the International Development Association (IDA), and the U.S. Agency for International Development (AID) has established similar kinds of criteria. Yet, as shown earlier, GNP in itself is not an adequate indicator of a country's condition or its requirements, because it does not tell anything about benefits actually provided to the population or about a country's ability to organize itself to provide these benefits. The PQLI can complement per capita GNP in identifying the kind of international action called for.

Even the experts are not always able to discriminate sufficiently to offer appropriate policies for groups of countries, much less individual ones. For example, the 1976 report of the U.N. Committee for Development Planning identified black Africa and South Asia as the two poorest regions in the world. Even though this report acknowledged that the regions differ in ways that invite different policy responses, it neglected the historically rooted structural differences that the PQLI research has suggested is of such enormous significance.[171] The failure to consider such differences has encouraged similar international policy responses for so-called "hard-core" countries that are as different as Mali and Ethiopia (with PQLIs of 15 and 20, respectively) and Sri Lanka (with a PQLI of 82), or as different as India (with a PQLI of 43) and Niger and Afghanistan (with PQLIs of 13 and 18, respectively).[172]

It is tempting to say that experts concerned with donor-country policies, whether they are in the donor countries or in international agencies, do not need the PQLI to help them differentiate the policies that might be needed in Gabon (PQLI = 21) and Guinea (20) *versus* Egypt (43), India (43), Sri Lanka (82), and the Philippines (71) *versus* Brazil (68), Mexico (73), and Venezuela (79). This may be true. However, even where they recognize the need for differentiated policy responses, technicians find their ability to channel resources and to shape appropriate policies sharply confined. National and international legislative bodies seeking to guarantee that their objectives and purposes as donors of development assistance are not frustrated, often impose rules and standards that are not sufficiently discriminating. Gabon (with a per capita GNP of $2,123) and Venezuela (with a per capita GNP of $2,171) now are treated similarly, even though (with PQLIs of 21 and 79, respectively) they are in quite different straits and require different policies. The same is true of Guinea and India, which have similar per capita incomes and very different PQLIs. The introduction of PQLI standards to complement per capita GNP standards could help experts to make more precise decisions about the policies that ought to be applied to the various types of developing countries.

The kinds of policies needed to address the various combinations of GNP and PQLI levels is a subject for further research and for discussion in various international forums and in donor countries. One classification for distinguishing among types of countries needing assistance is suggested below, merely as an example. "Low income" refers to the countries with per capita GNPs below $700; "high income" is used for those developing countries with per capita GNPs of $700 or more; the dividing line between "low" and "high" PQLI is 77, which is the equivalent of the Tinbergen-group's RIO report recommendations (see below).

Class	Per Capita GNP Level	PQLI Level
I	High	High
II	High	Low
III	Low	High
IV	Low	Low

Class I countries (e.g., Costa Rica with a per capita GNP of $884 and a PQLI of 85) do not need concessional assistance to improve their PQLIs but might require support (as many do now) to improve or sustain their per capita GNP growth rate. Class II countries—which include Turkey (per capita GNP, $789; PQLI, 55), Gabon (per capita GNP, $2,123; PQLI, 21) and a number of high-income oil producers of the Middle East—are in a position to finance their own PQLI improvements, but may require special types of technical and financial assistance tailored to help speed up the rate at which PQLI improves. Class III countries—Cuba (per capita GNP, $640; PQLI 84), the Republic of Korea ($464, 82), and Sri Lanka ($179, 82) are good examples—provide the structures through which high PQLIs are produced, but may require concessional assistance to strengthen their economic bases. Economic assistance may have to be provided under different standards than those required by orthodox lending policies so that the "growth" emphasis does not endanger continued PQLI improvement.[173] Class IV countries—Afghanistan ($137, 18) and many black African countries are among these—do not have the social infrastructure from which either high PQLI or satisfactory per capita GNP levels flow and thus require special international attention.[174]

Countries with low PQLIs—whether in Class II or in Class IV—pose particular development problems that derive from general absorptive constraints. Even within these classes, attention needs to be paid to each country's particular needs. Gabon, with a PQLI of 21, has a much smaller absorptive capacity than, for example, Brazil, with its PQLI of 68, even though Gabon's income is more than twice as large. To the extent that equity is as important a goal as growth, this problem is magnified, making it increasingly important that resource transfers be based on concepts with which the very poor are familiar and institutional arrangements in which they can participate.[175] This prescription presumes, of course, that the countries themselves place a high priority on raising the PQLI.

A Tool for Targeting and Measuring Progress

A third use of the PQLI is to establish targets and to measure progress toward the targets. Two recent international proposals, the Tinbergen-group report *Reshaping the International Order* and the Declaration of Amsterdam, suggested the universal achievement of internationally agreed to targets. The RIO report called for the "attainment of the following national objectives for all countries by the end of this century": a life expectancy at birth of sixty-five years or more; an infant mortality rate of 50 or fewer deaths per thousand births; a literacy rate of at least 75 percent; and a birth rate of 25 or fewer per thousand population.[176]

The PQLI provides one useful way of measuring overall progress toward these targets. The specific RIO targets, when converted into the PQLI's component indicators, imply that a PQLI of 77 should be the year 2000 target for every country.[177] This represents a more explicit and meaningful goal than one specified in terms of getting beyond absolute poverty lines defined by income, e.g., getting beyond $50 or $75 per capita GNP levels.

At the present time, only 32 percent of the world's population live in countries that have achieved the RIO targets. What might the situation be in the year 2000 if the world population is distributed in the same proportions as currently? If all countries currently below the RIO target have 1 percent average annual rates of improvement for twenty years, 39 percent of the world's population will live in countries with a PQLI of 77 or more. If they have 3 percent rates of improvement, 87 percent of the world population will live in countries with a PQLI of 77 or more. If they have 5 percent rates of improvement, 93 percent of the world population will live in countries with a PQLI of 77 or more. Thus over a twenty-year period, at 1, 3, and 5 percent average annual rates of improvement, countries that currently have PQLIs as low as 63, 43, and 29 could reach a minimum PQLI of 77.

The PQLI does not provide any information about how improvement can be brought about. By offering a sense of the rates of improvement that would be required to achieve an objective, however, it can introduce a sense of realism into discussions that sometimes lack it. For example, if the RIO proposals are taken at face value, countries with very low PQLIs will have to achieve extremely high rates of improvement to get to a PQLI of 77 in twenty years. Guinea-Bissau (with a PQLI of 12) would have to achieve a six-fold increase in its PQLI. Is such a multi-fold improvement possible? If this is the goal, what obligations does it impose on the international community as well as on Guinea-Bissau?

The signatories of the Amsterdam Declaration suggested a different year 2000 target.[178] The declaration calls for the "reduction by half" by the year 2000 of the disparities in levels of life expectancy, infant mortality, and literacy that now exist between individual developing countries and the most developed countries. Here, too, the PQLI offers both a convenient way of specifying diverse objectives in a composite measure and a means of measuring progress toward these objectives. The declaration's target is somewhat vaguely expressed in terms of the disparity between current developing-country performance and the performance of "the most developed countries." The PQLI of 100 (the best performance expected for any country in the year 2000) enables this somewhat vaguely defined target to be expressed more specifically in terms of a reduction by half in the disparity between current performance and the best possible PQLI of 100.

Progress toward the objectives of the Amsterdam Declaration can be measured in a number of different ways. It can be measured in absolute terms, or it can be measured in relative terms as either a percentage improvement over a base level performance, an annual rate of improvement, or a rate of reduction in the disparity between the existing PQLI and the target. Table 21 shows the number of ways in which the concept "halving the disparity" might be recorded, using the PQLI as the measure of performance.

If existing disparities (column 3) are reduced by half, countries that currently have different PQLIs will have differing PQLIs at the end of twenty years (column 4). Their percentages of improvement (column 6) and their average annual rates of improvement (column 7) also will vary. What will not vary among countries is the average rate at which the present disparity is reduced by half (column 8); over a twenty-year period reducing any disparity by half requires an average annual disparity reduction rate of 3.4 percent.

None of the rates of change in Table 21 is *the* correct rate. Each reflects different characteristics. Neither the different amounts of change in column 6 nor the different rates of change in column 7 reflects the ease or difficulty countries will encounter in attempting to "halve the disparity." The results are purely arithmetic (not substantive) manifestations of starting from different bases. Each of the rates can be used for specific purposes. The Disparity Reduction Rate in column 8 has the advantage of making the Amsterdam Declaration's target of "halving the disparity" a constant rate for all countries—3.4 percent over a twenty-year period—whether countries have high or low base levels.

Table 22 illustrates the use of the DRR to measure country performance over time; it also shows the quite different result obtained with the average annual rate of improvement. The table shows for fourteen countries the rate at which disparities—i.e., the differences between actual PQLIs and 100—were reduced in approximately twenty years. In approximately the period 1950 to 1970, Puerto Rico and Taiwan had the highest DRRs; Algeria and Brazil had the lowest. The average annual percentage rate of improvement gives quite a different impression, with India's performance (5.1 percent) outstripping other countries. This is a function of the low PQLI level from which it started.

It is, of course, significant that in the twenty-one years between 1949 and 1970, India increased its PQLI at an average annual rate of 5.1 percent. But it is also important that after twenty-one years of effort, India's PQLI was only

Table 21. Three Ways of Measuring the Amsterdam Declaration Goal of "Halving the Disparity" in Twenty Years

(1)	(2)	(3)	(4)	(5)	(6)	(7)	(8)
	Start of Twenty-Year Period		End of Twenty-Year Period		Total Percent Improvement[1]	Average Annual Rate of Improvement[2]	Average Annual DRR[3]
Country	PQLI	Disparity	PQLI	Disparity	(%)	(%)	(%)
A	90	10	95	5	5.6	0.27	3.41
B	70	30	85	15	21.4	0.98	3.41
C	50	50	75	25	50.0	2.05	3.41
D	20	80	60	40	200.0	5.65	3.41

[1]Percentage change between Col. 2 and Col. 4
[2]Average annual rate at which change from Col. 2 to Col. 4 is achieved.
[3]Average annual rate at which change from Col. 3 to Col. 5 is achieved.

Table 22. PQLI Performance, DRR, and Average Annual Rate of Improvement for Selected Countries, circa 1950 to circa 1970 (ranked in descending order of "1950" PQLI)

	PQLI		Average Annual DRR	Average Annual Rate of Improvement
	circa 1950	circa 1970	(%)	(%)
United States (1950, 1971)	89	93	2.1	0.2
Hungary (1951, 1972)	80	90	3.2	0.6
Argentina (1950, 1970)	77	85	2.1	0.5
Puerto Rico (1950, 1970)	74	91	5.2	1.0
Sri Lanka (1953, 1969)	65	80	3.4	1.3
Taiwan (1950, 1970)	63	87	5.1	1.6
Chile (1952, 1970)	62	77	2.8	1.2
Philippines (1950, 1971)	55	72	2.2	1.3
Mexico (1951, 1970)	55	71	2.3	1.4
Thailand (1949, 1972)	55	70	1.7	1.1
Brazil (1950, 1970)	53	66	1.6	1.1
Algeria (1950, 1970)	34	41	0.6	0.9
Turkey (1950, 1971)	30	55	2.1	2.9
India (1949, 1970)	14	40	1.7	5.1

NOTE: Average annual DRRs and rates of improvement are calculated for the actual number of years between "1950" and "1970" PQLI.

SOURCE: Appendix C, Table 1.

40. It is equally intriguing that over the same period, countries that started with superior PQLI and per capita income levels—Algeria, Brazil, Thailand—did so poorly. The DRR is a measure that can stimulate research on why some countries achieve more rapid progress toward a fixed goal than others.

Just as international groups have recommended general targets for GNP improvement—e.g., the U.N. General Assembly recommended a 3.5 percent average annual per capita GNP growth rate as a target for developing countries in the 1970s—the DRR enables a common target to be set for both high and low PQLI countries. At the same time, the PQLI encourages a more self-conscious examination of the targets that are set. In comparing the efforts individual countries will have to make to meet the two targets that have been suggested for the year 2000—the RIO target of a 77 PQLI for all countries and the Amsterdam Declaration target of "halving the disparity"—it is clear that in many cases they will require quite different levels of effort. Table 23 shows that—even if it "halves its disparity" in twenty years (a DRR of 3.4 percent per annum)—Mali, with a PQLI of 15, will only achieve a PQLI of 57. To reach the 77 PQLI target in twenty years (i.e., approximately by the end of the century), Mali will need

Table 23. DRRs Needed to Reach Year 2000 PQLI Targets Implied by Amsterdam Declaration and RIO Proposal, Selected Countries

	Current PQLI	Current Disparity	Amsterdam Declaration "Halving the Disparity" (DRR = 3.4%)		RIO Proposal	
			Year 2000 PQLI Target	Year 2000 Disparity	Year 2000 PQLI Target	DRR needed to reach Year 2000 Target
						(%)
Mali	15	85	57	42	77	6.4
Nigeria	25	75	63	37	77	5.7
Bangladesh	35	65	68	32	77	5.1
India	43	57	72	28	77	4.4
Guatamala	54	46	77	23	77	3.4
Brazil	68	32	84	16	77	1.6
Philippines	71	29	86	14	77	1.2
Mexico	73	27	87	13	77	0.8
Korea, Rep.	82	18	91	9	1	1
Jamaica	84	16	92	8	1	1
United States	94	6	97	3	1	1
Sweden	97	3	99	1	1	1

[1]Not relevant.

NOTE: "Current PQLIs" are those in Appendix A; DRRs assume that effort starts in 1980, giving twenty years to achieve the target PQLI.

to achieve an average annual DRR of 6.4 percent, almost twice the rate needed to halve its disparity.[179]

A Stimulus for Research

The PQLI's usefulness as a measuring device, as a criterion for decision making, and as a target does not explain why countries are at specific levels or have experienced specific rates of change. This is also true of the individual components of the PQLI and of GNP. An important difference between PQLI and GNP, however, is that there are theories that purport to explain how levels and (more specifically) rates and patterns of economic change are reflected in the GNP and other parts of the system of national accounts. The theories are recognized to be inadequate, but they do give decision makers some sense of confidence about the policies they recommend and the consequences expected to flow from those policies.[180]

While there are ways, particularly at the lower levels of performance, to increase literacy and life expectancy and to reduce infant mortality (if only by throwing ever larger quantities of resources at the problems), there are no satisfactory policies nor is there any coherent theory linking changes in these three features in any causal fashion with changes in economic performance. The discipline of economics has never been interested in these relationships. To the extent that economists have thought about them at all, they have assumed that rising life expectancy and declining infant mortality were the automatic (and therefore uninteresting) consequences of economic growth. Literacy has been of somewhat more explicit concern; the classical economists, profoundly influenced by Benthamite Utilitarianism, considered education to be a precondition of development. In the last few years, economists and economic historians have begun once again to attach considerable weight to the role of education in economic growth because of their assessment of the value of human capital in the growth process. There have been no satisfactory attempts, however, to link infant mortality and life expectancy performance to the growth process.[181]

Recently some modest attention has been paid to infant mortality, life expectancy, and literacy not merely as ends of development but also as factors that affect the nature, pace, and scope of economic growth and development. Such efforts, however, invariably have approached the issues in a partial fashion, treating literacy, health, longevity, nutrition, etc., separately, largely because incorporating all these elements into a general theory of economic development is a complex process. Yet the importance of an integrated analysis is increasing as pressure to provide all humans with at least a minimum level of social benefits increases. A theory is needed that will help to estimate both the cost of producing such benefits and the synergistic contribution they make to the rate of economic growth. The need for such a theory is not merely academic. If some relatively precise sense of alternative mixes and tradeoffs among policies can be established, it may be possible for developing countries to adapt policies to their factor proportions in ways that will generate benefits for their great majorities much more swiftly than they could otherwise.[182]

The PQLI can have more than a general hortatory effect on research. The index poses important questions about the performance of individual countries as well as groups of countries. Sri Lanka provides the most dramatic example of a country that has been able to achieve remarkable life-quality results at startlingly low levels of income. While the results in the Indian state of Kerala are not as dramatic, they are certainly noteworthy, particularly when compared with the all-India average. Examination of these and other "deviant" cases suggests that they did not achieve these results as quickly as may seem to be the case. Prolonged periods of various kinds of institution-building seem to have preceded. Are such long spans of time necessary or can lessons be learned and borrowed? If so, what are they? How can they be transferred? Answers to such questions will require detailed studies of individual countries.

Lessons should be learned not merely from the success stories, but from the experiences of all countries. Why do the Sahelian African countries perform so differently than, for example, the North African and South Asian countries? Do these differing experiences express meaningful structural differences of the sort—

tribal and village pasts—suggested in Chapter 6? If so, does this imply that, while region is important, it is not decisive in determining the countries to which specific policies might be appropriate? Does it suggest that Upper Volta and Afghanistan have more in common with one another than Upper Volta does with Egypt, or Afghanistan with India? Does it indicate that Egypt and India have similar policy needs? Are there perhaps differences in the policies required *within* large countries, if some groups have tribal backgrounds and others have village traditions (Iran, India, and Pakistan are obvious examples)? In addition, numerous research possibilities arise from the evidence of differential performance between males and females, among ethnic groups, and between urban and rural settings.

Considerable investigating and experimenting will be needed to determine how to collect the required data rapidly and at low cost. Moreover, the PQLI may be helpful in ways not even foreshadowed in this volume, for example, in the continuing effort to transform GNP into a measure of welfare. This may occur as techniques are developed to use the two indicators in complementary relationships, or as the PQLI stimulates further thought on how to incorporate the results it measures into GNP.

Even though the index begins to be "used up" among those developed countries which come close to a PQLI of 100, its very existence may stimulate a willingness to think about modified or transformed versions. For example, among many of the countries that already have PQLIs of 95 or more, literacy is nearly 100. A more demanding definition of literacy that nevertheless retained comparability among such countries would make the PQLI a still useful tool. Or perhaps a different type of Physical Quality of Life Index—with different components—should be created for those countries approaching 100 on the current PQLI. While there is no special reason to keep the index functioning—its present usefulness does not depend on its ability to work forever—the index suggests the potential value in developing other measures with limited objectives.

The PQLI is a measure, not a method. It was developed to measure somewhat more sensitively than has previously been possible the degree to which societies provide certain important social benefits. But the use of the PQLI for this purpose is certainly not meant to imply that "poor is happy," or that less developed countries should be satisfied merely with high PQLIs. Nor does it necessarily suggest that "small is beautiful" or that "basic human needs" strategies are the only paths along which poor countries should proceed. A whole range of alternative development choices is available from which to select, and the PQLI can be used to measure specific features of progress in all of them. It should be remembered that, whatever strategy is pursued, improvement in the quality of life is the ultimate justification of all development activity.

Notes

Chapter 1

[1]The following readings offer some specific evidence of the fundamental shift that is now underway: ILO International Labour Office, *Employment, Growth and Basic Needs: A One-World Problem* (New York: Praeger Publishers, 1977), see particularly the Introduction by James P. Grant, which offers a brief history of changing ideas about policy; *Reshaping the International Order: A Report to the Club of Rome*, coordinated by Jan Tinbergen (New York: E. P. Dutton and Co., 1976); Hollis B. Chenery, Montek S. Ahluwalia, C. L. G. Bell, John H. Duloy, and Richard Jolly, *Redistribution with Growth*, published for the World Bank and the Institute of Development Studies, University of Sussex (London: Oxford University Press, 1974); Robert S. McNamara, President of the World Bank, speech before the World Bank/International Monetary Fund Board of Governors meeting, Washington, D.C., September 25, 1977; U. S. House of Representatives, Committee on International Relations, *New Directions in Development Aid: Excerpts from the Legislation* (June 1976); U.S. Agency for International Development, *Implementation of "New Directions" in Development Assistance*, Report to the Committee on International Relations on Implementation of Legislative Reforms in the Foreign Assistance Act of 1973 (95th Congress, First Session), July 22, 1975; Mahbub ul Haq, *The Poverty Curtain: Choices for the Third World* (New York: Columbia University Press, 1976), particularly Part I; and Irma Adelman and Cynthia Taft Morris, *Economic Growth and Social Equity in Developing Countries* (Stanford, Calif.: Stanford University Press, 1973), particularly Introduction and Chapter 5. For a general recent survey of the field and literature, see Bruce F. Johnston, "Food, Health, and Population in Development," *Journal of Economic Literature*, Vol. 15, No. 3 (September 1977), pp. 879-907.

[2]Examples of these different emphases are Irma Adelman, "Strategies for Equitable Growth," *Challenge*, Vol. 17, No. 2 (May-June 1974), p. 44, and Denis Goulet, *The Cruel Choice: A New Concept in the Theory of Development* (New York: Atheneum, 1975).

[3]See, for example, a paper prepared in 1962 in the Indian Planning Commission, entitled "Perspective of Development—1961 to 1976: Implications of Planning for a Minimum Standard of Living." It has been reprinted in T. N. Srinivasan and P. K. Bardhan, eds., *Poverty and Income Distribution in India*

(Calcutta: Statistical Publishing Society, 1974). The paper apparently had no influence when it was written.

[4]Chapter 2 of this study discusses the limitations of GNP as a measure of performance.

[5]This figure is based on the optimistic assumption of an average annual per capita GNP growth rate of 3.17 percent for the twenty-five year period. While the per capita income of developing countries as a group did grow at nearly 3 percent per year between 1950 and 1975, the poorest countries generally grew much more slowly, at only about 1.5 percent. If this lower growth rate is assumed for 1975-2000, the low-income countries, containing 1.2 billion people in 1975, could only expect to attain an average per capita income of $220 in the year 2000. See Martin M. McLaughlin and the Staff of the Overseas Development Council, *The United States and World Development: Agenda 1979* (New York: Praeger Publishers, 1979), Table A-11, p. 177.

[6]From the letter of President Gerald R. Ford to the National Academy of Sciences, quoted in *World Food and Nutrition Study: The Potential Contributions of Research* (Washington, D.C.: National Academy of Sciences, 1977), p. iii.

[7]"Study Team 12: New Approaches to the Alleviation of Hunger," *Supporting Papers: World Food and Nutrition Study,* Vol. 4 (Washington, D.C.: National Academy of Sciences, 1977), pp. 75ff.

[8]*World Food and Nutrition Study,* Vol. 4, p. 89. The Study Team defined "poor countries" as those with per capita incomes of less than $700 in 1973; this definition includes those countries referred to throughout this study as "lower middle-income" countries ($300-$699).

[9]See John W. Sewell and the Staff of the Overseas Development Council, *The United States and World Development: Agenda 1977* (New York: Praeger Publishers, 1977), pp. 147-52 and 160-71. A somewhat more detailed working paper had earlier been circulated informally for professional criticism.

Chapter 2

[10]For a general evaluation of GNP, see, e.g., F. Thomas Juster, "On the Measurement of Economic and Social Performance," *National Bureau of Economic Research: 50th Annual Report* (New York, 1970), pp. 3-24. For the problems posed by attempts at cross-national and intertemporal comparison, see two important essays by Simon Kuznets, "National Income and Industrial Structure" and "National Income and Economic Welfare," reprinted in Simon Kuznets, *Economic Change* (New York: W. W. Norton, 1953), Chapters 6 and 7. See also Dudley Seers, "The Political Economy of National Accounting," in Alec Cairncross and Mohinder Puri, eds., *Employment, Income Distribution and Development Strategy: Problems of the Developing Countries* (New York: Holmes and Meier, 1976), pp. 193-209.

[11]Kuznets, "National Income and Industrial Structure," pp. 178 and 172-73.

[12]Kuznets, "National Income and Economic Welfare," p. 206.

[13]William Nordhaus and James Tobin, "Is Growth Obsolete?," in Milton Moss, ed., *The Measurement of Economic and Social Performance.* Studies in

Income and Wealth No. 38 (New York: National Bureau of Economic Research, 1973), p. 512.

[14]See, for example, Edward F. Denison, "Welfare Measurement and the GNP," *Survey of Current Business,* Vol. 51, No. 1 (January 1971), p. 13; and Arthur M. Okun, "Should GNP Measure Social Welfare?" *The Brookings Bulletin,* Vol. 8, No. 3, pp. 4-7.

[15]For a different approach to the problem of measuring welfare, see U.S. Department of Health, Education, and Welfare, *Toward a Social Report* (Washington, D.C.: HEW, 1969); and a subsequent discussion by Mancur Olson, Jr., "The Plan and Purpose of a Social Report," *The Public Interest,* No. 15 (Spring 1969), pp. 85-97.

[16]Moses Abramovitz, "The Welfare Interpretation of Secular Trends in National Income and Product," in Moses Abramovitz et al., *The Allocation of Economic Resources: Essays in Honor of Bernard Francis Haley* (Stanford, Calif.: Stanford University Press, 1959), p. 21. See also J. D. Gould, *Economic Growth in History: Survey and Analysis* (London: Methuen, 1972), pp. 5-11.

[17]Dan Usher, "An Imputation to the Measure of Economic Growth for Changes in Life Expectancy," in Moss, *Measurement of Economic and Social Performance,* pp. 193-226. See also the "Comment" by Robert J. Willis, *ibid.,* pp. 226-32.

[18]This analysis draws liberally from Kuznets, "National Income and Industrial Structure"; Kuznets, "National Income and Economic Welfare"; Dan Usher, *Rich and Poor Countries: A Study in Problems of Comparisons of Real Income* (London: The Institute of Economic Affairs, 1966); Paul Studenski, *The Income of Nations* (New York University Press, 1958); Wilfred Beckerman, *International Comparisons of Real Incomes* (Paris: Development Centre, Organisation for Economic Co-operation and Development, 1966); Irving B. Kravis, Zoltan Kenessey, Alan Heston, and Robert Summers, *A System of International Comparisons of Gross Product and Purchasing Power* (Baltimore and London: The Johns Hopkins University Press, 1975); and Oskar Morgenstern, *On the Accuracy of Economic Observations,* 2nd ed. (Princeton: Princeton University Press, 1963).

[19]Calculations by H. Stark reproduced in Theodore Morgan, *Economic Development: Concept and Strategy* (New York: Harper and Row, 1975), p. 69.

[20]Robin Barlow, "A Test of Alternative Methods of Making GNP Comparisons," *The Economic Journal,* Vol. 87 (September 1977), pp. 450-59.

[21]For a discussion of the International Comparison Project, see Kravis et al., *System of International Comparisons.* For a later discussion including more countries, see Irving B. Kravis, Alan W. Heston, and Robert Summers, "Real GDP Per Capita for More than One Hundred Countries," *The Economic Journal,* Vol. 88 (June 1978), pp. 215-42.

[22]*World Bank Atlas, 1977* (Washington, D.C.), p. 31.

[23]See Kravis et al., *System of International Comparisons,* pp. ix-xi, for a brief history of the International Comparison Project since 1967.

[24]*World Bank Atlas, 1977,* p. 2.

[25]See, for example, Montek S. Ahluwalia, "Inequality, Poverty, and Development," *Journal of Development Economics,* Vol. 3, No. 4 (December 1976),

particularly p. 7, footnote 8. According to information kindly provided by Dr. Hollis Chenery, Ahluwalia and his colleagues at the World Bank are beginning to examine this issue.

[26]The figures are derived from data in Appendix B, Table 1.

[27]Hollis Chenery et al., *Redistribution with Growth*, pp. 10-13. These figures differ slightly from those generally used in this study. Unfortunately, there is no single agreed-upon set of numbers that can be used for all purposes. The numerical differences, however, do not affect the point being made.

[28]The calculations of still preliminary work on Colombia by Marcelo Selowsky are the basis for these somewhat crude estimates for India. Marcelo Selowsky, "The Distributive Effect of Government Expenditure," World Bank Document No. RPO-670-96 (Washington, D.C., 1976), Table V.

[29]See also P. T. Bauer, *Dissent on Development* (Cambridge, Mass.: Harvard University Press), particularly pp. 55-60.

[30]Kuznets, "National Income and Industrial Structure," p. 179.

[31]Kuznets has noted another troublesome issue, the difficulties of comparing urban and rural incomes, particularly in countries which are rapidly urbanizing. Some part of increasing income may be merely the result of consumers shifting from low-priced, rural areas to high-priced, urban area—with little if any increase in consumption or welfare. See Simon Kuznets, "Problems in Comparing Recent Growth Rates for Developed and Less Developed Areas," *Economic Development and Cultural Change*, Vol. 10, No. 2 (January 1972), pp. 185-209.

[32]These remarks bypass the data problems on which Morgenstern so vigorously expatiated in *On the Accuracy of Economic Observations* (2nd ed.). For a useful example of the implications of these problems, see Arun Shourie, "National Accounts and the Regression Enthusiast - Sri Lanka: A Study," *Economic and Political Weekly*, Vol. 9, No. 52, December 28, 1974, pp. 2141-45.

[33]The nature of assumptions and conventions is conveniently discussed in Seers, "The Political Economy of National Accounting." Some inkling of the changes in the American economy that have been weakening the consensus can be found in the Introduction by the editor in Moss, *Measurement of Economic and Social Performance;* and F. Thomas Juster, "Alternatives to GNP as a Measure of Economic Progress," in *U.S. Economic Growth from 1976 to 1986: Prospects, Problems, and Patterns*, Vol. 10, prepared for U.S. Congress, Joint Economic Committee (95th Congress, First Session), May 20, 1977, p. 12-24.

[34]See, for example, Lee Schipper and A. J. Lichtenberg, "Efficient Energy Use and Well-Being: The Swedish Example," *Science,* December 3, 1976, pp. 1001ff.; and criticisms by Chauncy Starr and Stanford Field, as well as the response by Schipper and Lichtenberg, *Science,* April 8, 1977, pp. 194-96.

[35]Kuznets, "National Income and Industrial Structure," pp. 177-78.

Chapter 3

[36]Okun, "Should GNP Measure Social Welfare?," p. 5.

[37]Juster, "Alternatives to GNP," p. 12.

[38]See, for example, the essay by Hollis Chenery, "The World Bank and World Poverty," in William Loehr and John P. Powelson, eds., *Economic Development, Poverty, and Income Distribution* (Boulder, Colo.: Westview Press, 1977), p. 33. See also Anne V. White, "Water Supply and Income Distribution in Developing Countries," *ibid.*

[39]D. V. McGranahan, C. Richard-Proust, N. V. Sovani, and M. Subramanian, *Contents and Measurement of Socioeconomic Development*, Staff Study for the U.N. Research Institute for Social Development (New York: Praeger Publishers, 1972); Irma Adelman and Cynthia Taft Morris, *Society, Politics, and Economic Development* (Baltimore: Johns Hopkins Press, 1971); and Hollis Chenery and Moises Syrquin, with the assistance of Hazel Elkington, *Patterns of Development, 1950-1970* (London: Oxford University Press, 1975).

[40]McGranahan et al., *Contents and Measurement*, p. 97.

[41]*Ibid.*, p. 138.

[42]A useful introduction to the "social indicators" field, which consists of an already large and rapidly growing body of literature, is a recent article by Robert Parke and David Seidman, "Social Indicators and Social Reporting," in *The Annals of the American Academy of Political and Social Science* (January 1978), pp. 1-22. While the article is U.S.-focused, the references provide an introduction to the literature relating to other countries. *Social Indicators Newsletter*, published by the Social Science Research Council, Center for Coordination of Research on Social Indicators, Washington, D.C. is an up-to-date source of information on work in other countries. It should be noted that there is considerable disagreement on how social indicators should be used. For two sharply divergent views, see Olson, "The Plan and Purpose"; and Eleanor Bernert Sheldon and Howard E. Freeman, "Notes on Social Indicators: Promises and Potential," in *Policy Sciences*, Vol. 1, No. 1 (1970), pp. 97-111.

[43]See Angus Campbell, Philip E. Converse, William C. Rodgers, *The Quality of American Life: Perceptions, Evaluations, and Satisfactions* (New York: Basic Books/Russell Sage Foundation, 1976); and Richard A. Easterlin, "Does Economic Growth Improve the Human Lot? Some Empirical Evidence," in Paul A. David and Melvin W. Reder, eds., *Nations and Households in Economic Growth: Essays in Honor of Moses Abramovitz* (Chicago: Academic Press, 1974), pp. 89-125.

[44]See Joseph S. Davis, "Standards and Content of Living," in *American Economic Review*, Vol. 35, March 1, 1945, pp. 1-15; and M. K. Bennett, "International Disparities in Income Levels," in *American Economic Review*, Vol. 41, September 4, 1951, pp. 632-49; and *Report on International Definition and Measurement of Standards and Levels of Living* (New York: United Nations, March 1954), Doc. No. E/CN.3/179-E/CN.5/299.

[45]*International Definition*, pp. iv and vi.

[46]*International Definition and Measurement of Levels of Living: An Interim Guide* (New York: United Nations, 1961). Doc. No. E/CN.3/270/REV .1-E/CN. 5/353.

[47]*Measuring Social Well-Being: A Progress Report on the Development of Social Indicators* (Paris: Organisation for Economic Co-operation and Development, 1976), p. 26.

[48]OECD, *Measuring Social Well-Being*, p. 27.

[49]Jan Drewnowski, *Studies in the Measurements of Levels of Living and Welfare.* Report No. 70.3 (Geneva: United Nations Research Institute for Social Development, 1970).

[50]There have been many other efforts to create a real index of "welfare," but none has been able to resolve or evade the difficulties enumerated and discussed by the U.N. and UNRISD reports. Richard Ellsworth Eddy, "Measuring Levels of Living" (unpublished Ph.D. dissertation, University of Illinois, 1972), has carefully examined the literature and the issues. For a recent collection of essays, see *The Use of Socio-Economic Indicators in Development Planning* (Paris: The UNESCO Press, 1976), particularly the Introduction by Nancy Baster.

[51]Amilcar O. Herrera et al., *Catastrophe or New Society? A Latin American World Model* (Ottawa, Canada: International Development Research Centre, 1976); and Wassily Leontief et al., *The Future of the World Economy* (New York: Oxford University Press, 1977). A useful survey of various kinds of global models is John M. Richardson, Jr., "Global Modeling: A Survey and Appraisal," an unpublished report from the Center for Technology and Administration, College of Public Affairs, The American University, December 1977.

Chapter 4

[52]ILO, *Employment, Growth and Basic Needs,* pp. 191-92. The ILO resolution, in effect, says that the standards to be set and the goals to be achieved have to be defined by each country. Moreover, "basic needs" will change as a country progresses.

[53]The fact that the PQLI may be applicable to economically more developed countries as well is pure serendipity.

[54]Karl Marx, *Capital* (Chicago: Charles H. Kerr and Company, 1906), Vol. I, p. 13.

[55]W. W. Rostow, *The Stages of Economic Growth: A Non-Communist Manifesto* (New York: Cambridge University Press, 1961); Adelman and Morris, *Society, Politics, and Economic Development;* and McGranahan et al., *Contents and Measurement.*

[56]Kravis et al., *System of International Comparisons,* pp. 1-2.

[57]Marx, *Capital,* pp. 14-15.

[58]Even in the United States—with fewer and less sharp political cleavages than exist in many developing countries—attempts to improve the conditions of ethnic minorities, blacks, Mexican Americans, and Native Americans, and to improve conditions in such depressed regions as Appalachia, have encountered implacable difficulties.

[59]Phyllis Deane, *The First Industrial Revolution* (Cambridge: Cambridge University Press, 1965), pp. 6-7, made the rather bold but reasonable estimate that in the 1750s the per capita income of England and Wales in real terms was about three times that of India in the early 1960s. Given what we know about wages and other sources of income and the fact that migration between Britain and the American colonies was substantial, it is probable that per capita incomes in the United States were at least as high.

For a stimulating recent attempt to identify the significant similarities and differences between eighteenth and early nineteenth century North Atlantic economies and modern Fourth World countries, see K. N. Raj, "Poverty, Politics, and Development: Western Europe in the First Half of 19th Century and South Asia in Second Half of 20th," *Economic and Political Weekly*, Annual Number, Vol. 12 (February 1977), pp. 185-204; and the critique by Arun Majumdar, "Poverty, Politics and Development: A Comment," *Economic and Political Weekly*, Vol. 12 (May 7, 1977), pp. 773-74.

[60]Population Reference Bureau, *1977 World Population Data Sheet* (Washington, D.C.).

[61]Gunnar Myrdal, *Asian Drama: An Inquiry Into the Poverty of Nations* New York: Pantheon, 1968), Vol. 1, p. 552.

[62]From a review of *Asian Drama* in *Economic and Political Weekly*, Vol. 4, No. 5, February 1, 1969, pp. 289-90. Italics in the original.

[63]Myrdal, *Asian Drama*, Vol. 1, p. 552.

[64]Witness Aubrey Menen's South Indian grandmother in whose Nayar group it was thought that only low-class (and probably immoral) women would cover their breasts. Aubrey Menen, *Dead Man In the Silver Market* (New York: Scribner, 1953), p. 22. For a witty and chastening characterization of ethnocentricities in general, *passim.*

[65]Even in the United States, there is no commonly accepted minimum standard for housing. As the U.S. Department of Health, Education and Welfare pointed out in a recent report to Congress, it is not known "what kind or how much housing is necessary for the basic health of occupants, although there may be some relationship." The entire report is a salutory reminder of the difficulty of establishing satisfactory definitions of poverty even in a single society. See U.S. Department of Health, Education and Welfare, *The Measure of Poverty: A Report to Congress as Mandated by the Education Amendments of 1974* (Washington, D.C.: HEW, April 1976), p. 23.

[66]Popular wisdom long has assumed that reduced mortality rates since the late eighteenth century are the result of improved medical treatment. Now, however, current discussion among demographers and medical historians emphasizes the insignificance of medical and hospital contributions. For a statement of what now may be becoming the new orthodoxy, see Thomas McKeown, *The Modern Rise of Population* (New York: Academic Press, 1976). For an important review, see Etienne van de Walle, *Science*, Vol. 197, August 12, 1977, pp. 652-53. See also W. H. McNeill, *Plagues and People* (Garden City, N.J.: Anchor Press/Doubleday, 1976). For one examination of the relationship between economic development and mortality, see Samuel H. Preston, "The Changing Relation Between Mortality and Level of Economic Development," *Population Studies*, Vol. 19, No. 2 (July 1975), pp. 231-48.

[67]For an elaboration, see P. R. Payne, "Nutrition Planning and Food Policy," *Food Policy* (February 1976), pp. 114-15; and *World Food and Nutrition Study*, Vol. 4. See also P. V. Sukhatme, *Malnutrition and Poverty*, Ninth Annual Bahadur Shastri Memorial Lecture, New Delhi, Indian Agricultural Research Institute, January 29, 1977; Roger J. Williams, "Nutritional Individuality," *Human Nature*, Vol. 1, No. 6 (June 1978), pp. 46-53; and Daniel G. Freedman, "Ethnic Differences in Babies," *Human Nature*, Vol. 2, No. 1 (January 1979), pp. 36-43. The argument presented here about the inadequacy of knowledge about calorie requirements applies to protein requirements as well. For a general survey of the history of changing protein standards, see Dorothy Hollingsworth,

"How Much Protein Do We Need?", *British Nutrition Foundation Bulletin*, No. 16 (January 1976), pp. 226-39.

[68] On the implicit bias favoring proteins of animal origin, see, for example, P. G. K. Panikar, "Economics of Nutrition," in *Economic and Political Weekly*, Annual Number, Vol. 7 (February 1972), pp. 414-30. On the technical requirements, see Hollingsworth, "How Much Protein Do We Need?," p. 233.

[69] Myrdal, *Asian Drama*, Vol. 3, particularly pp. 1534-36. See also Schlomo Reutlinger and Marcello Selowsky, *Malnutrition and Poverty: Magnitudes and Policy Options*, World Bank Staff Occasional Paper, No. 23 (Washington, D.C.: 1976), p. 8.

[70] Reutlinger and Selowsky, *Malnutrition and Poverty*, pp. 14ff; David Morawetz, *Twenty-Five Years of Economic Development, 1950 to 1975* (Washington, D.C.: The World Bank, 1977), pp. 54-58. See also Helen C. Farnsworth, "National Food Consumption of Fourteen Western European Countries and Factors Responsible for Their Differences," *Food Research Institute Studies*, Vol. 13, No. 1 (1974), pp. 77-94.

[71] Kazushi Ohkawa and Nobukiyo Takamatsu, "Report of the Survey on Japanese Experiences of Changes in Food Habits in Relation to Production Pattern." A study for the Asia Productivity Organization, APO Project SUV-111-70. Cited in Raj, "Poverty, Politics, and Development," p. 187, footnote 20.

Another study estimates that while per capita income virtually tripled between 1883/87 and 1933/40, calories consumed increased no more than one third, rising from 1,811 calories at the beginning to a peak of 2,417 in 1918-22 and then slowly declining thereafter. Carl Mosk, "Fecundity, Infanticide, and Food Consumption in Japan" (unpublished manuscript, May 1978). See also Harry T. Oshima, "Food Consumption, Nutrition, and Economic Development in Asian Countries," *Economic Development and Cultural Change*, Vol. 15, No. 4 (July 1967), pp. 385-97. It has been argued that the Japanese not only did not increase their calorie intake significantly, but also did not change the composition of their diet much in the decades before World War II. Hiromitsu Kaneda, "Long-Term Changes in Food Consumption Patterns in Japan," in Kazushi Ohkawa, Bruce F. Johnston, Hiromitsu Kaneda, eds., *Agricultural and Economic Growth: Japan's Experience* (Princeton: Princeton University Press, 1969), pp. 398-429.

[72] On declining per capita food availability in India during the interwar period, see George Blyn, *Agricultural Trends in India, 1891-1947: Output, Availability, and Productivity* (Philadelphia: University of Pennsylvania Press, 1966), pp. 240-43; for evidence of the stability of per capita food availability between 1950-51 and 1973-74, see James D. Gavin and John A. Dixon, "India: A Perspective on the Food Situation," in *Science*, Vol. 188, No. 4188, May 9, 1975, p. 542. Between 1921 and 1971, life expectancy at birth rose from 21 years to approximately 44 years. Sudhansu Bhusan Mukherjee, *The Age Distribution of the Indian Population: A Reconstruction for the States and Territories, 1881-1961* (Honolulu: Hawaii University Press, 1977), pp. 221-40.

[73] *FAO Production Yearbook* (Rome: Food and Agriculture Organization), various years.

[74] See *World Food and Nutrition Study*, Vol. 4. pp. 80-81. Food (whether measured as calories or more complexly) is being treated here as it is typically considered in discussions of "welfare"—not as an end in itself but as a necessity

to achieve other ends. However, food and the act of eating—what we will and will not eat as well as who we will and will not eat with—are vital elements in social relationships. This ritual, ceremonial function is probably of greatest importance; however, it lies outside the range of this discussion.

[75] Some sense of the difficulties involved in deriving agreed upon conclusions about what has happened to income distribution within the United States can be found in Peter H. Lindert and Jeffrey G. Williamson, "Three Centuries of American Inequality," in Paul Uselding, ed., *Research in Economic History,* Vol. 1 (Greenwich, Conn., JAI Press, 1976), pp. 69-123. Problems of measurement for less developed countries are, of course, even more formidable. See Ahluwalia, "Inequality, Poverty, and Development," pp. 7 and 33.

[76] Morawetz, *Twenty-Five Years,* pp. 28-29.

[77] United Nations, *International Definition: An Interim Guide;* Adelman and Morris, *Society, Politics, and Economic Development;* Adelman and Morris, *Economic Growth and Social Equity in Developing Countries;* UNRISD, "Compilation of Indicators for 1970," Vol. 1 of *Research Bank of Development Indicators* (Geneva: UNRISD, June 1970), Report No. 76.1; and OECD, *Measuring Social Well-Being.*

[78] United Nations, Department of Economic and Social Affairs, Population Branch, "The Statistics," Vol. 1 of *Foetal, Infant and Early Childhood Mortality* (New York: United Nations, 1954), Doc. No. ST/SOA/Series A, No. 13, p. 29. See also Iwao M. Moriyama and Susan O. Gustavus, *Cohort Mortality and Survivorship United States Death Registration States, 1900-1968, Analytical Studies,* U.S. Department of Health, Education, and Welfare, National Center for Health Statistics, Series 3, No. 16 (November 1972), p. 2; and Walsh McDermott, "Environmental Factors Bearing on Medical Education in the Developing Countries," *Journal of Medical Education,* Vol. 41, No. 9 (September 1966), Part 2, pp. 137-62.

[79] Literacy is not the only indicator for which equality of the sexes can be questioned. There are also societies where the survival of girl babies and of women generally is a matter of lower social value than is the survival of males. These cultural differences suggest how deep-rooted and complex the problem of ethnocentricity is.

[80] Ahluwalia discusses the different impacts of basic literacy and secondary education in a way that is consistent with the view presented here. See Ahluwalia, "Inequality, Poverty, and Development," pp. 17-19.

[81] For a useful discussion of the complexities economists encounter in measuring income distribution, see Richard Szal and Sherman Robinson, "Measuring Income Inequality," in Charles R. Frank, Jr., and Richard C. Webb, eds., *Income Distribution and Growth in the Less Developed Countries* (Washington, D.C.: Brookings Institution, 1977), Appendix I, pp. 491-533.

[82] 8 people live   25 years, for a total of 200 years
      2 people live 100 years, for a total of 200 years
                     total years lived = 400 years
              Average life expectancy =   40 years

[83] One does not have to accept McKeown's particular interpretation *(The Modern Rise of Population)* to come to this conclusion. See Etienne van de

Walle's review in *Science*, Vol. 197, August 12, 1977, pp. 652-53, for some alternative possibilities.

[84]Ahluwalia, "Inequality, Poverty, and Development," p. 16; see also McGranahan et al., *Contents and Measurement*, p. 19.

[85]The prime purpose of this essay is to explore the intellectual requirements of a PQLI, making use of whatever data are available. To the extent that the index is accepted, one of its virtues will be to point to the most important data improvements that are required. The PQLI can be an economizing device; it can reduce the amount of data required to produce answers to certain kinds of questions. Because the emphasis is placed on where individual nations stand in reference to absolute objectives rather than on performance relative to other countries, differences in definitions among countries are not particularly critical as long as the definitions remain consistent over time.

[86]This refers to the notion of a "cutting score," one that establishes the fact of literacy rather than levels attained. See Thomas F. Donlow, W. Miles McPeek, and Lois R. Chatham, "The Development of the Brief Test of Literacy," *Vital and Health Statistics*, U.S. Department of Health, Education, and Welfare, National Center for Health Statistics, Series 2, No. 27 (September 1974).

[87]A good general summary is found in D. V. Glass and C. Grebenik, "World Population: 1800-1950," in H. J. Habakkuk and M. Postan, eds., *The Industrial Revolution and After: Incomes, Population, and Technological Change (I)*, Vol. 6, Part 1, of *The Cambridge Economic History of Europe* (Cambridge: Cambridge University Press, 1965), pp. 70ff. The evidence on this point is widespread but not easily pulled together. An excellent comparison of mortality improvements in France and Germany between 1861 and 1910 is found in E. A. Wrigley, *Industrial Growth and Population Change* (Cambridge: Cambridge University Press, 1961). Scotland is a case where general mortality declined slowly during the second half of the nineteenth century, as did the death rate of children ages one to five, while infant mortality continued to rise until the very end of the century. See Charlotte A. Douglas, "Infant and Perinatal Mortality in Scotland," *Vital and Health Statistics, Analytical Studies*, U.S. Department of Health, Education, and Welfare, National Center for Health Statistics, Series 3, No. 5 (November 1966), p. 39. See also the data in the collected essays of United Nations, *Proceedings of the World Population Conference, 1954, Papers*, Vol. 1, Doc. No. E/Cont. 13/413.

[88]See also Mortimer Spiegelman, "Mortality Trends and Prospects and Their Implications." *The Annals of the American Academy of Political and Social Science*, Vol. 316 (March 1958), pp. 25-28; and George J. Stolnitz, "A Century of International Mortality Trends: II," *Population Studies*, Vol. 10, No. 1 (July 1956), pp. 34-42. This point is further supported by the correlation coefficients in Table 4.

[89]Pierre Cantrelle, "Is There a Standard Pattern of Tropical Mortality?" in Pierre Cantrelle et al., eds., *Population in African Development*, Vol. 1 (Liège, Belgium: International Union for the Scientific Study of Population, n.d.), pp. 33-42. See also Remy Clarin, "The Assessment of Infant and Child Mortality from the Data Available in Africa," in John Charles Caldwell and Chukuka Okonjo, eds., *The Population of Tropical Africa* (New York: Columbia University Press, 1968), pp. 199-213. Death rates in India among children and young adults appear to be higher than standardized life tables would lead one to

expect. See Mukherjee, *The Age Distribution of the Indian Population,* p. 173.

[90] For a useful discussion, see Brian MacMahon, "Infant Mortality in the United States," in Carl L. Erhardt and Joyce E. Berlin, eds., *Mortality and Morbidity in the United States* (Cambridge, Mass.: Harvard University Press, 1974), pp. 189-282.

[91] This is true even in very similar societies. For example, a recent report cited in *New York Times,* September 4, 1977, noted that Scotsmen aged 35 to 44 tend to die of heart disease at more than three times the rate of Swedish males of the same age group.

[92] McDermott, "Environmental Factors." See also a forthcoming study by Michelle B. McAlpin on economic and demographic patterns in western India, from 1872 to 1931, which indicates that the 1918/19 influenza epidemic killed many more females than males in India and was also very age-specific.

[93] On the other hand, women in South Asia, particularly of childbearing age, seem to be significantly less prone to deaths during famine periods. See McAlpin, forthcoming.

[94] Stolnitz, "A Century of International Mortality Trends," pp. 22-25; and Bernard Benjamin and H. W. Haycocks, *The Analysis of Mortality and Other Actuarial Statistics* (Cambridge: Cambridge University Press, 1970), pp. 8-9.

[95] Donald J. Bogue, *Principles of Demography* (New York: John Wiley and Sons, Inc., 1969), pp. 580-81. Stolnitz, "A Century of International Mortality Trends," p. 33, remarked that "Judged by the standards of current research in fertility, recent mortality analysis by demographers has been infrequent and even casual." More than twenty years have passed, but there has been relatively little reason to modify that opinion.

[96] Bogue, *Demography,* p. 585. McDermott, "Environmental Factors," has a useful set of medical classifications that help clarify the distinction made here.

[97] Cited in W. P. D. Logan, "The Measurement of Infant Mortality," *Population Bulletin of the United Nations,* No. 3 (October 1953), Doc. No. ST/SOA/Ser.N/3, p. 53.

[98] For example, Stolnitz, "A Century of International Mortality Trends," pp. 34-42; Wrigley, *Industrial Growth;* and E. A. Wrigley, *Population and History* (New York: McGraw-Hill, 1969), pp. 164-80.

[99] Ansley J. Coale and Paul Demeny, *Regional Model Life Tables and Stable Populations* (Princeton: Princeton University Press, 1967), and United Nations, *Methods of Estimating Basic Demographic Measures from Incomplete Data,* Manual IV of *Manuals on Methods of Estimating Population* (New York: United Nations, 1967). See also United Nations, *The Concept of Stable Population: Application to the Study of Countries with Incomplete Demographic Statistics* (New York: United Nations, 1968).

[100] Arjun Adlakha, "Model Life Tables: An Empirical Test of their Applicability to Less Developed Countries," *Demography,* Vol. 9, No. 4 (November 1972), pp. 589-601. Clarin, "The Assessment of Infant and Child Mortality"; Cantrelle, "Is There a Standard Pattern?"; E. A. Wrigley, "Mortality in Pre-Industrial England: The Example of Colyton, Devon, Over Three Centuries," *Daedalus* (Spring 1969), pp. 570-71; United Nations, Department of Economic and Social Affairs, *Methods for Population Projections by Sex and Age, Manual*

III of Manuals on Methods of Estimating Population (New York: United Nations, 1956), ST/SOA/Series A, Population Studies No. 25, p. 28.

[101]See Appendix A.

[102]S. Swaroop and K. Uemura, "Proportional Mortality of 50 Years and Above," *World Health Organization Bulletin,* No. 17 (1957), pp. 439-81.

[103]Values are extremely important. It is no accident that Utah, where the dominating Mormon Church strongly favors large families, has a birth rate of 29.9 per thousand, more than double the U.S. average of 14.5. And as evidence of the swings in public attitudes, one can refer to the concern over the decline in the birth rate in Western Europe between the two wars. See, for example, Richard Titmuss and Kathleen Titmuss, *Parents Revolt* (London: Seeker and Warburg, 1942), where Britain's sixty-year decline is treated as a "public danger." There is also growing concern currently among some groups in the Federal Republic of Germany over the long-run implications of the very low birth rate. See John Dornberg, "Are German People Facing Extinction?," *Boston Sunday Globe,* June 18, 1978, p. A-3.

[104]Daniel F. Sullivan, *Conceptual Problems in Developing an Index of Health* (Washington, D.C.: HEW, National Center for Health Statistics, 1966). Iwao M. Moriyama, "Problems in the Measurement of Health Status," in Eleanor B. Sheldon, and Wilbert E. Moore, eds., *Indicators of Social Change* (New York: Russell Sage Foundation, 1968), particularly pp. 585–95.

[105]In the metaphysical sense, the danger that a longer life means a more miserable one afflicts us all, rich as well as poor.

[106]See W. Arthur Lewis, "Is Economic Growth Desirable?," the Appendix to *The Theory of Economic Growth* (Homewood, Ill.: Richard D. Irwin, 1955), pp. 420-35.

[107]No mention has been made of "freedom" because it is far too culturally (and politically) specific a concept to be easily captured in an international measure. While the Western developed world tends to associate freedom with the operation of particular types of parliamentary institutions, freedom poses far more complex questions of participation and control that are not exhausted by the presence or absence of a particular set of political arrangements and economic settings. Moreover, the problem of freedom is not merely national but depends also on the specific character of local organizations and relationships.

Chapter 5

[108]Dan Usher has made an interesting attempt to incorporate rising life expectancy into GNP. See Usher, "An Imputation," pp. 193-226. A major criticism is pointed at the valuation process. See also Willis, "Comment," pp. 226-32.

[109]The basic data available are crude. In order to avoid any spurious implication of an accuracy that does not exist, PQLI has been rounded. This would still not be considered sufficiently cautious by Morgenstern, but it is at least a nod of recognition to the problem. See Morgenstern, *On the Accuracy of Economic Observations.*

[110]Bogue, *Demography,* p. 559.

[111]While the estimates of infant mortality for sixteenth and seventeenth century Europe vary greatly for time and place, Cipolla cited Sweden between 1718 and 1782 with an average infant mortality of 212 per thousand as a typical example. See Carlo Cipolla, *Before the Industrial Revolution* (New York, W. W. Norton, 1976), pp. 150 and 286-87.

[112]The formula used to approximate the life table value at age one was:

$$e_1 = \frac{e_0 - 1 + q_0 (1 - k_0)}{1 - q_0}$$

where e_0=life expectancy at birth, q_0=infant mortality per thousand live births, and k_0=estimated average length of life of infants who died before age one. Reasonable assumptions about the distribution of infant deaths through the first year affect life expectancy at age one very little.

[113]For example, India would have generated negative life expectancy index numbers during the first two decades of the twentieth century. Indian life expectancies at birth for 1901, 1911, and 1921 are estimated to have been 23.8, 22.9, and 20.1 years, respectively. With infant mortalities of 205 per thousand in 1901 and 1911, and of 198 in 1921, life expectancy at age one would have been 28.4, 27.3, and 23.6 years, respectively. Data are from Kingsley Davis, *The Population of India and Pakistan* (Princeton, N.J.: Princeton University Press, 1951), pp. 34 and 36. Davis did not give an infant mortality figure for 1901, so the 1911 rate was used.

[114]Benjamin and Haycocks, *Analysis of Mortality*, pp. 21-23. This particular concept adopts as the limit of "normal" life that age in the life table by which 90 percent of persons have died.

[115]Benjamin and Haycocks, *Analysis of Mortality*, pp. 23-26.

[116]See Glass and Grebenik, "World Population," p. 81; and I. M. Moriyama, "The Change in Mortality Trend in the United States," *Vital and Health Statistics, Analytical Studies*, U.S. Department of Health, Education, and Welfare, National Center for Health Statistics, Series 3, No. 1 (March 1964), p. 38.

[117]This is an average life expectancy at age one for men and women together. In countries having long life expectancies, female life expectancy tends to be much higher than that of males. For example, in Sweden, it is seventy-eight years for women and only seventy-two years for men. Some consideration was given to setting the upper limit for the life expectancy at age one indicator at the female level (78 = 100) or slightly higher. Because, for the most part, a combined male-female average is used, this would only leave empty space at the upper end of the scale and unnecessarily compress the spread of countries within the range. Chapter 6 considers this issue in greater detail.

[118]Appendix A provides data for 150 countries.

[119]For example, more attention is paid to the fact that the "income gap" between developed and less developed countries is increasing over time than to the fact that real per capita incomes in virtually all developing countries rose between 1950 and 1975. Morawetz, *Twenty-Five Years*, Table A-1.

[120]In OECD countries, where PQLI ranges from 93 to 97, poverty is defined relatively or as a phenomenon affecting *les marginaux*. See Organisation for Economic Co-operation and Development (OECD), *Public Expenditures on In-*

come Maintenance Programmes, OECD Studies in Resource Allocations, No. 3 (Paris: OECD, July 1976), pp. 61ff.

[121]Chenery et al., *Redistribution with Growth,* Chapter 2. Todaro, writing favorably about the World Bank effort, comments that, "Although the choice of welfare weights in an index of development is purely arbitrary, it does represent and reflect important social 'value judgments' about goods and objectives for a given society." He goes on to point out that the GNP measure is itself not neutral, that "so long as the growth rate of GNP is explicitly or implicitly used to compare development performance, we know that a 'wealthy weights' index is actually being employed." Michael P. Todaro, *Economic Development in the Third World* (London: Longman Group Ltd., 1977), pp. 115-16.

[122]For convincing evidence that there is no unique mathematical solution to the weighting problem, see Z. Hellwig, "On the Problem of Weighting in International Comparisons," in Zygmunt Gostkowski, ed., *Toward a System of Human Resources Indicators for Less Developed Countries* (Ossolineum, Institute of Philosophy and Sociology, Polish Academy of Sciences, 1972), pp. 110-11. See also other articles in the same volume.

[123]Gerald M. Meier, *Leading Issues in Economic Development,* 3rd ed. (New York: Oxford University Press, 1976), pp. 7-8. The usefulness of market prices is also limited by their inability to reflect external diseconomies or social costs.

[124]Hollis Chenery, "The World Bank and World Poverty," in William Loehr and John P. Powelson, eds., *Economic Development, Poverty, and Income Distribution* (Boulder, Colorado: Westview Press, 1977), p. 33. See also Montek S. Ahluwalia and Hollis Chenery, "The Economic Framework," in Chenery et al., *Redistribution with Growth,* pp. 38-51.

[125]Weights and scales can be changed in a large number of ways. Each variation would produce a slightly different ranking of countries. There is no particular virtue to such a game. Nor does the fact that such variations are possible "prove" anything. The major requirement is that once a pattern of weights and scales has been selected, it is used consistently.

[126]This problem becomes an important issue only if the object is to determine a "normal" path of development, as in McGranahan et al., *Contents and Measurement,* pp. 127-28. The PQLI, however, is an instrument to help identify and explore diversity. If at some future time it could be determined how relatively difficult improvement at different levels actually is, such an "arduousness" factor could be incorporated into the PQLI.

[127]See Davidson R. Gwatkin and James P. Grant, "Using Targets to Help Improve Child Health," a paper presented to the National Council on International Health Conference on Child Health in a Changing World, New York, May 15, 1978 (Washington, D.C.: Overseas Development Council, 1978); and James P. Grant, *Disparity Reduction Rates in Social Indicators: A Proposal for Measuring and Targeting Progress in Meeting Basic Needs,* Monograph No. 11 (Washington, D.C.: Overseas Development Council, 1978).

[128]Morawetz, *Twenty-Five Years,* pp. 54-58, agrees with this conclusion.

[129]It is also likely that some of the correlation is a function of assumptions made in the construction of the data on which the PQLI is based.

[130]According to Hollis Chenery, the World Bank currently is involved in research on this repricing issue.

Chapter 6

[131]Unless otherwise noted, data are taken from Appendix A. PQLIs are for the years 1970-75. Per capita GNPs are also for the years 1970-75 in constant 1974-76 U.S. dollars. Where aggregated by region or by income group, PQLI and GNP data are weighted by population. Population data also are averages for the years 1970-75.

[132]See Appendix B for rankings of 150 countries according to per capita GNP and according to PQLI.

[133]In some cases of this sort—Angola is a good example—the low PQLI may point to the possibility of a serious flaw in the per capita GNP estimate.

[134]As noted earlier, a 3- to 5-point margin of error is assumed throughout. In other words, Iran could have a PQLI as high as 48; India could have one as low as 38. However, a ninefold difference in per capita income probably is significant. In this circumstance, the similarity in PQLIs tells something about how social benefits are distributed in the two societies. It is probably equally significant that Iran, Panama, and Uruguay have nearly identical per capita incomes but grossly different PQLIs (43, 80, and 87, respectively).

[135]A lower rate of growth in per capita income would indicate that an even larger proportion of the human race would not achieve a PQLI of 90 by the end of the century.

[136]Tinbergen, *Reshaping the International Order,* p. 130. See Chapter 7 for a discussion of how the Tinbergen group goals were converted into a PQLI rating.

[137]This estimate is based on the fact that the average PQLI for the thirty-two "upper middle-income countries," having a weighted average per capita GNP of $1,047, is only 68 (see Table 7 and Appendix A).

[138]The paucity of studies presently makes it difficult to link the flow of income and the movement of the PQLI. But what evidence there is does seem to support the point. It will be interesting to see how long it takes tiny systems —Qatar (with a population of 180,000), the United Arab Emirates (with a population of 320,000), Bahrain (with a population of 232,000), Oman (with a population of 720,000)—to raise their PQLIs after they have become social service paradises. The larger states—Iraq, Iran, Libya—are likely to have more difficulty.

[139]Dr. Stanley Heginbotham of the Congressional Research Service has made an interesting preliminary attempt to estimate the factors that may account for the distribution of PQLIs. See Stanley J. Heginbotham, "Measuring Social and Economic Human Rights Conditions," *Human Rights Conditions in Selected Countries and the U.S. Response,* Appendix A. U.S. House of Representatives, Committee on International Relations, July 25, 1978 (Washington, D.C.).

[140]Colonial experience in itself cannot account for low PQLI levels, as the cases of Guyana and Sri Lanka (with PQLIs of 85 and 82, respectively) indicate. Nor was independent status a historical guarantee of high PQLI levels, as Afghanistan (with a PQLI of 18), Ethiopia (20), and Liberia (26) show.

[141]See, for example, I. M. Lewis, "Tribal Society," *International Encyclopedia of the Social Sciences,* Vol. 16 (New York: The Macmillan Company and the Free Press, 1968), pp. 146-51.

[142]It appears that not only the Caribbean countries, but many other island nations with colonial pasts have fairly high PQLIs. This may reflect not only the duration of colonial status but also the ease with which imperial powers were able to impose their own institutional arangements on small systems with the ultimate effect (even where not consciously intended) of bringing improvements to social conditions to something close to the level of the metropolitan power.

[143]The slave trade was a self-defeating activity if the Europeans were interested in generating other surpluses.

[144]For an excellent survey of the conceptual and practical problems involved, see Gary S. Fields, "Assessing Progress Toward Greater Equality of Income Distribution," in William McGreevey, ed., *Measuring Development Progress* (New York: Praeger Press, forthcoming).

[145]Chenery et al., *Redistribution with Growth,* pp. 10-13.

[146]Nor is there any difference (except slightly to favor Niger) in the World Bank's measures of absolute poverty. Each country has 33 percent of its population living with an annual per capita income of less than U.S. $50 per person. Niger has 60 percent and Sri Lanka has 63 percent of its population living below an annual per capita income of U.S. $75. Ibid.

[147]For a brief discussion of strong assumptions that have to be made in using cross-sectional data as a surrogate for historical data, see Morgan, *Economic Development,* pp. 46-48.

[148]Even if historical data were available for much longer periods, there is probably some point in the past when the PQLI might cease to be terribly interesting. For example, literacy would be very low and virtually unchanging. Infant mortality and life expectancies would be fairly volatile but not improving. One would have to judge whether under such circumstances it might not be better to use individual components. However, at the moment, any data that contribute to the construction of a historical series will be important because of the added understanding that will flow from them.

[149]The DRR for PQLI is calculated according to the formula:

$$\text{DRR}_t^{t+n} = \left(\frac{X_{t+n}}{X_t} \right)^{\frac{1}{n}} - 1$$

where X is the disparity between actual PQLI performance and 100 in time t and in time t+n. The calculation yields a negative number when the disparity is being reduced. However, for the convenience of discussion, the rate at which the gap between actual PQLI and 100 is narrowing is shown as a positive number. A negative rate indicates that the PQLI is declining—that the disparity is becoming greater. The uses to which the DRR can be put are indicated in Chapter 7. For a more complete discussion of the DRR, see Grant, *Disparity Reduction Rates.*

[150]See Appendix C for data sources and a discussion of problems associated with their use.

[151]India data are from Appendix A of this volume.

[152]Income growth rate calculated from Morawetz, *Twenty-Five Years,* Table A-1.

[153]A similar phenomenon may help explain Israel's slow PQLI improvement between 1950 and 1970. See Table 13.

[154]These figures are 1970 per capita personal income figures. U.S. Bureau of the Census, *Historical Statistics of the United States, Colonial Time to 1970,* Bicentennial Edition, Part II (Washington, D.C.: Government Printing Office, 1975), pp. 243-45.

[155]In addition, infant mortality data for Egypt in 1970 and for Cyprus in 1973 also show the female rate as worse than the male rate. The lack of other data makes it impossible to construct PQLIs for these years.

[156]It is not clear what effect large increases in female literacy would have on social performance, specifically on life expectancy and infant mortality.

[157]Ingrid Waldron, "Why Do Women Live Longer than Men?", *Social Science and Medicine,* Vol. 10 (1976), pp. 349-62, examines the state of the debate and provides an extensive bibliography. Waldron herself attributes higher male mortality largely to social-cultural factors.

[158]See the remarks by Glass and Grebenik, "World Population," p. 79, footnote 2. Problems of urban-rural definition are crucial for demographers but are probably less troublesome for the uses to which the PQLI will be put.

[159]Glass and Grebenik, "World Population," remark that "in some of the western countries, at least, differences between urban and rural mortality appear to have been diminishing since the First World War. In England and Wales, 1950-52, the expectation of life at birth was slightly higher in Greater London than in the country as a whole. But in other large urban areas, mortality was above the national average, while in rural districts it was below that average."

[160]Samir S. Basta, "Nutrition and Health in Low Income Urban Areas of the Third World," *Ecology of Food and Nutrition,* Vol. 6 (1977), pp. 113-24, stresses the adversities of urban life. Nevertheless, his data show that urban health performance, particularly infant mortality, is better than rural. Basic literacy rates tend to be higher in urban areas.

[161]See, for example, Adna Ferris Weber, *The Growth of Cities in the Nineteenth Century* (Ithaca, N.Y.: Cornell University Press, 1963), pp. 343 ff; Deane, *The First Industrial Revolution,* Chapters 13 and 15; and C. Arnold Anderson, "Literacy and Schooling on the Development Threshold: Some Historical Cases," in C. Arnold Anderson and Mary Jean Bowman, eds., *Education and Economic Development* (London: Frank Cass and Co., 1956), pp. 347-62.

[162]The task of comparison is extremely complex, as Basta, "Nutrition and Health," makes obvious. One point that Basta does not take into account is that it is not enough to compare "poor" in urban areas with "poor" in rural areas. One also must consider the conditions of the various *types* of poor people in the two sectors. A recent study tentatively suggests that "what distinguished urban from rural areas [in early modern Europe] was not a radical discrepancy in mortality conditions, but differences in the proportions married, generated by distinct migration and occupational patterns." See Allan Sharlin, "Natural Decrease in Early Modern Cities: A Reconsideration," in *Past and Present,* No. 79 (May 1978), pp. 126-38. If Sharlin is correct that urban death rates of earlier times were somewhat exaggerated, this may help resolve the puzzle of why urban motality rates in developing countries tend to be so much more favorable than in the nineteenth-century North Atlantic world.

[163]Michael P. Todaro, "A Model of Labor Migration and Urban Unemployment in Less Developed Countries," *American Economic Review,* Vol. 59, No. 1 (March 1969), pp. 138-48; and J. R. Harris and M. P. Todaro, "Migration, Unemployment, and Development: A Two Sector Analysis," *American Economic Review,* Vol. 60, No. 1 (March 1970), pp. 126-42.

Chapter 7

[164]"Rich" and "poor" are put in quotation marks to remind the reader that money is not all, that whatever may be happening to per capita GNP, the gradual realization of PQLI standards is in itself a process of enrichment.

[165]U.N. Economic and Social Council, "The International Development Strategy: First Over-all Review and Appraisal of Issues and Policies," Preliminary Report of the Secretary General, Doc. No. E/AC.54/1.60, March 14, 1973, p. 7. Prepared for the Ninth Session of the Committee for Development Planning. Although the specific reference was to the desirability of a physical consumption measure, the PQLI certainly seems to satisfy the specifications.

[166]It should not be forgotten that the individual components are themselves composite measures.

[167]A satisfactory theory defines and specifies significant relationships in a way that makes it possible to predict the consequences that will flow from changes in any of the elements. In operational form, a theory permits the design of policies that will bring about specified changes by making changes in one or more variables. Current economic theory does not satisfy these requirements.

[168]The thermometer, when developed, merely described certain bodily responses. It did not provide a theory. But it encouraged the search for a theory that would explain the complex interrelationships which it summarizes. If the PQLI prompts a similar search for theory, it will perform a useful task.

[169]U.S. Congress, *Foreign Assistance Act of 1973,* Public Law 93-189.

[170]See, for example, U.N. Economic and Social Council, "Developing Countries and Levels of Development," paper prepared by the Secretariat, Doc. No. E/AC.54/L.81, October 15, 1975. Prepared for the Twelfth Session of the Committee for Development Planning, March 29 - April 9, 1976; and the Working Group on Hard-Core Developing Countries and Related Policy Issues, December 8-12, 1975.

[171]U.N. Economic and Social Council, Committee for Development Planning, "Report on the Twelfth Session (29 March - 7 April 1976)," Official Records, Sixty-first Session, Supplement No. 6 (United Nations: New York, 1976), Doc. No. E/5793, pp. 21ff.

[172]See, for example, U.N. Economic and Social Council, "Economic Growth and Main Streams of Production: Some Basic Problems in Hard-Core Developing Countries," paper prepared by the Secretariat, Doc. No. E/AC.54/L.86, November 17, 1975. Prepared for the Twelfth Session of the Committee for Development Planning, March 29 - April 9, 1976, and the Working Group on Hard-Core Developing Countries and Related Policy Issues, December 8-12, 1975.

[173]To the extent that countries are perceived to be constrained by an "equity

versus growth" choice, development programs should strive to minimize or eliminate this contradiction.

[174]For another classification of countries, see Grant, *Disparity Reduction Rates,* pp. 42-44.

[175]See *World Food and Nutrition Study,* Vol. 4, pp. 94-100.

[176]Tinbergen, *Reshaping the International Order,* p. 130.

[177]The RIO "life expectancy at birth" target had to be adjusted to "life expectancy at age one" in order to be consistent with the requirements of the PQLI. The RIO infant mortality target of 50 deaths per thousand live births implies a life expectancy at age one objective of 67.4 years. The individual targets for life expectancy, infant mortality, and literacy were then indexed and the indexes averaged, to obtain a PQLI of 77.

[178]Statement of the Participants, *Amsterdam Symposium on Food and Basic Needs,* Amsterdam, The Netherlands, February 26, 1978.

[179]For a full discussion of the DRR, see Grant, *Disparity Reduction Rates.*

[180]For some harsh cautionary qualifications, see Oskar Morgenstern, "Does GNP Measure Growth and Welfare?" *Business and Society Review,* No. 15 (Fall 1975), pp. 23-31.

[181]As late as 1958, Jan Tinbergen noted that while education is an important condition of development, it is not relevant to the development of economic policy. See Jan Tinbergen, *The Design of Development* (Baltimore: Johns Hopkins Press, 1958), p. 5. For a different view, see Myrdal, *Asian Drama,* Vol. 3, for his strictures on the neglect by economists not merely of education but of all these relationships.

[182]This proposition is based on the conclusion that there are no quick, cheap technological solutions that can be invented in one country and transferred to another. The large sustainable declines in infant mortality and the sustainable increases in life expectancy, literacy, etc. are primarily the result of effective social organization within the countries concerned. This means that if rapid progress is to be made in ways that largely benefit the "lower orders," it certainly must be organized around conceptual systems and institutional procedures that are indigenous to the particular area.

Population, Per Capita GNP, PQLI, and Component Indicators (Actual Data and Index Numbers) for 150 Countries, by Income Groups, early 1970s

NOTE TO APPENDIX A

The basic PQLI refers not to a specific year but to the "early 1970s," that is, to the period from 1970 to 1975. This derives from the characteristics of the available data, which were obtained from the most generally accepted sources. Population data typically are collected at decennial censuses; annual figures are extrapolated from these data. The accuracy of the intra-censal figures depends on the accuracy of assumptions about birth, death, fertility, etc. Countries with highly developed statistical capabilities not only produce fairly accurate decennial censuses but generally also have elaborate birth and death registration systems that record actual births and mortality ages. Registration systems in most countries—certainly in most developing countries—are inadequate, if they exist at all. Birth and death data often are the products of heroic estimation and/or periodic surveys. Literacy figures typically are produced only occasionally. Thus for many countries, the PQLI is constructed from three indicators that do not relate to the same year. Similarly, the data of one or more of the indicators do not necessarily relate to the same year for all countries. Where this was a problem, every effort was made to find data that relate to a close cluster of years within the period 1970 to 1975. The precise dates for the component indicators of all countries are available in the sources cited below.

Most sources report life expectancy at birth. In order to avoid double counting infant deaths, since the infant mortality rate is also a PQLI component, the PQLI uses life expectancy at age one. These data were derived from life expectancy at birth and infant mortality figures according to the following formula:

$$e^1 = \frac{e^0 - 1 + q^0 (1-k_0)}{1 - q^0}$$

where q^0 is the infant mortality rate per thousand live births;
k^0 is the average survival period (0.2 years) during the first year;
e^0 is life expectancy at birth; and
e^1 is life expectancy at age one.

Because the data from which the PQLIs are constructed often relate to more than a single year and to different years for different countries, average populations and per capita GNPs are given for the years 1970 to 1975, rather than for a single year, as well. Population estimates for all countries are average estimates provided by the United Nations for the period 1970 to 1975. However, obtaining average annual per capita GNP figures calculated in constant dollars for this same period was more difficult. The World Bank is the obvious source of such information. But because the published Bank sources use different base years for determining average domestic prices and average exchange rates, it is not possible merely to apply a U.S. dollar deflator to the figures provided by those sources to derive constant dollar figures for the required years. The Economic Analysis and Projections Department of the World Bank generously made available its unpublished "Derived Atlas Series," which calculates country per capita GNPs in current U.S. dollars and uses the same base year for average domestic prices and exchange rates. Applying the Bank's 1974-76 dollar deflator to these data produced constant dollar estimates for each year in the period 1970 to 1975. The figures used in this study are the averages of these six years.

Column 1 data of the Appendix table are from United Nations, *World Population Prospects as Assessed in 1973*, Population Studies No. 60, Publication Sales No. E.76.X11.4 Column 2 data are calculated in 1974-76 U.S. dollars from World Bank, Economic Analysis and Projections Department, "Derived Atlas Series" (unpublished). Column 3 is the simple average of Columns 4, 5, 6. Column 4 is based on a life expectancy at age one scale that ranges from 38 to 77 years; the formula used is:

$$\frac{\text{Column } (7) - 38}{0.39}$$

Column 5 is based on infant mortality rates ranging from 7 to 229 per thousand live births; the formula used is:

$$\frac{229 - \text{Column } (8)}{2.22}$$

Column 6 is from U.N. Educational, Scientific, and Cultural Organization, *Statistical Yearbook, 1973* and *Statistical Yearbook, 1976;* these data represent percentages of populations aged fifteen and over that are literate. Because these numbers are percentages, they also serve as the literacy index. Column 7 is calculated from life expectancy at birth and infant mortality data (column 8) in *1977 World Population Data Sheet,* published by the Population Reference Bureau, Inc. (Washington, D.C.); see above for the formula used. See Chapter 5 of this volume (pp. 41-56) for a fuller discussion of how the Physical Quality of Life Index is constructed.

Appendix A: Population, Per Capita GNP, PQLI, and Component Indicators

	(1)	(2)	(3)	(4)	(5)	(6)	(7)	(8)
	Population, 1970-75 Average	Per Capita GNP, 1970-75 Average	Physical Quality of Life Index	Life Expectancy at Age One Index	Infant Mortality Index	Literacy (aged 15 and over)	Life Expectancy at Age One	Infant Mortality Rate
	(thousands)	($)[1]				(%)	(years)	(per 1,000 live births)
Low-Income Countries (42) (per capita GNP under $300)								
Afghanistan	18,129	137	18	25.4	21.2	8	47.9	182
Bangladesh	70,719	92	35	38.7	43.7	22	53.1	132
Benin	2,880	124	23	29.0	19.8	20	49.3	185
Burma	29,494	105	51	46.7	46.4	60	56.2	126
Burundi	3,558	111	23	20.5	35.6	14	46.0	150
Cameroon	6,117	273	27	21.8	41.4	19	46.5	137
Central African Empire	1,701	226	18	29.7	17.6	7	49.6	190
Chad	3,832	113[2]	18	15.9	31.1	6	44.2	160
Comoro Islands	288	230[2]	43	40.3	31.1	58	53.7	160
Egypt	35,436	245	43	50.8	50.9	26	57.8	116
Ethiopia	26,415	97	20	31.3	21.6	6	50.2	181
Gambia	486	153	25	35.1	28.8	10	51.7	165
Guinea	4,169	126	20	27.4	24.3	9	48.7	175
Guinea-Bissau	506	120[2]	12	22.8	9.5	5	46.9	208
Haiti	4,394	176	36	50.8	35.6	23	57.8	150
India	578,175	133	43	45.9	48.2	34	55.9	122
Indonesia	127,756	203[2]	48	42.6	41.4	60	54.6	137
Kampuchea (Cambodia)	7,585	70[2]	40	32.1	45.9	42	50.5	127

Kenya	12,249	213	39	45.4	49.5	23	55.7	119
Laos	3,133	70[2]	31	16.9	47.7	28	44.6	123
Lesotho	1,096	131	48	33.1	51.8	59	50.9	114
Madagascar	7,476	204	41	25.6	57.2	39	48.0	102
Malawi	4,638	115	30	28.5	39.2	22	49.1	142
Mali	5,372	90	15	20.0	18.5	5	45.8	188
Mauritania	1,223	287	17	19.7	18.9	11	45.7	187
Nepal	11,902	102	25	35.6	27.0	13	51.9	169
Niger	4,304	132	13	21.5	13.1	5	46.4	200
Nigeria	58,999	297	25	28.2	22.1	25	49.0	180
Pakistan	65,505	155	38	48.7	48.6	16	57.0	121
Rwanda	3,940	97	27	21.3	43.2	16	46.3	133
Sierra Leone	2,814	203	27	30.5	41.9	10	49.9	136
Somalia	2,980	111	19	27.7	23.4	5	48.8	177
Sri Lanka	13,250	179	82	82.6	82.9	81	70.2	45
Sudan	16,982	241	36	52.1	39.6	15	58.3	141
Tanzania	14,355	154	31	34.6	30.2	28	51.5	162
Togo	2,104	250	27	20.3	45.9	16	45.9	127
Uganda	10,580	265	40	52.6	31.1	35	58.5	160
Upper Volta	5,708	99	16	19.0	21.2	8	45.4	182
Vietnam	41,279	189	54	44.9	51.4	65	55.5	115
Yemen Arab Rep.	6,218	180[2]	27	35.9	34.7	10	52.0	152
Yemen, People's Rep.	1,548	260	33	35.9	34.7	27	52.0	152
Zaire	23,062	136	32	34.1	31.1	31	51.3	160
Population Total	1,242,357							
Mean		164.3	31	33.8	35.7	24.3	51.2	149.8
Weighted Average		155.4	40	42.8	43.7	33.8	54.7	132.0

	(1) Population, 1970-75 Average	(2) Per Capita GNP, 1970-75 Average	(3) Physical Quality of Life Index	(4) Life Expectancy at Age One Index	(5) Infant Mortality Index	(6) Literacy (aged 15 and over)	(7) Life Expectancy at Age One	(8) Infant Mortality Rate
	(thousands)	($)[1]				(%)	(years)	(per 1,000 live births)
Lower Middle-Income Countries (38) (per capita GNP $300-$699)								
Albania	2,126	530[2]	75	88.2	64.0	72	72.4	87
Angola	6,012	601	16	22.1	11.7	13	46.6	203
Bolivia	5,095	332	43	35.1	54.5	40	51.7	108
Botswana	654	316	51	59.0	59.5	33	61.0	97
Cape Verde	282	470[2]	48	39.2	67.6	37	53.3	79
China, People's Rep.	605,322	300[2]	69	68.2	78.4	60[4]	64.6	55
Colombia	23,283	526	71	73.1	59.5	81	66.5	97
Congo	1,268	465	27	37.4	22.1	20	52.6	180
Cuba	9,023	640	84	84.9	90.1	78	71.1	29
Dominican Rep.	4,731	630	64	64.9	59.0	68	63.3	98
Ecuador	6,561	505	68	66.9	68.0	68	64.1	78
El Salvador	3,812	432	64	57.9	77.0	57	60.6	58
Equatorial Guinea	298	354	28	35.1	28.8	20	51.7	165
Ghana	9,251	595	35	45.6	32.9	25	55.8	156
Grenada	106[3]	465	77	66.9	88.7	76	64.1	32
Guatemala	5,714	540	54	47.7	67.1	46	56.6	80
Guyana	750	559	85	81.5	85.1	87	69.8	40
Honduras	2,795	359	51	56.7	50.5	45	60.1	117

Ivory Coast	4,598	506	28	34.9	29.3	20	51.6	164
Jordan	2,484	452	47	50.5	59.5	32	57.7	97
Korea, Republic of	32,335	464	82	74.9	82.0	88	67.2	47
Liberia	1,616	415	26	37.2	31.5	10	52.5	159
Malaysia	11,280	692	66	74.6	69.4	53	67.1	75
Mauritius	862	552	71	69.2	82.4	61	65.0	46
Morocco	16,315	436	41	56.2	44.6	21	59.9	130
Mozambique	8,737	333	25	35.1	28.8	11	51.7	165
Nicaragua	2,144	650	54	54.9	47.7	58	59.4	123
Papua New Guinea	2,565	460	37	46.2	31.5	32	56.0	159
Paraguay	2,474	533	75	70.0	73.9	80	65.3	65
Philippines	41,021	342	71	60.5	69.8	83	61.6	74
Rhodesia	5,792	529	46	51.8	48.2	39	58.2	122
Senegal	4,172	355	25	34.1	31.5	8	51.3	159
Swaziland	439	353	35	32.6	36.0	36	50.7	149
Syria	6,753	662	54	61.0	61.3	40	61.8	93
Thailand	38,919	318	68	63.1	63.1	79	62.6	89
Tunisia	5,442	626	47	61.0	46.8	32	61.8	125
Western Somoa	153[3]	300[2]	84	68.2	85.1	98	64.6	40
Zambia	4,659	415	28	40.3	31.1	14	53.7	160
Population Total	1,080,743							
Mean		472	53	55.4	55.7	47.9	59.6	105.3
Weighted Average		340	67	66.2	73.7	60.1	63.8	65.4

Upper Middle-Income Countries (32)
(per capita GNP $700-$1,999)

Algeria	15,561	780	41	58.2	39.2	26	60.7	142
Argentina	24,565	1,285	85	85.4	76.6	93	71.3	59
Bahrain	232[3]	1,370	61	75.1	68.0	40	67.3	78
Barbados	242	1,352	89	83.8	86.0	98	70.7	38

Appendix A (continued)

	(1) Population, 1970-75 Average (thousands)	(2) Per Capita GNP, 1970-75 Average ($)[1]	(3) Physical Quality of Life Index	(4) Life Expectancy at Age One Index	(5) Infant Mortality Index	(6) Literacy (aged 15 and over) (%)	(7) Life Expectancy at Age One (years)	(8) Infant Mortality Rate (per 1,000 live births)
Brazil	102,467	912	68	70.3	66.2	66	65.4	82
Bulgaria	8,642	1,780[2]	91	86.4	92.8	95	71.7	23
Chile	9,811	1,137	77	74.9	68.5	88	67.2	77
Costa Rica	1,866	884	85	81.3	86.0	89	69.7	38
Cyprus	653	1,481	85	87.4	90.1	76	72.1	29
Fiji	549	989	80	83.3	93.7	64	70.5	21
Guadeloupe	342	1,240[2]	76	61.0	83.3	83	61.8	44
Hong Kong	4,084	1,624	86	85.1	95.5	77	71.2	17
Iran	30,641	1,260	43	51.8	40.5	37	58.2	139
Iraq	10,212	999	45	50.8	58.6	26	57.8	99
Jamaica	1,956	1,037	84	79.0	91.4	82	68.8	26
Lebanon	2,669	822	79	74.4	76.6	86	67.0	59
Malta	320[3]	1,050[2]	87	83.1	94.6	83	70.4	19
Martinique	351	1,540[2]	83	72.1	88.7	88	66.1	32
Mexico	54,759	996	73	72.8	73.4	74	66.4	66
Netherlands Antilles	234[3]	1,642	82	63.6	90.5	93	62.8	28
Panama	1,568	1,240	80	76.2	85.1	78	67.7	40
Peru	14,287	701	62	61.3	53.6	72	61.9	110
Portugal	8,695	1,535	80	83.8	86.0	71	70.7	38
Réunion	470	1,550[2]	73	69.5	82.0	68	65.1	47

Romania	20,711	1,100[2]	90	83.3	87.4	99	70.5	35
South Africa	23,082	1,205	53	51.0	50.5	57	57.9	117
Surinam	397	1,282	83	74.4	89.6	84	67.0	30
Taiwan	15,424[3]	847	86	81.5	91.4	85	69.8	26
Trinidad and Tobago	982	1,867	85	75.1	87.8	92	67.3	34
Turkey	37,557	789	55	65.9	49.5	51	63.7	119
Uruguay	3,032	1,268	87	87.9	82.9	90	72.3	45
Yugoslavia	20,847	1,341	84	81.5	85.1	84	69.8	40
Population Total	417,209							
Mean		1,216	76	74.1	77.8	74.8	66.9	56.2
Weighted Average		1,047	68	70.5	66.8	67.7	65.5	80.6

High-Income Countries (38)
(per capita GNP $2,000 and over)

Australia	13,181	5,449	93	85.1	95.9	98	71.2	16
Austria	7,493	4,529	93	85.9	93.7	98	71.5	21
Bahamas	190[3]	3,284	84	75.4	87.4	90	67.4	35
Belgium	9,742	5,845	93	85.1	95.9	97	71.2	16
Canada	21,924	6,527	95	90.0	96.4	98	73.1	15
Czechoslovakia	14,548	3,330[2]	93	85.9	93.7	100	71.5	21
Denmark	4,978	6,606	96	92.1	97.7	99	73.9	12
Finland	4,629	4,984	94	83.8	98.6	99	70.7	10
France	51,792	5,585	94	86.9	97.7	97	71.9	12
Gabon	513	2,123	21	27.7	23.0	12	48.8	178
German Dem. Rep.	17,126	3,710[2]	93	85.1	95.9	99	71.2	16
Germany, Fed. Rep.	61,191	6,507	93	85.6	94.1	99	71.4	20
Greece	8,862	2,148	89	89.2	92.3	84	72.8	24
Hungary	10,436	2,180[2]	91	85.6	88.3	98	71.4	33
Iceland	211	5,708	96	91.8	98.2	99	73.8	11
Ireland	3,043	2,354	93	85.1	95.5	98	71.2	17

Appendix A (continued)

	(1)	(2)	(3)	(4)	(5)	(6)	(7)	(8)
	Population, 1970-75 Average	Per Capita GNP, 1970-75 Average	Physical Quality of Life Index	Life Expectancy at Age One Index	Infant Mortality Index	Literacy (aged 15 and over)	Life Expectancy at Age One	Infant Mortality Rate
	(thousands)	($)[1]				(%)	(years)	(per 1,000 live births)
Israel	3,188	3,579	89	88.7	93.2	84	72.6	22
Italy	54,294	2,756	92	88.5	93.7	94	72.5	21
Japan	107,726	4,146	96	91.5	98.6	98	73.7	10
Kuwait	923	13,787	74	85.1	83.3	55	71.2	44
Libya	2,097	4,402	45	62.1	44.6	27	62.2	130
Luxembourg	341	6,054	92	82.3	96.4	98	70.1	15
Netherlands	13,316	5,558	96	91.8	98.2	98	73.8	11
New Zealand	2,926	4,222	94	87.7	95.9	98	72.2	16
Norway	3,942	6,221	96	91.8	98.2	99	73.8	11
Poland	33,157	2,510[2]	91	84.1	91.9	98	70.8	25
Puerto Rico	2,823	2,230[2]	90	89.2	92.3	89	72.8	24
Qatar	180[3]	11,779	31	39.5	41.0	13	53.4	138
Saudi Arabia	8,353	3,529	29	35.9	34.7	15	52.0	152
Singapore	2,162	2,111	83	76.9	96.8	75	68.0	14
Spain	34,606	2,485	91	87.2	96.8	90	72.0	14
Sweden	8,167	7,668	97	93.8	99.5	99	74.6	8
Switzerland	6,401	8,569	95	89.5	97.7	98	72.9	12
U.S.S.R.	248,903	2,380[2]	91	82.1	90.5	100	70.0	28
United Arab Emirates	320[3]	14,368	34	39.5	41.0	21	53.4	138

United Kingdom	55,954	3,658	94	87.7	95.9	99	72.2	16
United States	209,402	7,024	94	87.7	95.9	99	72.2	16
Venezuela	11,386	2,171	79	75.1	81.1	82	67.3	49
Population Total	1,040,426							
Mean		5,054	84	80.5	86.9	84.1	69.4	36.1
Weighted Average		4,404	92	85.9	93.8	97.0	71.5	20.8
World Population	3,780,735							
World Mean		1,706	60	59.7	62.7	56.2	61.3	89.7
World Weighted Average		1,476	65	64.4	68.6	62.5	63.1	76.7

[1] 1974-76 U.S. dollars.
[2] 1974 per capita GNP at market prices. *World Bank Atlas, 1976.*
[3] *World Bank Atlas, 1975.* 1973 figure.
[4] Estimate by Evelyn Rawsky, University of Pittsburgh.

SOURCES: See Note to Appendix A (p. 126).

150 Countries Ranked by Increasing Per Capita GNP (Table 1) and by Increasing PQLI (Table 2)

Appendix B

Table 1. 150 Countries Ranked by Per Capita GNP, early 1970s

Rank in Per Capita GNP among 150 Countries	Per Capita GNP ($)	PQLI	Cumulative Population (thousands)
1. Kampuchea	70	40	7,585
2. Laos	70	31	10,718
3. Mali	90	15	16,090
4. Bangladesh	92	35	86,809
5. Ethiopia	97	20	113,224
6. Rwanda	97	27	117,164
7. Upper Volta	99	16	122,872
8. Nepal	102	25	134,774
9. Burma	105	51	164,268
10. Burundi	111	23	167,826
11. Somalia	111	19	170,806
12. Chad	113	18	174,638
13. Malawi	115	30	179,276
14. Guinea-Bissau	120	12	179,782
15. Benin	124	23	182,662
16. Guinea	126	20	186,831
17. Lesotho	131	48	187,927
18. Niger	132	13	192,231
19. India	133	43	770,406
20. Zaire	136	32	793,468
21. Afghanistan	137	18	811,597
22. Gambia	153	25	812,083
23. Tanzania	154	31	826,438
24. Pakistan	155	38	891,943
25. Haiti	176	36	896,337
26. Sri Lanka	179	82	909,587
27. Yemen Arab Rep.	180	27	915,805
28. Vietnam	189	54	957,084
29. Indonesia	203	48	1,084,840
30. Sierra Leone	203	27	1,087,654
31. Madagascar	204	41	1,095,130
32. Kenya	213	39	1,107,379
33. Central African Emp.	226	18	1,109,080
34. Comoro Islands	230	43	1,109,368
35. Sudan	241	36	1,126,350
36. Egypt	245	43	1,161,786
37. Togo	250	27	1,163,890
38. Yemen, People's Rep.	260	33	1,165,438
39. Uganda	265	40	1,176,018
40. Cameroon	273	27	1,182,135
41. Mauritania	287	17	1,183,358
42. Nigeria	297	25	1,242,357
43. China, People's Rep.	300	69	2,047,679
44. Western Somoa	300	84	2,047,832

(continued on p. 140)

Appendix B
Table 2. 150 Countries Ranked by PQLI, early 1970s

Rank in PQLI among 150 Countries	PQLI	Per Capita GNP ($)	Cumulative Population (thousands)
1. Guinea-Bissau	12	120	506
2. Niger	13	132	4,810
3. Mali	15	90	10,182
4. Angola	16	601	16,194
5. Upper Volta	16	99	21,902
6. Mauritania	17	287	23,125
7. Chad	18	113	26,957
8. Afghanistan	18	137	45,086
9. Central African Emp.	18	226	46,787
10. Somalia	19	111	49,767
11. Ethiopia	20	97	76,182
12. Guinea	20	126	80,351
13. Gabon	21	2,123	80,864
14. Benin	23	124	83,744
15. Burundi	23	111	87,302
16. Senegal	25	355	91,474
17. Gambia	25	153	91,960
18. Mozambique	25	333	100,697
19. Nigeria	25	297	159,696
20. Nepal	25	102	171,598
21. Liberia	26	415	173,214
22. Congo	27	465	174,482
23. Rwanda	27	97	178,422
24. Yemen Arab Rep.	27	180	184,640
25. Togo	27	250	186,744
26. Cameroon	27	273	192,861
27. Sierra Leone	27	203	195,675
28. Equatorial Guinea	28	354	195,973
29. Ivory Coast	28	506	200,571
30. Zambia	28	415	205,230
31. Saudi Arabia	29	3,529	213,583
32. Malawi	30	115	218,221
33. Tanzania	31	154	232,576
34. Laos	31	70	235,709
35. Qatar	31	11,779	235,889
36. Zaire	32	136	258,951
37. Yemen, People's Rep.	33	260	260,499
38. United Arab Emirates	34	14,368	260,819
39. Ghana	35	595	270,070
40. Bangladesh	35	92	340,789
41. Swaziland	35	353	341,228
42. Sudan	36	241	358,210
43. Haiti	36	176	362,604
44. Papua New Guinea	37	460	365,169

(continued on p. 141)

Rank in Per Capita GNP among 150 Countries	Per Capita GNP ($)	PQLI	Cumulative Population (thousands)
45. Botswana	316	51	2,048,486
46. Thailand	318	68	2,087,405
47. Bolivia	332	43	2,092,500
48. Mozambique	333	25	2,101,237
49. Philippines	342	71	2,142,258
50. Swaziland	353	35	2,142,697
51. Equatorial Guinea	354	28	2,142,995
52. Senegal	355	25	2,147,167
53. Honduras	359	51	2,149,962
54. Zambia	415	28	2,154,621
55. Liberia	415	26	2,156,237
56. El Salvador	432	64	2,160,049
57. Morocco	436	41	2,176,364
58. Jordan	452	47	2,178,848
59. Papua New Guinea	460	37	2,181,413
60. Korea, Rep.	464	82	2,213,748
61. Grenada	465	77	2,213,854
62. Congo	465	27	2,215,122
63. Cape Verde	470	48	2,215,404
64. Ecuador	505	68	2,221,965
65. Ivory Coast	506	28	2,226,563
66. Colombia	526	71	2,250,546
67. Rhodesia	529	46	2,256,338
68. Albania	530	75	2,258,664
69. Paraguay	533	75	2,261,138
70. Guatemala	540	54	2,266,852
71. Mauritius	552	71	2,267,714
72. Guyana	559	85	2,268,464
73. Ghana	595	35	2,277,715
74. Angola	601	16	2,283,727
75. Tunisia	626	47	2,289,169
76. Dominican Rep.	630	64	2,293,900
77. Cuba	640	84	2,302,923
78. Nicaragua	650	54	2,305,067
79. Syria	662	54	2,311,820
80. Malaysia	692	66	2,323,100
81. Peru	701	62	2,337,387
82. Algeria	780	41	2,352,948
83. Turkey	789	55	2,390,505
84. Lebanon	822	79	2,393,174
85. Taiwan	847	86	2,408,598
86. Costa Rica	884	85	2,410,464
87. Brazil	912	68	2,512,931
88. Fiji	989	80	2,513,480
89. Mexico	996	73	2,568,239
90. Iraq	999	45	2,578,451

(continued on p. 142)

Rank in PQLI among 150 Countries	PQLI	Per Capita GNP	Cumulative Population
		($)	(thousands)
45. Pakistan	38	155	430,674
46. Kenya	39	213	442,923
47. Uganda	40	265	453,503
48. Kampuchea	40	70	461,088
49. Madagascar	41	204	468,564
50. Morocco	41	436	484,879
51. Algeria	41	780	500.440
52. Egypt	43	245	535,876
53. India	43	133	1,114,051
54. Iran	43	1,260	1,144,692
55. Comoro Islands	43	230	1,144,980
56. Bolivia	43	332	1,150,075
57. Libya	45	4,402	1,152,172
58. Iraq	45	999	1,162,384
59. Rhodesia	46	529	1,168,176
60. Tunisia	47	626	1,173,618
61. Jordan	47	452	1,176,102
62. Cape Verde	48	470	1,176,384
63. Indonesia	48	203	1,304,140
64. Lesotho	48	131	1,305,236
65. Botswana	51	316	1,305,890
66. Honduras	51	359	1,308,685
67. Burma	51	105	1,338,179
68. South Africa	53	1,205	1,361,261
69. Nicaragua	54	650	1,363,405
70. Guatemala	54	540	1,369,119
71. Vietnam	54	189	1,410,398
72. Syrian Arab Rep.	54	662	1,417,151
73. Turkey	55	789	1,454,708
74. Bahrain	61	1,370	1,454,940
75. Peru	62	701	1,469,227
76. Dominican Rep.	64	630	1,473,958
77. El Salvador	64	432	1,477,770
78. Malaysia	66	692	1,489,050
79. Brazil	68	912	1,591,517
80. Ecuador	68	505	1,598,078
81. Thailand	68	318	1,636,997
82. China, People's Rep.	69	300	2,442,319
83. Mauritius	71	552	2,443,181
84. Philippines	71	342	2,484,202
85. Colombia	71	526	2,508,185
86. Réunion	73	1,550	2,508,655
87. Mexico	73	996	2,563,414
88. Kuwait	74	13,787	2,564,337
89. Paraguay	75	533	2,566,811
90. Albania	75	530	2,569,137

(continued on p. 143)

Rank in Per Capita GNP among 150 Countries	Per Capita GNP ($)	PQLI	Cumulative Population (thousands)
91. Jamaica	1,037	84	2,580,407
92. Malta	1,050	87	2,580,727
93. Romania	1,100	90	2,601,438
94. Chile	1,137	77	2,611,249
95. South Africa	1,205	53	2,634,331
96. Panama	1,240	80	2,635,899
97. Guadeloupe	1,240	76	2,636,241
98. Iran	1,260	43	2,666,882
99. Uruguay	1,268	87	2,669,914
100. Surinam	1,282	83	2,670,311
101. Argentina	1,285	85	2,694,877
102. Yugoslavia	1,341	84	2,715,724
103. Barbados	1,352	89	2,715,966
104. Bahrain	1,370	61	2,716,198
105. Cyprus	1,481	85	2,716,851
106. Portugal	1,535	80	2,725,546
107. Martinique	1,540	83	2,725,897
108. Réunion	1,550	73	2,726,367
109. Hong Kong	1,624	86	2,730,451
110. Netherlands Antilles	1,642	82	2,730,685
111. Bulgaria	1,780	91	2,739,327
112. Trinidad and Tobago	1,867	85	2,740,309
113. Singapore	2,111	83	2,742,471
114. Gabon	2,123	21	2,742,984
115. Greece	2,148	89	2,751,846
116. Venezuela	2,171	79	2,763,232
117. Hungary	2,180	91	2,773,668
118. Puerto Rico	2,230	90	2,776,491
119. Ireland	2,354	93	2,779,534
120. U.S.S.R.	2,380	91	3,028,437
121. Spain	2,485	91	3,063,043
122. Poland	2,510	91	3,096,200
123. Italy	2,756	92	3,150,494
124. Bahamas	3,284	84	3,150,684
125. Czechoslovakia	3,330	93	3,165,232
126. Saudi Arabia	3,529	29	3,173,585
127. Israel	3,579	89	3,176,773
128. United Kingdom	3,658	94	3,232,727
129. German Dem. Rep.	3,710	93	3,249,853
130. Japan	4,146	96	3,357,579
131. New Zealand	4,222	94	3,360,505
132. Libya	4,402	45	3,362,602
133. Austria	4,529	93	3,370,095
134. Finland	4,984	94	3,374,724
135. Australia	5,449	93	3,387,905
136. Netherlands	5,558	96	3,401,221

(continued on p. 144)

Rank in PQLI among 150 Countries	PQLI	Per Capita GNP ($)	Cumulative Population (thousands)
91. Guadeloupe	76	1,240	2,569,479
92. Chile	77	1,137	2,579,290
93. Grenada	77	465	2,579,396
94. Lebanon	79	822	2,582,065
95. Venezuela	79	2,171	2,593,451
96. Panama	80	1,240	2,595,019
97. Portugal	80	1,535	2,603,714
98. Fiji	80	989	2,604,263
99. Korea, Rep.	82	464	2,636,598
100. Sri Lanka	82	179	2,649,848
101. Netherlands Antilles	82	1,642	2,650,082
102. Surinam	83	1,282	2,650,479
103. Singapore	83	2,111	2,652,641
104. Martinique	83	1,540	2,652,992
105. Yugoslavia	84	1,341	2,673,839
106. Western Somoa	84	300	2,673,992
107. Jamaica	84	1,037	2,675,948
108. Bahamas	84	3,284	2,676,138
109. Cuba	84	640	2,685,161
110. Cyprus	85	1,481	2,685,814
111. Guyana	85	559	2,686,564
112. Argentina	85	1,285	2,711,130
113. Trinidad and Tobago	85	1,867	2,712,112
114. Costa Rica	85	884	2,713,978
115. Hong Kong	86	1,624	2,718,062
116. Taiwan	86	847	2,733,486
117. Malta	87	1,050	2,733,806
118. Uruguay	87	1,268	2,736,838
119. Greece	89	2,148	2,745,700
120. Israel	89	3,579	2,748,888
121. Barbados	89	1,352	2,749,130
122. Romania	90	1,100	2,769,841
123. Puerto Rico	90	2,230	2,772,664
124. Hungary	91	2,180	2,783,100
125. U.S.S.R.	91	2,380	3,032,003
126. Poland	91	2,510	3,065,160
127. Spain	91	2,485	3,099,766
128. Bulgaria	91	1,780	3,108,408
129. Italy	92	2,756	3,162,702
130. Luxembourg	92	6,054	3,163,043
131. Austria	93	4,529	3,170,536
132. Belgium	93	5,845	3,180,278
133. Ireland	93	2,354	3,183,321
134. Australia	93	5,449	3,196,502
135. Germany, Federal Rep.	93	6,507	3,257,693
136. Czechoslovakia	93	3,330	3,272,241

(continued on p. 145)

Appendix B, Table 1 (continued)

Rank in Per Capita GNP among 150 Countries	Per Capita GNP ($)	PQLI	Cumulative Population (thousands)
137. France	5,585	94	3,453,013
138. Iceland	5,708	96	3,453,224
139. Belgium	5,845	93	3,462,966
140. Luxembourg	6,054	92	3,463,307
141. Norway	6,221	96	3,467,249
142. Germany, Fed. Rep.	6,507	93	3,528,440
143. Canada	6,527	95	3,550,364
144. Denmark	6,606	96	3,555,342
145. United States	7,024	94	3,764,744
146. Sweden	7,668	97	3,772,911
147. Switzerland	8,569	95	3,779,312
148. Qatar	11,779	31	3,779,492
149. Kuwait	13,787	74	3,780,415
150. United Arab Emirates	14,368	34	3,780,735

SOURCE: Based on Appendix A.

Appendix B, Table 2 (continued)

Rank in PQLI among 150 Countries	PQLI	Per Capita GNP ($)	Cumulative Population (thousands)
137. German Dem. Rep.	93	3,710	3,289,367
138. Finland	94	4,984	3,293,996
139. New Zealand	94	4,222	3,296,922
140. France	94	5,585	3,348,714
141. United States	94	7,024	3,558,116
142. United Kingdom	94	3,658	3,614,070
143. Canada	95	6,527	3,635,994
144. Switzerland	95	8,569	3,642,395
145. Netherlands	96	5,558	3,655,711
146. Japan	96	4,146	3,763,437
147. Denmark	96	6,606	3,768,415
148. Iceland	96	5,708	3,768,626
149. Norway	96	6,221	3,772,568
150. Sweden	97	7,668	3,780,735

SOURCE: Based on Appendix A.

PQLI and Component Indicators for Seventy-Four Countries, by Sex

Although Appendix A has data for 150 countries, it does not provide information for females and males separately. By using other sources (noted below), it was possible to collect separate male and female data for seventy-three countries. For forty-three of these, it was possible to construct male and female PQLIs for two or three years. Taiwan is included in this Appendix as the seventy-fourth country, even though there are no separate male/female data, because the data permit construction of total PQLIs for three different years.

As with the basic PQLI in Appendix A, the data for the three indicators for a country are not necessarily for the same year. The general rule was to use data from years as close together as possible, preferably with no more than a five-year spread. The dates for the three components were averaged in order to give the PQLI a date, even if that date is somewhat arbitrary.[1] In the few cases where the PQLI is constructed from indicators that refer to dates more than five years apart, the PQLI is dated only by decade (e.g., 1950s, 1960s, or 1950s/60s, where the data overlaps two decades). The footnotes in Table 2 of this Appendix indicate precisely to what years the data refer. Where there are no specific notes, the data are for the year indicated in the "date" column of the table.

The purpose of this Appendix is to show the possibilities of using the PQLI for making comparisons between males and females and for conducting historical analysis. Examination will make it obvious that there are often differences between PQLIs for the 1970s in this Appendix and PQLIs listed in Appendix A. This occurs because of the difference in data sources; caution should be exercised in trying to link the results from the two appendices. Moreover, even in using only the data from this Appendix, great caution should be exercised in moving from data to interpretation. For example, Algeria shows a steadily worsening infant mortality rate between 1950 and 1970. It is possible, however, that this is due to improved reporting rather than to actually deteriorating conditions. It is also possible that the decision to use data clustered around a specific year produced some unrepresentative results.

Table 1 of this Appendix lists male, female, and total PQLIs, and Table 2 shows the basic data for life expectancy, infant mortality, and literacy on which the PQLIs are based.

The data sources in this Appendix generally provide life expectancy at age one information. Where life expectancy at birth, rather than at age one, was provided, life expectancy at age one was calculated according to the formula described in the note to Appendix A (p. 126), using an infant mortality rate for a year as close as possible to the life expectancy at birth figure. Except where otherwise footnoted, the data for life expectancy at age one and for infant mortality are from United Nations, *Demographic Yearbook* (1957, 1965, 1966, 1974, and 1976), and literacy data are from U.N. Educational, Scientific, and Cultural Organization, *Statistical Yearbook* (1965, 1973, and 1976).

---

[1]One reason for assuming the PQLI refers to a specific year is to make it possible to explore the use of the Disparity Reduction Rate. See p. 74.

Appendix C

Table 1. PQLI, by Sex, for Seventy-Four Countries, Various Years, 1947 to 1973

	Date	Male	Female	Total
AFRICA				
Algeria	1950	34	35	34
	1964	38	34	36
	1970	—	—	41
Botswana	1960s	34	40	37
Burundi	1960s	23	23	23
Cameroon	1965	28	20	24
Central African Emp.	1960s	10	13	11
Chad	1960s	10	14	11
Egypt	1947	33	31	32
	1960	45	39	42
Ethiopia	1967	15	18	17
Gabon	1962	13	25	18
Gambia	1960/70s	12	16	14
Ghana	1970	35	35	35
Kenya	1960s	38	37	37
Liberia	1960/70s	31	21	26
Malawi	1969	27	27	27
Mauritius	1952	57	53	55
	1962	69	66	67
Réunion	1954	44	52	48
	1963	56	65	60
	1970	66	74	70
Rhodesia	1960s	45	45	44
Togo	1961	18	23	20
Uganda	1960s	41	39	40
Zambia	1969	37	30	33
ASIA				
Afghanistan	1960/70s	13	13	13
Burma	1955	47	36	41
	1962	49	40	45
Cyprus	1948	75	69	72
	1960	85	80	82
Hong Kong	1960	79	74	76
	1971	87	85	86
India	1949	17	10	14
	1959	34	25	30
	1970	45	35	40
Indonesia	1971	51	47	49

	Date	Male	Female	Total
Israel	1950	84	84	84
	1960	87	86	86
Japan	1960	87	91	89
Jordan	1961	61	48	54
Korea, Rep.	1957	57	58	58
	1968	76	76	76
Kuwait	1972	70	68	70
Malaysia	1949	51	42	47
	1960	48	46	47
	1970	69	65	67
Pakistan	1960s	38	32	35
Philippines	1950	53	57	55
	1960	58	62	60
	1971	71	74	72
Sri Lanka	1953	70	60	65
	1963	78	72	75
	1969	82	78	80
Taiwan	1950	—	—	63
	1960	—	—	77
	1970	—	—	87
Thailand	1949	59	52	55
	1960	59	58	58
	1972	69	71	70
Turkey	1950	—	—	30
	1960	—	—	42
	1971	59	52	55
LATIN AMERICA				
Argentina	1950	75	79	77
	1960	79	85	82
	1970	82	88	85
Bahamas	1960s	82	87	85
Barbados	1949	65	70	68
	1960	82	87	85
Brazil	1950	51	55	53
	1960	—	—	63
	1970	64	68	66
Chile	1952	60	64	62
	1960	61	68	65
	1970	75	79	77
Colombia	1951	47	49	47
	1964	64	67	66

	Date	Male	Female	Total
Costa Rica	1950	66	68	67
	1963	76	80	78
	1973	—	—	86
Cuba	1950/60s	80	85	83
Dominican Rep.	1951	46	49	47
	1960	62	63	62
	1968	61	65	63
Ecuador	1952	48	48	48
	1962	60	60	60
El Salvador	1950	50	51	51
	1961	60	62	61
	1973	63	65	64
Grenada	1947	59	62	61
Guadeloupe	1954	65	69	67
	1961	76	79	78
	1965	80	84	82
Guatemala	1950	38	36	36
	1961	44	44	44
	1970	53	50	52
Guyana	1949	64	65	64
	1960	75	77	76
Jamaica	1951	65	71	68
	1960	77	83	80
	1970	—	—	87
Martinique	1954	69	74	72
	1960	76	81	78
	1970	83	88	86
Mexico	1951	54	56	55
	1959	64	65	65
	1970	70	73	71
Nicaragua	1950	—	—	42
	1963	52	56	53
Panama	1950	67	69	68
	1960	71	74	73
	1971	80	82	81
Peru	1961	62	55	58
Puerto Rico	1950	74	76	74
	1960	81	85	84
	1970	—	—	91
Surinam	1963	77	82	79
Trinidad and Tobago	1950	68	69	69
	1960	80	83	81
	1971	85	88	87

	Date	Male	Female	Total
Uruguay	1966	82	88	85
Venezuela	1950	58	59	58
	1961	69	70	69
	1971	78	80	79
NORTH AMERICA, EUROPE, AND OCEANIA				
Bulgaria	1950	75	73	74
	1956	79	79	79
	1965	89	89	89
Greece	1955	85	79	82
	1961	86	82	84
	1972	89	88	88
Hungary	1951	78	82	80
	1960	85	90	87
	1972	87	93	90
Italy	1952	79	81	80
	1960	85	89	87
Poland	1951	73	79	76
	1972	88	95	92
Portugal	1950	62	62	62
	1960	68	70	69
Romania	1956	76	78	77
United States	1950	86	92	89
	1960	88	95	91
	1971	90	97	93
Western Samoa	1965	82	86	84
Yugoslavia	1950	65	63	64
	1960	74	72	73
	1972	84	84	84

SOURCE: Based on data in Appendix C, Table 2.

Appendix C

Table 2. Life Expectancy at Age One, Infant Mortality, and Literacy, by Sex, for Seventy-Four Countries, Various Years, 1947 to 1973

	Date	Life Expectancy at Age One (years)			Infant Mortality (per 1,000 live births)			Literacy (%)		
		Male	Female	Total	Male	Female	Total	Male	Female	Total
AFRICA										
Algeria	1950	45.4	46.9	46.2[2,13]	93.4	78.4	86.2	21.2	14.5	17.8[8]
	1964	52.5	54.8	53.6[2,23]	123.8	114.7	119.4[23]	29.9	8.0	18.8[26]
	1970	—	—	58.7[2,30]	—	—	130.7[1,30]	41.8	12.6	26.4[31]
Botswana	1960s	44.3	47.2	45.8[2,30]	103.0	91	97.0[1,31]	30.1	34.8	32.7[24]
Burundi	1960s	42.6	45.5	44.0[2,30]	147	133	140.0[1,31]	21.0	7.0	13.9[22]
Cameroon	1965	40.0	41.0	40.5	122	130	126[1,27]	31.0	7.0	18.9[22]
Central African Emp.	1960s	40.0	43.0	41.5[20]	201	178	190[1,30]	13.0	2.0	7.4[22]
Chad	1960s	34.0	40.0	37.0[23]	170	150	160[1,30]	12.1	0.6	5.6[24]
Egypt	1947	47.1	53.2	50.2	131.7	127.3	129.6	31.5	8.7	20.9
	1960	56.8	59.9	58.4	104.4	114.9	109.3	31.9	8.6	20.5
	1970	—	—	—	111.2	121.7	116.3	—	—	—
Ethiopia	1967	43.2	46.3	44.7[2,28]	174	164	169[1,29]	8.0	4.0	6.0[25]
Gabon	1962	34.0	52.0	43.0[21]	172	153	163[1,25]	22.2	4.8	12.4[21]
Gambia	1960/70s	48.9	51.2	50.0[2,33]	230	204	217[1,33]	9.0	3.0	6.0[22]
Ghana	1970	48.1	50.4	49.3[2]	167	142	156[1]	51.7	33.8	43.7
Kenya	1960s	52.6	56.6	54.6[29]	126	112	119[1,29]	30.0	10.0	19.5[22]
Liberia	1960/70s	52.1	52.7	52.4[31]	137	183	160[1,31]	13.9	4.2	8.9[22]
Malawi	1969	44.7	46.0	45.3[2,30]	164	121	142[1,31]	33.7	12.3	23.0[26]
Mauritius	1952	54.7	56.7	55.7	88.3	73.0	80.8	63.6	39.9	51.8
	1962	61.9	64.4	63.2	66.9	53.1	60.1	72.5	50.6	61.6

153

Appendix C, Table 2 (continued)

	Date	Life Expectancy at Age One (years)			Infant Mortality (per 1,000 live births)			Literacy (%)		
		Male	Female	Total	Male	Female	Total	Male	Female	Total
Réunion	1954	53.8	59.3	56.5[13]	108.2	96.9	102.6	37.0	41.6	39.4
	1963	59.8	66.3	63.1[25]	92.2	76.7	84.4[22]	48.9	54.2	51.7[21]
	1970	61.8	66.2	64.0[2]	55.4	44.6	50.1	59.7	65.9	62.9[29]
Rhodesia	1960s	54.9	59.9	56.6[2,30]	131.2	125.8	128.5[1,29]	48.0	31.0	39.4[22]
Togo	1961	36.4	42.9	39.7	140.7	113.8	127.0	17.0	4.0	9.7[22]
Uganda	1960s	54.0	57.4	55.8[2,30]	144.7	138.0	141.4[1,29]	44.0	26.0	34.9[22]
Zambia	1969	42.4	45.6	44.0[30]	144.3	147.5	145.9	61.0	34.5	47.3
ASIA										
Afghanistan	1960/70s	49.1	48.4	48.8[2,30]	230.0	204.0	217.0[1,31]	12.0	1.0	6.4[25]
Burma	1955	49.8	51.6	50.7[14]	168.3	142.5	155.8[17]	83.4	33.8	58.6[14]
	1962	50.1	52.5	51.2[23]	147.3	130.9	139.3	80.0	40.0	59.7
Cyprus	1948	67.3	72.6	70.0[9]	67.2	66.6	66.9	77.7	44.2	60.5[6]
	1960	67.8	71.9	69.8[2]	29.4	30.4	29.9	88.2	64.4	75.9
	1973	70.5	74.8	72.5[2,30]	25.4	31.7	28.4	—	—	—
Hong Kong	1960	62.6	70.5	66.4[2]	44.6	38.2	41.5	90.2	51.8	71.4[21]
	1971	68.0	75.3	71.6	22.5	17.0	19.2[30]	90.1	64.1	77.1
India	1949	39.0	37.3	38.2[5]	190.0	175.0	182.5[10]	29.4	8.4	19.3[11]
	1959	48.4	46.0	47.2[15]	153.0	138.0	145.5[20]	41.5	13.2	27.8[21]
	1970	55.3	54.3	54.9[2]	131.0	138.0	135.0[1]	45.3	21.5	33.4[31]
Indonesia	1971	52.4	54.2	53.3[2,30]	132.3	118.3	125.3[1]	70.8	49.0	59.6

Country	Year									
Israel	1950	66.7	68.2	67.9[2,13]	49.7	41.4	45.7	96.8	90.3	93.7[8]
	1960	68.5	71.2	69.8[2]	32.0	30.0	31.0	92.8	82.9	87.9[21]
	1970	71.1	73.8	72.4[33]	23.6	20.4	22.0	—	—	—
Japan	1960	66.8	71.4	69.0[2]	33.6	27.6	30.7	99.0	96.7	97.8
Jordan	1961	58.2	58.2	58.2	49.0	58.3	53.5	50.1	15.2	32.4
Korea, Rep.[3]	1957	52.6	57.5	55.1[18]	125.0	103.0	114.0[18]	87.4	66.7	76.8[15]
	1968	66.0	69.0	67.5	94.0	81.0	87.5	94.4	81.0	87.6[30]
Kuwait	1972	68.3	73.9	71.1[30]	78.6	75.0	76.8[1,35]	63.4	41.9	55.0[30]
Malaysia	1949	50.8	52.9	51.9[2,13]	89.0	71.7	80.6	55.9	16.3	37.8
	1960	54.5	57.2	55.9[2]	77.3	60.1	68.9	32.3	11.9	22.3
	1970	58.0	61.1	59.5[2]	46.4	35.5	41.0	72.1	49.6	60.8
Pakistan	1960s	53.5	52.5	53.1[2,28]	131.3	116.1	124.3[28]	28.9	7.4	18.8[21]
Philippines	1950	54.7	58.6	56.7[8]	112.4	90.1	101.7	64.1	56.2	60.0
	1960	53.8	55.6	54.6[2]	97.6	72.2	84.6	74.2	69.5	71.9
	1971	60.5	62.8	61.6[2,32]	75.3	59.7	67.9[32]	84.6	82.2	83.3[30]
Sri Lanka	1953	61.4	58.4	59.9[2]	77.0	65.1	71.2	80.5	52.7	67.6
	1963	66.1	65.9	66.0[2]	57.2	48.2	52.8[22]	85.9	63.7	75.1
	1969	67.4	68.9	68.2[27]	51.5	43.3	47.4[30]	89.4	72.4	80.9
Taiwan[4]	1950	—	—	55.6	—	—	35.2[11]	—	—	56.0
	1960	—	—	65.7	—	—	35.0	—	—	72.9
	1970	—	—	68.8	—	—	16.9	—	—	85.3
Thailand	1949	52.0	55.2	53.6[8]	70.2	59.9	65.3	68.6	35.6	52.0[7]
	1960	52.2	56.9	54.5[2]	95.4	75.3	85.4	79.3	56.1	67.7
	1972	60.0	63.6	61.7[2,33]	91.9	59.6	75.7[1,34]	87.2	70.3	78.6[30]
Turkey	1950	51.1	55.0	53.0[11]	—	—	187	47.7	16.7	31.9
	1960	—	—	58.9[2]	—	—	152	54.9	21.1	38.1
	1971	62.7	65.3	63.9[2,33]	133.7	115.5	124.6[1,33]	69.1	33.6	51.4[30]

Appendix C, Table 2 (continued)

	Date	Life Expectancy at Age One (years)			Infant Mortality (per 1,000 live births)			Literacy (%)		
		Male	Female	Total	Male	Female	Total	Male	Female	Total
LATIN AMERICA										
Argentina	1950	64.1	68.5	66.2[2, 13]	72.4	63.8	68.2	87.9	84.8	86.4[7]
	1960	66.2	71.8	69.0	67.1	57.5	62.4	92.5	90.3	91.4
	1970	68.1	74.1	71.0[2]	64.0	53.8	58.9	93.5	91.7	92.6
Bahamas	1960s	65.6	70.4	68.0[30]	38.7	34.1	36.4	90.1	89.4	89.7[23]
Barbados	1949	61.3	65.6	63.4[6]	132.0	118.2	125.2	92.8	89.8	91.3[12]
	1960	67.0	71.2	69.1	63.8	56.8	60.4	98.4	98.2	98.2
Brazil	1950	56.8	62.7	59.8[2]	118.6	99.0	109.1	54.8	44.2	49.4
	1960	—	—	60.2[2]	100.6	—	70.0	64.4	57.4	60.7
	1970	63.1	68.9	66.0[2]	100.6	91.3	96.0	69.4	63.1	66.2
Chile	1952	56.8	60.6	58.7	119.7	104.9	112.4[13]	82.0	78.6	80.2
	1960	61.1	66.1	63.6	140.4	122.6	125.1	84.9	82.4	83.6
	1970	64.9	70.1	67.5	78.8	78.9	78.8	88.9	87.2	88.1
Colombia	1951	50.4	51.1	50.8	128.5	110.8	119.9	65.0	59.8	62.3
	1964	59.4	62.0	60.7[2, 24]	90.2	76.2	83.3	74.8	69.5	73.0
	1967	—	—	—	85.2	71.2	78.3	—	—	—
Costa Rica	1950	60.0	61.6	60.6	94.8	85.0	90.2	80.1	78.6	79.4
	1963	66.8	68.9	67.8	73.6	59.5	66.7	84.7	84.0	84.3
	1973	68.9	72.9	71.4[2]	48.8	40.6	44.8	—	—	89.1
Cuba	1950/60s	69.3	72.3	70.8[2, 28]	40.2	33.2	36.8[28]	75.8	80.0	77.9[13]
Dominican Rep.	1951	45.8	48.5	47.1[2, 13]	69.4	57.4	63.4[16]	44.7	41.1	42.9[10]
	1960	62.9	63.4	63.2	109.0	91.7	100.6	66.7	62.4	64.5
	1968	57.7	60.8	59.3[2, 28]	87.0	75.1	81.1[28]	68.8	65.7	67.2[30]

156

Country	Year									
Ecuador	1952	51.2	53.8		123.6	112.3	118.0	62.1	49.7	55.7[10]
	1962	57.1	59.0		101.1	90.5	95.9	72.1	63.1	67.5
	1972	62.7	65.3	63.9[2,33]	86.5	77.2	81.9	—	—	—
El Salvador	1950	54.3	56.4	55.3	85.0	77.1	81.2	43.6	37.2	40.4
	1961	60.8	63.9	62.3	76.5	63.2	70.0	53.9	44.5	49.0
	1973	58.8	62.1	60.4[2]	64.0	54.0	59.1	60.8	55.6	57.1
Grenada	1947	52.2	56.9	54.6[6]	91.1	89.2	90.1[10]	77.2	75.9	76.4[6]
Guadeloupe	1954	58.1	61.4	59.8[13]	59.9	47.8	53.9	65.8	64.7	65.2
	1961	63.1	67.3	65.1[12,20]	39.9	39.8	39.8	79.0	77.9	78.4
	1965	65.0	69.4	67.2[26]	38.5	34.8	36.7[24]	83.5	82.9	83.2[27]
Guatemala	1950	48.3	47.2	47.7	113.9	99.5	106.8	34.4	26.0	29.4
	1961	52.5	53.4	52.9[24]	98.8	84.5	91.9[20]	36.0	27.0	31.5[20]
	1970	55.0	55.9	55.4[2]	93.4	80.5	87.1	53.9	38.5	46.1
Guyana	1949	57.4	59.8	58.6[11]	91.8	79.6	85.8[10]	81.5	70.5	76.0[6]
	1960	61.7	65.3	63.5	66.3	56.7	61.5	91.2	83.2	87.1
Jamaica	1951	59.9	62.4	61.1	87.0	75.3	81.2	73.8	79.7	77.0
	1960	65.6	69.2	67.4	48.9	45.6	48.8	78.6	84.8	81.9
	1970	—	—	69.9[2]	—	—	32.2	—	—	91.3
Martinique	1954	59.5	62.6	60.9[2,13]	53.2	42.9	46.7	72.8	74.9	73.9
	1960	64.3	67.9	66.0[2]	58.5	48.9	53.8	84.9	84.3	84.6[21]
	1970	68.1	71.5	69.8[2]	38.9	29.1	34.0	87.4	88.2	87.8[29]
Mexico	1951	54.5	56.9	55.6[2,13]	96.5	82.7	89.8[12]	60.4	53.4	56.8
	1959	59.6	62.2	60.9[16]	79.7	68.4	74.2[20]	70.2	60.7	65.4[20]
	1970	63.1	66.6	64.8	77.1	65.0	71.1	78.2	70.4	73.2
Nicaragua	1950	—	—	45.8[2]	—	—	82.0	38.0	38.7	38.4
	1963	49.0	52.2	50.5[2]	59.6	49.1	54.5	50.1	49.2	49.6
Panama	1950	60.9	63.3	62.1[2,13]	70.9	66.0	68.4	70.9	69.0	69.9
	1960	62.8	65.3	64.1	62.0	51.7	57.0	74.2	72.4	73.3
	1971	66.4	69.4	67.9[30]	34.9	32.4	33.7[6]	79.0	77.8	78.3[30]
Peru	1961	57.7	58.8	58.2	96.0	87.8	92.1	74.4	48.3	61.1

Appendix C, Table 2 (continued)

	Date	Life Expectancy at Age One (years)			Infant Mortality (per 1,000 live births)			Literacy (%)		
		Male	Female	Total	Male	Female	Total	Male	Female	Total
Puerto Rico	1950	67.0	69.9	68.0[2]	74.3	60.4	67.5	77.0	69.6	73.3
	1960	69.0	74.2	71.6[2]	48.0	38.4	43.3	83.0	77.1	80.6
	1970	70.1	76.9	73.5	26.6	21.8	24.2	—	—	89.2
Surinam	1963	64.4	68.3	66.4	52.2	43.6	48.0[2]	84.0	83.3	83.7[24]
Trinidad and Tobago	1950	60.7	63.1	61.8[2,13]	85.9	74.6	80.3	81.8	73.0	77.4
	1960	64.6	68.4	66.5	50.3	40.2	45.4	92.0	85.0	88.5
	1971	65.6	69.3	67.4[30]	28.2	18.6	23.2[33]	94.0	90.0	92.0[30]
Uruguay	1966	68.1	73.7	70.8[24]	53.7	45.0	49.4[1,30]	90.2	90.7	90.5[23]
Venezuela	1950	55.1	59.0	57.0[2,13]	70.5	62.8	66.7	57.2	47.2	52.2
	1961	60.9	64.3	62.3[2]	57.6	48.1	52.9[20]	69.8	61.7	65.8
	1971	65.4	68.7	67.0[2,30]	54.1	44.3	49.3	85.9	78.8	82.4
NORTH AMERICA, EUROPE, AND OCEANIA										
Bulgaria	1950	67.2	70.2	68.7[2,13]	88.2	72.9	80.8[13]	85.8	65.9	75.8[6]
	1956	68.2	71.2	69.6[2,15]	77.7	65.9	72.0	92.7	78.1	85.3
	1965	70.3	73.8	72.1[26]	32.7	27.3	30.8	95.2	85.3	90.2
Greece	1955	69.7	72.8	71.2[17]	39.3	38.3	38.7[16]	88.1	61.4	74.1[11]
	1961	70.5	73.5	72.0	41.9	37.6	39.8	91.7	70.0	80.4
	1972	70.5	74.6	72.5[2,33]	25.8	21.8	23.9	93.3	76.3	84.4[31]
Hungary	1951	67.5	70.2	68.7[2,13]	92.2	75.1	83.9	96.2	94.6	95.3[9]
	1960	68.4	72.3	70.3[2]	52.6	42.3	47.6	97.4	96.4	96.8
	1972	68.3	73.6	70.9[2,33]	38.2	29.1	33.8[33]	98.4	97.6	98.0[30]

158

Italy	1952	68.0	71.0	69.5[2,13]	67.7	59.0	63.5	88.7	83.4	85.9
	1960	69.3	73.4	71.4[2]	47.6	39.9	43.9	93.4	89.9	91.6
	1972	—	—	—	29.9	23.8	27.0	—	—	—
Poland	1951	64.3	69.0	66.7[13]	104.4	85.6	95.3[12]	95.2	92.5	93.8[10]
	1972	67.8	74.6	71.3	29.7	21.7	25.8[33]	98.7	96.9	97.8[30]
Portugal	1950	62.2	66.9	64.4[2]	100.2	87.5	94.1	64.9	48.0	55.9
	1960	65.0	70.2	67.5[2]	83.4	71.2	77.5	69.4	55.4	61.9
Romania	1956	65.7	68.6	67.2[2,15]	87.1	75.6	81.5	93.9	85.7	88.6
United States	1950	66.7	71.8	69.3[2]	32.8	25.5	29.2	96.4	97.1	96.8[13]
	1960	67.7	74.1	70.9[2]	29.3	22.6	26.0	97.5	98.2	97.8
	1971	67.9	75.5	71.6[2,30]	20.8	16.0	18.5[32]	98.9	99.0	99.0[29]
Western Samoa	1965	63.8	67.6	65.7[23]	46.0	38.3	42.5	97.4	97.5	97.5[26]
Yugoslavia	1950	63.0	66.5	64.6[2,13]	125.5	111.1	118.6	83.8	62.3	72.9[8]
	1960	66.0	70.7	68.8[2]	91.7	83.5	87.7	87.6	66.4	76.5[21]
	1972	68.7	73.6	71.2[2,31]	45.6	43.2	44.4	91.9	76.7	83.5[31]

[1] Infant mortality rate estimate generously provided by the International Population Office, U.S. Bureau of the Census.
[2] Life expectancy at age one calculated according to the formula described in Appendix A (p. 126), using infant mortality figures shown in this table and life expectancy at birth figures from United Nations, World Population Prospects as Assessed in 1973, Population Studies No. 60, Publication Sales No. E.76.XIII.4 (New York: 1977).
[3] Tai Hwan Kwon et al., The Population of the Republic of Korea, The Population Development Center, Seoul National University (1975).
[4] National Health Administration, Executive Yuan, "A Review of Progress in Public Health in Taiwan Area, Republic of China" (Taiwan: 1976).

[5] 1945.
[6] 1946.
[7] 1947.
[8] 1948.
[9] 1949.
[10] 1950.

[11] 1951.
[12] 1952.
[13] 1953.
[14] 1954.
[15] 1955.

[16] 1956.
[17] 1957.
[18] 1958.
[19] 1959.
[20] 1960.

[21] 1961.
[22] 1962.
[23] 1963.
[24] 1964.
[25] 1965.

[26] 1966.
[27] 1967.
[28] 1968.
[29] 1969.
[30] 1970.

[31] 1971.
[32] 1972.
[33] 1973.
[34] 1974.
[35] 1975.

SOURCES: See Note to Appendix C (p. 148).

Appendix D

United States: Historical Data by Race (Table 1) and by State (Table 2)

Appendix D.

**Table 1. Historical U.S. PQLI and Component Indicators,
by Race, 1900-1974**

	PQLI	Life Expectancy at Age One Index	Infant Mortality Index	Literacy	Life Expectancy at Age One (years)	Infant Mortality (per 1,000 live births)
Total U.S.						
1900	56.1	42.1	36.8	89.3	54.4	147.3
1910	61.8	46.4	46.6	92.3	56.1	125.5
1915	68.9	55.1	58.6	93.2	59.5	99.9
1920	70.1	51.8	64.5	94.0	58.2	85.8
1930	77.8	63.6	74.1	95.7	62.8	64.6
1940	82.8	69.2	82.0	97.1	65.0	47.0
1947	87.6	76.9	88.7	97.3	68.0	32.2
1950	88.9	80.0	90.0	96.8	69.2	29.2
1952	89.6	81.0	90.4	97.5	69.6	28.4
1959	91.1	84.1	91.3	97.8	70.8	26.4
1969	92.4	84.4	93.7	99.0	70.9	20.9
1974	94.0	87.5	95.6	99.0	72.1	16.7
Whites						
1915	70.3	56.7	58.7	95.5	60.1	98.6
1920	71.8	53.2	66.2	96.0	58.7	82.1
1930	80.2	67.4	76.1	97.0	64.3	60.1
1940	84.6	72.0	83.7	98.0	66.1	43.2
1947	88.8	78.7	89.6	98.2	68.7	30.1
1950	90.4	82.0	91.1	98.2	70.0	26.8
1952	90.9	82.8	91.7	98.2	70.3	25.5
1959	92.2	85.5	92.7	98.4	71.4	23.2
1969	93.5	86.2	94.9	99.3	71.6	18.4
1974	95.0	89.2	96.5	99.3	72.8	14.8
Blacks and Other Races						
1915	38.8	21.7	21.5	73.3	46.5	181.2
1920	51.4	33.4	43.8	77.0	51.0	131.7
1930	59.5	36.8	58.2	83.6	52.3	99.9
1940	68.5	46.8	69.9	88.5	56.3	73.8
1947	77.1	60.9	81.3	89.0	61.7	48.5
1950	78.5	63.1	83.1	89.4	62.6	44.5
1952	79.0	65.1	82.0	89.8	63.4	47.0
1959	82.4	71.4	83.3	92.5	65.8	44.0
1969	85.2	70.4	88.3	96.4	65.5	32.9
1974	88.2	76.2	91.9	96.4	67.7	24.9

SOURCES: Life expectancy at age one was calculated, using the formula described in Appendix A, from life expectancy at birth data in U.S. Bureau of the Census, *Social Indicators, 1976* (Washington, D.C.). Infant Mortality data for 1900 through 1970 are from U.S. Bureau of the Census, *Historical Statistics of the United States: Colonial Times to 1970,* Part I (Washington, D.C.). Since there were no national data until much later, Massachusetts data were used for 1900 (average of 1895-99 and 1900-04) and 1910 (average of 1905-09 and 1910-14). The 1974 infant mortality rate comes from U.S. Bureau of the Census, *Social Indicators, 1976.* Literacy data are from U.S. Bureau of the Census, *Historical Statistics.* The data for 1915 are the arithmetic mean of 1910 and 1920 rates. Since there are no data for 1974, the 1969 rate was used.

Table 2. U.S. Life Expectancy at Age One, Infant Mortality, and Literacy, by State, 1940-1970

	Life Expectancy at Age One (years)				Infant Mortality (per 1,000 live births)				Literacy (%)			
	1940	1950	1960	1970	1940	1950	1960	1970	1940	1950	1960	1970
Alabama	67.2	66.5	69.4	69.8	61.4	36.8	32.4	24.7	89.9	93.8	95.8	97.9
Alaska	—	—	69.4	69.7	—	51.8	40.5	20.1	86.6	93.7	97.0	98.5
Arizona	64.5	69.2	70.2	70.9	84.3	45.8	31.9	19.3	91.4	93.8	96.2	98.2
Arkansas	68.2	68.9	71.1	71.2	45.7	26.5	27.4	21.0	93.7	95.0	96.4	98.1
California	66.7	69.8	71.5	72.0	39.4	25.0	23.3	17.3	97.5	97.8	98.2	98.9
Colorado	67.1	70.5	71.8	72.5	59.8	34.4	27.5	19.6	97.5	98.0	98.7	99.3
Connecticut	67.3	70.6	71.6	72.7	34.1	21.8	21.1	17.1	95.9	96.9	97.8	98.4
Delaware	67.3	65.0	70.1	70.4	48.9	30.7	23.8	19.3	96.5	97.3	98.1	99.1
Florida	68.7	66.2	71.0	71.2	53.6	32.1	29.7	21.8	94.2	96.1	97.4	98.7
Georgia	68.0	65.2	69.2	69.1	57.9	33.5	33.0	22.1	91.4	93.1	95.5	98.0
Hawaii	—	70.2	72.3	73.9	—	24.0	23.2	17.9	87.1	91.6	95.0	98.0
Idaho	67.9	71.0	71.8	72.2	42.3	27.1	22.9	17.7	98.8	98.7	99.2	99.4
Illinois	66.4	69.8	70.4	70.7	35.3	25.6	25.0	21.7	97.9	98.0	98.4	99.1
Indiana	66.8	69.9	71.1	71.3	41.9	27.0	23.9	19.6	98.3	98.3	98.8	99.3
Iowa	69.6	71.8	72.5	72.9	36.7	24.8	21.9	18.4	99.1	99.1	99.3	99.5
Kansas	69.7	71.9	72.5	72.9	38.1	25.7	22.1	18.4	98.7	98.7	99.1	99.5
Kentucky	66.6	65.3	70.7	70.5	52.8	34.9	27.9	19.9	94.2	95.7	96.7	98.4
Louisiana	67.4	66.3	69.4	69.4	64.2	34.6	32.0	23.7	87.6	90.2	93.7	97.2
Maine	67.7	70.2	70.9	71.4	53.5	30.9	25.5	19.8	97.5	98.0	98.7	99.3
Maryland	66.3	65.8	69.7	70.6	49.6	27.0	27.3	19.0	96.6	97.3	98.1	99.0
Massachusetts	66.5	69.6	71.2	72.1	37.5	23.3	21.6	17.3	96.6	97.2	97.8	98.0
Michigan	66.8	69.9	70.9	71.1	40.7	26.3	24.1	20.1	97.9	98.0	98.4	99.1
Minnesota	69.3	71.8	72.4	73.2	33.3	25.1	21.6	17.1	98.6	98.5	99.0	99.4
Mississippi	67.7	66.5	69.6	69.1	54.3	36.7	41.6	29.3	89.1	92.9	95.1	97.0
Missouri	68.2	71.1	71.1	71.2	46.9	29.2	24.7	20.3	97.7	97.9	98.3	99.2

Appendix D, Table 2 (continued)

	Life Expectancy at Age One (years)				Infant Mortality (per 1,000 live births)				Literacy (%)			
	1940	1950	1960	1970	1940	1950	1960	1970	1940	1950	1960	1970
Montana	67.1	70.0	70.3	71.1	46.2	28.2	25.0	21.3	98.2	98.2	99.0	99.4
Nebraska	69.5	71.8	72.6	73.0	35.7	25.0	21.9	18.2	98.8	98.8	99.1	99.4
Nevada	65.4	68.6	68.5	69.6	51.9	37.9	30.1	22.0	96.5	97.8	98.9	99.5
New Hampshire	67.7	69.7	71.1	71.6	40.0	24.5	23.6	18.6	97.5	98.0	98.6	99.3
New Jersey	66.4	69.8	70.6	71.3	35.6	25.2	24.6	19.5	96.4	97.1	97.8	98.9
New Mexico	64.5	69.9	70.9	70.9	99.6	54.8	33.2	22.0	89.3	93.4	96.0	97.8
New York	66.5	69.8	70.3	71.0	37.2	24.7	24.1	19.6	96.2	96.5	97.1	98.6
North Carolina	68.0	66.3	69.6	69.9	57.4	34.5	31.7	23.8	91.5	94.5	96.0	98.2
North Dakota	70.2	71.9	72.5	72.9	45.1	26.6	24.8	15.4	98.0	97.7	98.6	99.2
Ohio	66.8	70.9	70.9	71.2	41.4	26.8	24.0	18.8	97.8	98.1	98.5	99.2
Oklahoma	68.5	67.1	71.7	71.9	49.7	30.2	25.5	20.1	97.2	97.5	98.1	98.9
Oregon	68.3	70.6	71.5	72.4	32.9	22.5	23.2	17.3	98.9	98.8	99.2	99.4
Pennsylvania	66.0	68.9	70.2	70.9	44.7	27.6	24.5	19.9	96.9	97.3	98.0	99.0
Rhode Island	66.6	70.0	71.3	72.3	38.2	27.8	23.3	19.6	95.7	96.9	97.6	98.7
South Carolina	66.6	65.6	67.8	68.6	68.1	38.6	34.3	23.0	87.7	92.1	94.5	97.7
South Dakota	69.8	71.9	72.0	72.5	39.2	26.6	28.1	19.1	98.6	98.5	99.1	99.5
Tennessee	67.8	66.5	70.5	70.6	54.7	36.4	29.4	21.3	93.7	95.3	96.5	98.0
Texas	67.7	66.5	71.2	71.4	68.6	37.4	28.9	21.0	93.7	94.6	95.9	97.8
Utah	67.8	70.7	72.0	73.0	40.6	23.7	19.6	15.0	98.6	98.6	99.1	99.4
Vermont	67.1	69.7	71.1	71.9	45.0	24.5	24.1	17.5	98.0	98.3	98.9	99.4
Virginia	67.0	65.3	69.9	70.6	59.3	34.6	29.8	21.1	90.7	95.1	96.6	98.6
Washington	67.4	71.0	71.7	72.1	35.7	27.3	23.4	18.6	98.8	98.7	99.1	99.4
West Virginia	66.6	66.4	70.3	70.1	53.9	36.1	25.5	22.4	95.5	96.5	97.3	98.6
Wisconsin	68.6	70.8	71.8	72.7	37.2	25.7	21.8	16.7	98.1	98.3	98.8	99.3
Wyoming	67.2	70.3	70.9	71.0	46.3	32.5	28.2	23.7	98.3	98.3	99.1	99.4

District of Columbia	67.2	66.5	67.7	66.6	47.0	36.4	30.4	28.6	98.3	98.2	98.1	98.9
United States	**65.0**	**69.3**	**70.6**	**71.3**	**47.0**	**29.2**	**26.0**	**20.0**	**96.0**	**96.7**	**97.6**	**98.8**
Puerto Rico	—	68.0	71.6	73.5	—	67.5	43.3	24.2	—	73.3	80.6	89.2

NOTE: PQLIs of all the states are listed on Table 16, p. 80.

SOURCES: For 1940, 1950, and 1960 life expectancy at age one is calculated, using the formula described in Appendix A, from life expectancy at birth data and infant mortality data in Robert Grove and Alice Hetzel, *Vital Health Statistics in the United States* (Washington, D.C.: HEW, National Center for Health Statistics, 1976); life expectancy figures are averages for 1939-41 (white population only), 1949-51, and 1959-61. 1970 life expectancy at age one and infant mortality data are from HEW, National Center for Health Statistics, *U.S. Decennial Life Tables*, Vol. 11 (June 1975). Literacy data are from *Statistical Abstract of the United States*, 1975. There are no state literacy data for 1940 in the source. An average of the literacy for 1930 and 1950 is used instead.

Taiwan: Historical PQLI and Component Indicators, 1950-1976

Appendix E
Taiwan's Historical Performance in PQLI, Life Expectancy at Age One, Infant Mortality, and Literacy, 1950-1976

	PQLI	Life Expectancy at Age One Index	Infant Mortality Index	Literacy	Life Expectancy at Age One (years)	Infant Mortality (per 1,000 live births)
1950	63	45.1	87.3	56.0	55.57	35.16
1951	64	46.5	87.6	56.8	56.15	34.47
1952	66	57.2	83.0	57.9	60.29	44.71
1953	68	61.6	83.5	58.5	62.04	43.68
1954	70	65.5	85.2	60.3	63.55	39.90
1955	71	67.6	83.0	62.1	64.36	44.79
1956	72	67.4	84.4	62.9	64.27	41.55
1957	73	67.7	82.5	67.7	64.42	45.85
1958	75	71.7	84.7	79.1	65.95	41.00
1959	76	71.4	85.5	71.1	65.84	39.11
1960	77	71.1	87.4	72.9	65.74	35.99
1961	78	72.4	87.9	74.1	66.25	34.97
1962	79	72.7	89.0	75.2	66.35	31.41
1963	80	73.5	90.3	76.4	66.68	28.51
1964	81	75.0	91.5	77.5	67.24	25.94
1965	82	76.6	92.3	76.9	67.89	24.11
1966	82	75.3	93.4	76.9	67.37	21.69
1967	83	75.6	93.0	80.4	67.47	22.57
1968	84	74.5	93.8	83.6	67.04	20.71
1969	86	77.6	94.5	84.7	68.26	19.14
1970	87	79.0	95.6	85.3	68.81	16.85
1971	87	79.5	96.2	86.0	69.01	15.51
1972	89	82.3	96.8	86.7	70.08	14.02
1973	89	82.6	96.8	86.2	70.23	14.08
1974	89	83.0	97.2	86.7	70.37	12.94
1975	90	84.1	97.5	87.1	70.81	12.57
1976	90	84.6	98.6	87.9	71.98	10.06

SOURCE: Infant mortality from National Health Administration, Executive Yuan, "A Review of Progress in Public Health in Taiwan Area, Republic of China" (Taiwan: 1976); life expectancy at age one calculated from life expectancy at birth data provided by National Health Administration, Taiwan Provincial Health Department, Taipei City, Health Department, "Health Statistics, Republic of China" (Taiwan: 1976); and literacy data are from Ministry of the Interior, *Taiwan Demographic Fact Book* (Taiwan: 1976).

Index

Index includes substantive, but not bibliographic, notes. Therefore, see Notes (pp. 106-24) *for additional references. See also Appendices A through E* (pp. 125-68) *for additional data for all countries.*

Abramovitz, Moses, 9
Adelman, Irma, 1, 16, 22, 30
Afghanistan, 23, 66-71, 83, 97, 98
Africa, 23, 36, 93, 97
  regional PQLI data, 66-71, 68*T*
Agency for International Development (AID), 97
Agricultural societies, 68-71
Ahluwalia, Montek S., 12, 33
Albania, 64, 64*T*
Algeria, 76, 102, 75*T*, 84*T*, 102*T*
Amsterdam Declaration, 99-103
Angola, 60
Argentina, 10, 23, 75*T*, 88*T*, 102*T*
Asia, 93
  regional PQLI data, 67, 68*T*
  See also South Asia; Southeast Asia
Attitudinal measures, 17

Bangladesh, 66, 70, 103*T*
Barbados, 78
Bennett, M. K., 17
Birth rate, 39
Bolivia, 67
Bourgeois-Pichat, J., 37
Brazil, 23, 97, 98, 75*T*, 88*T*, 102*T*, 103*T*
Britain. *See* United Kingdom

Bulgaria, 62, 75*T*, 88*T*
Burma, 67, 72, 83, 73*T*, 84*T*

Cambodia. *See* Kampuchea
Cameroon, 84*T*
Campbell, Angus, 17
Canada
  See also North America
Caribbean, 67
  See also Latin America
Chad, 72, 73*T*
Chenery, Hollis, 1, 16, 50-51
Chile, 23, 75*T*, 88*T*, 102*T*
China, People's Republic, 64, 64*T*
Club Of Rome. *See Reshaping the International Order* report
Coale, Ansley J., 37
Colombia, 64, 11*T*, 64*T*, 75*T*, 109 *n*28
Colonial societies, 68-71
Costa Rica, 64, 98, 75*T*
Cuba, 63, 98, 63*T*
Cultural biases in measurement, 25-27
Cyprus, 75*T*, 84*T*, 120 *n*155
Davis, Joseph S., 17
Death rate. *See* Health issues; Infant mortality component (PQLI); Mortality rate
Demeny, Paul, 37

Developing countries, types, 22-24, 98
   See also Income distribution
Disparity Reduction Rate (DRR),
   74-92, 99-102
Dominican Republic, 67, 88*T*
Drewnowski, Jan, 18

Easterlin, Richard A., 17
Economic development measures,
   16-17
   See also Foreign assistance programs
Ecuador, 72, 64*T*, 73*T*, 75*T*
Egypt, 97, 75*T*, 84*T*, 122 *n*155
El Salvador, 75*T*
England, 36, 44, 116*n*100, 120*n*159
   See also United Kingdom
Ethiopia, 97
Ethnic differences in PQLI data, 66
Ethnocentric issues in measurement,
   22-27
Europe, 36, 68*T*, 117 *n*103
Exchange rates, 10-13, 68*T*

Foreign assistance programs, 96-99
Fourth World countries, definition,
   23-24
France, 11*T*, 113*n*87

GNP. *See* Gross National Product
Gabon, 43, 60, 97-98
Germany, Federal Republic, 11*T*,
   115 *n*87, 117 *n*103
Ghana, 91*T*
Great Britain. *See* United Kingdom
Greece, 78, 75*T*, 84*T*, 88*T*
Grenada, 63*T*
Gross National Product (GNP), 7-14
   and PQLI data, 41-42, 52-56, 60-66
Guatemala, 83, 87, 88*T*, 103*T*
Guinea, 97
Guinea-Bissau, 46, 99
Guyana, 63*T*

Haiti, 67
ul Haq, Mahbub, 1

Harris, J. R., 92
Health issues, 26-28, 35, 36, 39,
   66, 76
Honduras, 67, 72, 73*T*
Hong Kong, 64, 84*T*
Hungary, 62, 11*T*, 75*T*, 88*T*, 102*T*

Income distribution, 12-13, 29, 60-66,
   71-72, 73*T*
Income measures. *See* Gross National
   Product
India, 10-11, 12, 28, 49-50, 60, 61, 70,
   72-77, 83-86, 87, 97, 105,
   11*T*, 45*T*, 73*T*, 75*T*, 84*T*, 88*T*,
   90*T* 102*T*, 103*T*, 113*n*89,
   116 *n*92, 118 *n*113
   See also Kerala State (India)
Indonesia, 67, 84*T*, 91*T*
Industrialization, 87-92
Infant mortality component (PQLI)
   description, 30-37
   scale, 42-47
International Development Association
   (IDA), 97
International Labour Office (ILO), 1
Iran, 60, 72, 73*T*
Ireland, 36, 62
Israel, 78, 75*T*, 122 *n*153
Italy, 11*T*, 75*T*

Jamaica, 72, 73*T*, 75*T*, 103*T*
Japan, 28, 11*T*
Jordan, 84*T*

Kampuchea, 67
Kenya, 11, 79, 11*T*
Kerala State (India), 64, 74, 87, 104,
   64*T*, 90*T*
Korea, Republic, 63-64, 72, 98, 63*T*,
   73*T*, 103*T*
Kravis, Irving B., 12, 55
Kuwait, 61*T*
Kuznets, Simon, 8, 9, 12, 13-14

Laos, 66, 67

Latin America, 23, 93
regional PQLI data, 66-71, 68*T*
Lebanon, 23
Leontief, Wassily, 19
Liberia, 83, 84*T*, 91*T*
Libya, 61*T*
Life expectancy component (PQLI)
description, 30-37
scale, 42-47
Literacy component (PQLI)
description, 30-34, 37-38
scale, 42, 45-47
Low income countries, PQLI data,
60-66
See also Income distribution

McGranahan, D. V., 16, 22
Madan, T. N., 25
Malaysia, 67, 72, 73*T*, 75*T*, 84*T*, 88*T*
Mali, 97, 102, 103*T*
Malta, 78
Martinique, 75*T*, 88*T*
Marx, Karl, 22
Mauritius, 64*T*, 75*T*
Measure of Economic Welfare (MEW),
9
Meier, Gerald M., 50
Men, PQLI data, 82-87
Mexico, 23, 97, 75*T*, 88*T*, 102*T*, 103*T*
Middle East, 23
regional PQLI data, 60-62, 66-71,
68*T*
Migration, 82
Minority groups. *See* Ethnic differences
in PQLI data
Morbidity rate, 39
See also Health issues
Morris, Cynthia Taft, 1, 16, 22, 30
Mortality rate, 9-10, 35-37, 38-39
See also Infant mortality component
(PQLI)
Myrdal, Gunnar, 25

National Academy of Sciences, 2-3

National income measures. *See* Gross
National Product
Nepal, 66
Nicaragua, 75*T*
Niger, 72, 97, 73*T*
Nigeria, 45*T*, 103*T*
Nordhaus, William, 9
North America
regional PQLI data, 68*T*
Nutrition measures, 27-29, 66

Oceania
regional PQLI data, 68*T*
Okun, Arthur, 15
Organisation for Economic Co-
operation and Development
(OECD), 3, 18, 21, 30
Overseas Development Council, 2, 74

PQLI. *See* Physical Quality of Life
Index
Pakistan, 70, 84*T*, 118 *n*113
Panama, 75*T*, 88*T*, 120 *n*134
Paraguay, 64*T*
Peru, 72, 73*T*, 84*T*
Philippines, 64, 67, 72, 97, 64*T*, 73*T*,
75*T*, 88*T*, 102*T*, 103*T*
Physical Quality of Life Index (PQLI).
See also countries and regions by
name for PQLI data
applications, 96-105
components, 42-47
description, 30-38
selection, 21-30
construction, 41-55
definition, 3-6
ethnic differences, 78-82
and Gross National Product data,
42, 52-56, 60-66
historical data, 72-78
limitations, 57-60, 94-96
projections, 99-102
regional data, 66-71
rural-urban differences, 87-92
scaling, 49-52

sex differences, 82-87
weighting, 47-52
Poland, 88*T*
Portugal, 75*T*
Poverty. *See* Income distribution
Puerto Rico, 62, 100, 75*T*, 102*T*
Purchasing power parity method,
   10-12, 55

Qatar, 66, 61*T*

Regional differences in PQLI data,
   66-71
Reshaping the International Order
   (RIO) report, 62, 63, 98-99
Réunion, 75*T*, 88*T*
Romania, 62
Rostow, W. W., 22
Rural-urban differences in PQLI data,
   87-92
Russia. *See* U.S.S.R.

Saudi Arabia, 60, 66, 61*T*
Scotland, 115 *n*87, 116 *n*91
  See also United Kingdom
Senegal, 72, 73*T*
Sex differences in PQLI data, 82-87
Singapore, 67
Social systems, 22-24, 39, 66-71
Social welfare measures, 9-10, 17-19
South Africa, 23, 79
South Asia, 23, 36, 67, 83, 116 *n*93
  See also Asia
  regional PQLI data, 66-71
Southeast Asia, 23
  regional PQLI data, 67, 71
  See also Asia
Spain, 62
Sri Lanka, 29, 38, 53, 63, 64, 72,
   76-77, 97, 104-105, 63*T*, 73*T*,
   75*T*, 76*T*, 84*T*, 88*T*, 102*T*
Sussex University, Institute of Develop-
   ment Studies, 1
Sweden, 36, 38, 42-46, 62, 103*T*,
   116 *n*91, 118 *n*111

Switzerland, 62
Syrquin, Moises, 16

Taiwan, 72, 76, 77, 100, 73*T*, 75*T*,
   102*T*, Appendix E
Thailand, 67, 102, 64*T*, 75*T*, 84*T*,
   88*T*, 102*T*
Third World countries, definition, 24
Tinbergen report. *See Reshaping the*
   International Order (RIO) report
Tobin, James, 9
Todaro, Michael, P., 92
Tribal societies, 70-71
Trinidad, 75*T*, 88*T*
Turkey, 23, 98, 75*T*, 84*T*, 102*T*

U.S.S.R., 62
Uganda, 79
ul Haq, Mahbub, 1
United Arab Emirates, 66, 61*T*
United Kingdom, 15, 23, 36, 42, 44,
   62, 91, 11*T*
  See also England; Scotland; Wales
United Nations, 1, 3, 21, 30, 37, 42,
   94, 97, 102
United Nations Educational, Scientific,
   and Cultural Organization
   (UNESCO), 34
United Nations International Compari-
   son Project, 10
United Nations Research Institute for
   Social Development (UNRISD),
   3, 16, 18, 21, 30
United States, 10-11, 15, 23, 28,
   36, 38, 60, 62, 78-82, 11*T*
   45*T*, 68*T*, 75*T*, 79*T*, 88*T*, 102*T*,
   103*T*, 111 *n*58, 114 *n*75, 117 *n*103,
   Appendix D
  PQLI data by state, 80*T*
Urbanization, 36, 87-92
Uruguay, 78, 120 *n*134
Usher, Dan, 9

Values in Measurement, 25-27
Venezuela, 97, 75*T*, 88*T*

Vietnam, 44, 67

Wales, 36, 44, 122 *n*159
   See also United Kingdom
Welfare measures, 9, 17-18
Western Samoa, 63*T*
Women, PQLI data, 82-87
World Bank, 1, 3, 10-11, 47, 50, 51,
   52, 53, 71-72
World Employment Conference, 20-21

Yemen Arab Republic, 66
Yemen, People's Republic, 66
Yugoslavia, 72, 73*T*, 88*T*

Zambia, 72, 73*T*, 84*T*

About the Overseas
Development Council
and the Author

The *Overseas Development Council* is an independent, nonprofit organization established in 1969 to increase American understanding of the economic and social problems confronting the developing countries and of the importance of these countries to the United States in an increasingly interdependent world. The ODC seeks to promote consideration of development issues by the American public, policymakers, specialists, educators, and the media through its research, conferences, publications, and liaison with U.S. mass membership organizations interested in U.S. relations with the developing world. The ODC's program is funded by foundations, corporations, and private individuals; its policies are determined by its Board of Directors. Theodore M. Hesburgh, C.S.C., is Chairman of the Board, and Edward J. Schlegel is its Vice Chairman. The Council's President is James P. Grant.

Morris David Morris is Professor of Economics at the University of Washington and a member of the Associated Staff of the Overseas Development Council. He has spent much of his academic career studying problems of growth, stagnation, and long-run change in Southern Asia, particularly as these compare with historical patterns elsewhere in the world. Since 1974, Dr. Morris also has been concerned with how various societies and groups within them cope with environmental conditions of high risk and uncertainty. In 1976-77, he was Lead Analyst for Panel 12 of the World Food and Nutrition Study of the National Academy of Sciences. This book, which developed from that experience, was written largely while he was a Visiting Fellow at the Overseas Development Council.

Overseas Development Council
1717 Massachusetts Ave., N.W.
Washington, D.C. 20036
(202) 234-8701

Board of Directors

Chairman: Theodore M. Hesburgh, C.S.C.
Vice Chairman: Edward J. Schlegel
Chairman, Administrative Committee: Davidson Sommers

Robert O. Anderson
William Attwood
*Marguerite Ross Barnett
Edward G. Biester, Jr.
Eugene R. Black
Harrison Brown
Lester R. Brown
Ronald B. Brown
Robert S. Browne
**Carleton D. Burtt
Wallace Campbell
Thomas P. Carney
Lisle C. Carter, Jr.
Kathryn Christopherson
Harlan Cleveland
Frank M. Coffin
Owen Cooper
Richard H. Demuth
Charles S. Dennison
John Diebold
*Thomas L. Farmer
Clarence Ferguson, Jr.
*Roger Fisher
*Albert Fishlow
Luther H. Foster
*J. Wayne Fredericks
*Orville L. Freeman
*Lester E. Gordon
*Lincoln Gordon
**James P. Grant (ex officio)
*Edward K. Hamilton
Arnold C. Harberger
*Susan Herter
**Theodore M. Hesburgh, C.S.C.
*Ruth J. Hinerfeld
Vernon E. Jordan
Nicholas deB. Katzenbach

Tom Killefer
*J. Burke Knapp
Peter F. Krogh
*Anne O. Krueger
*William J. Lawless
Walter J. Levy
David E. Lilienthal
*C. Payne Lucas
Harald B. Malmgren
Edwin M. Martin
Edward S. Mason
C. Peter McColough
*Lawrence C. McQuade
John Mellor
*Alfred F. Miossi
Thomas A. Murphy
*Randolph Nugent
William S. Ogden
F. Taylor Ostrander
Daniel S. Parker
James A. Perkins
John Petty
Samuel D. Proctor
*Charles W. Robinson
*William D. Rogers
Bruce W. Rohrbacher
Janeth R. Rosenblum
**Edward J. Schlegel
David H. Shepard
Eugene Skolnikoff
*Davidson Sommers
*Stephen Stamas
*C. M. van Vlierden
Clifton R. Wharton, Jr.
Charles W. Yost
*Barry Zorthian

*Member of Executive Committee
**Ex Officio Member of Executive Committee

Pergamon Policy Studies

No. 1 Laszlo—The Objectives of the New International Economic Order
No. 2 Link/Feld—The New Nationalism
No. 3 Ways—The Future of Business
No. 4 Davis—Managing and Organizing Multinational Corporations
No. 5 Volgyes—The Peasantry of Eastern Europe, Volume One
No. 6 Volgyes—The Peasantry of Eastern Europe, Volume Two
No. 7 Hahn/Pfaltzgraff—The Atlantic Community in Crisis
No. 8 Renninger—Multinational Cooperation for Development in West Africa
No. 9 Stepanek—Bangledesh—Equitable Growth?
No. 10 Foreign Affairs—America and the World 1978
No. 11 Goodman/Love—Management of Development Projects
No. 12 Weinstein—Bureacratic Opposition
No. 13 De Volpi—Proliferation, Plutonium, and Policy
No. 14 Francisco/Laird/Laird—The Political Economy of Collectivized Agriculture
No. 15 Godet—The Crisis in Forecasting and the Emergence of the "Prospective" Approach
No. 16 Golany—Arid Zone Settlement Planning
No. 17 Perry/Kraemer—Technological Innovation in American Local Governments
No. 18 Carman—Obstacles to Mineral Development
No. 19 Demir—Arab Development Funds in the Middle East
No. 20 Kahan/Ruble—Industrial Labor in the U.S.S.R.
No. 21 Meagher—An International Redistribution of Wealth and Power
No. 22 Thomas/Wionczek—Integration of Science and Technology With Development
No. 23 Mushkin/Dunlop—Health: What Is It Worth?
No. 24 Abouchar—Economic Evaluation of Soviet Socialism
No. 25 Amos—Arab-Israeli Military/Political Relations
No. 26 Geismar/Geismar—Families in an Urban Mold
No. 27 Leitenberg/Sheffer—Great Power Intervention in the Middle East
No. 28 O'Brien/Marcus—Crime and Justice in America
No. 29 Gartner—Consumer Education in the Human Services
No. 30 Diwan/Livingston—Alternative Development Strategies and Appropriate Technology
No. 31 Freedman—World Politics and the Arab-Israeli Conflict
No. 32 Williams/Deese—Nuclear Nonproliferatrion
No. 33 Close—Europe Without Defense?
No. 34 Brown—Disaster Preparedness
No. 35 Grieves—Transnationalism in Politics and Business

No. 36   Franko/Seiber—*Developing Country Debt*
No. 37   Dismukes—*Soviet Naval Diplomacy*
No. 38   Morgan—*The Role of U.S. Universities in Science and Technology for Development*
No. 39   Chou/Harmon—*Critical Food Issues of the Eighties*
No. 40   Hall—*Ethnic Autonomy—Comparative Dynamics*
No. 41   Savitch—*Urban Policy and the Exterior City*
No. 42   Morris—*Measuring the Condition of the World's Poor*
No. 43   Katsenelinboigen—*Soviet Economic Thought and Political Power in the USSR*
No. 44   McCagg/Silver—*Soviet Asian Ethnic Frontiers*
No. 45   Carter/Hill—*The Criminal's Image of the City*
No. 46   Fallenbuchl/McMillan—*Partners in East-West Economic Relations*
No. 47   Liebling—*U.S. Corporate Profitability*
No. 48   Volgyes/Lonsdale—*Process of Rural Transformation*
No. 49   Ra'anan—*Ethnic Resurgence in Modern Democratic States*